TALKING TO VIRGIL

A MISCELLANY

TALKING TO VIRGIL
A MISCELLANY

T.P. WISEMAN

University of Exeter Press

First published 1992 by the
University of Exeter Press
Reed Hall
Streatham Drive
Exeter, Devon EX4 4QR
UK

© T.P. Wiseman, 1992
University of Exeter

British Library Cataloguing in Publication Data

A catalogue record for this book is available
from the British Library

ISBN 0 85989 375 8

Typeset in 10/13pt Garamond
by Richards Typesetting Ltd, Exeter

Printed and bound in Great Britain
by Short Run Press Ltd, Exeter

For Miss Orchard
and all those like her

CONTENTS

List of illustrations.................................viii

Preface and acknowledgements........................xi

1. Killing Caligula.................................1
2. The Giants' Revenge............................14
3. Julius Caesar and the *mappa mundi*.....................22
4. Mortal Trash..................................43
5. The Centaur's Hoof.............................51
6. A Roman Villa.................................71
7. With Boni in the Forum........................111
8. Rediscovering a Benefactor........................149
9. Talking to Virgil.............................171
10. Uncivil Discourse..............................210

Appendices....................................227

Index..238

LIST OF ILLUSTRATIONS

Plates (between pp 116 and 117)

 I   The Hereford *mappa mundi*

 II (a) Detail from the *mappa mundi*: Augustus and the three surveyors

     (b) Augustus with a 'T-O' map

III (a) Excavation of a Roman house in the Villa Negroni

     (b) S. Maria Maggiore before 1870

 IV (a) The papal Stazione di Termini

     (b) Preparing the ground for development, 1874

  V Detail of the bronze doors of the Senate wing of the Capitol

 VI Mary Crawford, Mrs Hugh Fraser: (a) from the Washington group; (b) and (c) frontispiece portraits from her memoirs

VII (a) Group at the *lapis niger*, 1899

     (b) W. St Clair Baddeley, *c.* 1930

     (c) G. McN. Rushforth F.S.A., 1937

VIII 'J.K. at Caroline House 1953'

Figures

1. The Bay of Naples in antiquity 15

2. The Campus Martius in the time of Augustus 39

3. The site of ancient Rome and its walls 73

4. The area of the Villa Montalto in 1576 78

5. The Villa Montalto in 1748 79

6. 'Giustizia' 81

7. The *palazzo* of the Villa Montalto-Negroni 84

8. A wall-painting from the Roman house discovered in 1777 86

9. Plan of the Roman house excavated in 1777 87

10. The Villa Negroni-Massimo in 1869 94

11. The area of the Villa Negroni-Massimo in 1882 95

PREFACE AND ACKNOWLEDGEMENTS

I hope this is a book to be read for pleasure. It was certainly written for pleasure. It represents, in fact, twelve years of displacement activity—which is psychologists' jargon for something you do to avoid doing what you ought to be doing instead. Each of these essays was written for no better reason than that the subject interested me at the time, and they are collected here in the hope that readers may find them interesting too. I don't suppose the frontiers of knowledge have been very far advanced, but a good deal of curiosity has been satisfied.

For guidance off my usual beaten track, I am very grateful to Harold Baldry, Jean Branford, John D. Christie, Lucos Cozza, Michael Crawford, Tony Cubberley, Oswald Dilke, Robert L. Gale, Federico Guidobaldi, Judy Hallett, David Harrison, Graham Haslam, Christine Häuber, Anthony James, Roger Ling, Alan McWhirr, John C. Moran, Sarah Newton, John Pilkington, Gordon Poole, Maurice Pope, William Ravenhill, Michael Reeve and Valerie Scott.

'Mortal Trash' (1978) and 'Killing Caligula' (1988) first appeared in *Pegasus*, Exeter University's classical journal; so did 'Rediscovering a Benefactor' (1981), which was reprinted with notes, bibliography and illustration in the *Papers of the British School at Rome* under the title 'The First Director of the British School'. 'The Giants' Revenge' (1979) and an earlier version of 'Julius Caesar and the *Mappa mundi*' (1987) were first published in *History Today*, and 'The Centaur's Hoof' (1981) in *Classical and Modern Literature*. 'With Boni in the Forum' (1985) appears for the first time in English; an Italian translation was published in the *Rivista dell'Instituto Nazionale di Archaeologia e Storia dell'Arte*. I am grateful to the editors of all those journals for permission to reprint; also to the publications committee of the Exeter University School of Education, for the first section of 'Uncivil Discourse', which appeared in *Perspectives on the National Curriculum* (1987). 'Talking to Virgil'

xi

(1989) was a lecture to the Virgil Society; like 'A Roman Villa' and the greater part of 'Uncivil Discourse' (both 1990), it is published here for the first time.

For permission to reproduce the illustrations, thanks are due to the Dean and Chapter of Hereford (Plates I and IIa), The British School at Rome (IIIb, IVa and b, VIIa), The British Museum (fig. 8), The Tate Gallery (Plate IIIa), The Architect of the Capitol (V), The British Library (VIb and c), Gloucester County Library (VIIb), and Jean Creedy (VIII). Finally, it is a pleasure to thank Rodney Fry for drawing the maps, and Sandi Ellison for preparing the text.

Exeter, September 1991

1

KILLING CALIGULA

Late in AD 40, in the fourth year of the rule of Gaius Caesar (whom some called Caligula, but not to his face), a senior senator was accused by one of his enemies of treason against the emperor. When the case came before Gaius, the prosecutor called the senator's mistress, Quintilia, to give evidence. Quintilia was a stage performer, one of the *mimae* who acted, danced and bared their bodies to appreciative audiences at the *ludi scaenici* of the Roman festivals. She was also a brave woman, and refused to testify. The prosecutor demanded that she be interrogated under torture. Gaius ordered a senior guardsman to take her away and carry out the torture in person.

The officer concerned was a decent and honourable man whom the emperor had often criticised for being too soft; he would have to do a thorough job now, out of fear for his own life. He did—but Quintilia did not talk. What had been a glamorous showgirl was brought back to the imperial presence broken and ruined. Even the sadistic Gaius was affected. He dismissed the case and freed Quintilia with a gift of money 'as consolation for the maltreatment that marred her beauty and the intolerable agonies she had undergone'. As for the officer, Cassius Chaerea, it was that experience which made him resolve that Gaius must not be allowed to live.

This horrible story is part of one of the most important and neglected narratives in the whole of Roman imperial history.

Important, because the death of Gaius was a very critical moment. He was the last of the Iulii Caesares, and he left no heir. What did Chaerea and his friends expect to happen after the assassination? We know what *did* happen: Claudius, the forgotten man, was put in power by the Praetorian Guard, and managed to stay there for thirteen years. But that could not have been predicted. Augustus' dynasty ended with Gaius.

Claudius was closely related to it (his two grandmothers were Augustus' wife and Augustus' sister), and his brother, Germanicus, had become Augustus' grandson by adoption—but he himself was still a Claudius Nero, not a Iulius Caesar.

The events of January AD 41, both those that happened and those that might have happened, require a narrative with some historical perspective and political sophistication. But Tacitus' *Annals* are lost from AD 37 to 47; the relevant part of Cassius Dio's *History* survives only in Byzantine excerpts and epitomes; and Suetonius, as usual, offers anecdote and character description rather than historical insight or analysis. What we *do* have, however, and very unexpectedly too, is a lengthy account in book XIX of Flavius Josephus' *Antiquities of the Jews*, written in the nineties AD and evidently based on good, possibly even contemporary, Roman sources. Gaius' proposed desecration of the temple at Jerusalem, narrowly averted by his unexpected death, gave Josephus the motive to narrate in detail, as an example of the power and providence of God, the whole story of the assassination and of Claudius' eventual succession.

It is astonishing how little serious work has been done on this long and historically crucial narrative.[1] What I hope to show below is how the details it provides can give us an unexpected insight into Roman political thought.

As Josephus tells it, after the Quintilia affair, Chaerea, in anger and shame, went to the Praetorian Prefect and put it to him that the Guards were now no more than public executioners. 'We bear these arms,' he said, 'not for the freedom of the Romans, but to protect the man who enslaves them' (42). When the Prefect promised tacit support for the assassination plan, Chaerea went off to enrol Cornelius Sabinus, an officer of his own rank and like him a 'lover of liberty' (46). The two of them approached L. Annius Vinicianus, a distinguished senator with good reason to hate Gaius, to be the leader of their enterprise. To him Chaerea spoke of his anguish 'at the enslavement of our country, once the freest of all, now deprived of the power of its laws' (57).

Freedom from slavery is in itself a predictable enough ideal for a tyrannicide, but freedom with the addition of the *laws* makes the

---

1. That was true when this essay was first published. Since then I have tried to fill the gap myself: see Flavius Josephus, *Death of an Emperor* (Exeter Studies in History 30, Exeter 1991).

programme much more specific. It is not a merely casual reference. At the very beginning, Josephus' justification for the length and detail of his assassination narrative is that Gaius' death was a happy outcome for the *laws* and the security of all (15). And he makes it a recurring theme: Chaerea is a champion of the rule of law (74); Gaius has abolished the protection of the laws (156); the survival of his wife and child would be a menace to the city and the laws (190); Claudius is urged by the Senate to yield to the laws (230–1); and so on.

To a Roman, the combination of those two ideas—freedom and the laws, *libertas et leges*—could only mean one thing: the Republic. Remember the beginning of Livy's second book, after the expulsion of Tarquin the tyrant:

> *Liberi* iam hinc populi Romani res pace belloque gestas, annuos magistratus, imperiaque *legum* potientiora quam hominum peragam (II 1.1)

> The history of the free Roman people in peace and war, annual magistrates, and the commands of the laws more powerful than those of men—this shall be my subject from now on.

Similarly, Tacitus, at the beginning of the *Annals*, defines the Republic as 'freedom and the consulate' at its foundation and as 'the Senate, the magistrates, and the laws' at its usurpation by Augustus:

> *Libertatem* et consulatum L. Brutus instituit (I 1.1)
> Munia senatus magistratuum *legum* in se trahere (I 2.1).

It is true that *leges* alone might characterise a 'constitutional monarch'— Servius Tullius, perhaps, or even Augustus[2]—as opposed to a despot. But in combination with *libertas* the phrase can only mean the Republic.

Few things are so unhelpful to our understanding of Roman history as the firm line we like to draw between the Republic and the Principate. It is true, of course, that the Battle of Actium was a profoundly significant event; but the habit of using it to end or to begin a historical 'period' makes us less able to see the continuities. When, after all, did the Republic end? More important, when did the *idea* of the Republic as the natural constitution of Rome finally become obsolete?

---

2. Tac. *Ann.* III 26.6; Ovid *Fasti* II 142.

Already in 59 BC, under the *dominatio* of Caesar, Pompey and
Crassus, Cicero could describe constitutional government as totally
lost.[3] Caesar's dictatorship effectively extinguished it, and though it
resumed for a year or so after the Ides of March, it was abolished again by
the Triumvirate in 43. In 27, Augustus solemnly restored the *res publica*
to the Senate and People; in the speech Cassius Dio gives him on that
occasion, he defines what he is giving back as 'the armies, the *laws* and
the provinces', and more generally as '*liberty* and democracy'. His own
over-riding authority made that a somewhat disingenuous claim, but it is
clear enough from Augustus' actions in 23 that if he had died in that year,
as he very nearly did, the Republic would have resumed—with whatever
consequences—just as it had in 44.[4] What we call the Principate was still
thought of as a temporary expedient. The *princeps* was like a doctor,
urgently needed to cure the ills of the Republic, but not to replace it.[5]

Even the formal powers of the *princeps* were, in theory, revocable.
The *tribunicia potestas* was granted every year by popular vote, and in
principle there was nothing to prevent the assembly from declining to
grant it. Similarly, the Senate's vote of the *provincia* in which Augustus'
imperium was exercised—the command, that is, of the legionary
armies—was for limited periods, usually of ten years, and subject always
to renewal.[6] In practice, the renewal was a formality, as must have been
obvious from the very first time, in 18 BC, but the principle remained
important: as the Senate made clear over fifty years later, it was they who
granted the *princeps* his power.[7] The logical corollary was that if ever
they chose not to do so, the Republic would govern itself without
his guidance.

Some people, at least, regarded that as a practical possibility. Nero
Claudius Drusus, Tiberius' brother, thought that *libertas* and the
pristinus rei publicae status should be restored, and is said to have
written to Tiberius on the subject of 'compelling Augustus to bring back

3. *Ad Q. f.* I 2.15: 'rem publicam funditus amisimus'.
4. Dio LIII 4.3, 5.3 (27 BC); 31.1–4 (23 BC).
5. Dio LVI 39.2. See Ronald Syme, *Roman Papers* I (Oxford 1979) 205–217,
   and *The Augustan Aristocracy* (Oxford 1986) 439–454. On *libertas*, see
   P.A. Brunt, *The Fall of the Roman Republic and Related Essays* (Oxford
   1988) 281–350.
6. Dio LIII 16.2, 17.10.
7. Dio LVIII 24.1 (AD 34).

liberty'. Drusus died in 9 BC, but twenty years later there were still some who shared his opinion, including—so it was thought—his son Germanicus.[8]

Tiberius himself, when reluctantly taking on the burden of Augustus' responsibilities, begged the Senate not to think of it as a permanent arrangement: 'I will do it,' he said, 'until I reach the age when you may be able to think it right to give my old age some rest.' In AD 23, with both his heirs untimely dead, he evidently thought the time was getting close. Commending his grandsons to the Senate's protection, he went on to speak of restoring the Republic and handing over power to the consuls: 'de reddenda re publica, utque consules seu quis alius regimen susciperent.' Despite Tacitus' sneer, there is no reason to suppose he didn't mean it.[9]

In the end, like his predecessor, he couldn't take the risk. Holding power, he used to say, was like holding a wolf by the ears (Suet. *Tib.* 25.1). But the idea was always there, the possibility always real in the mind. For Cassius Chaerea, it was real enough to inspire him to kill. Remove the tyrant, and liberty and the laws would automatically resume.

Like the idea of the free Republic, so its corollary, the idea of justifiable tyrannicide, can be traced through several generations both before and after that illusory and artificial boundary line of 31 BC.

Consider, for instance, the optimate version of the death of Tiberius Gracchus, as reported in Valerius Maximus (III 2.17):

> When Tiberius Gracchus in his tribunate usurped the People's favour with lavish bribery and held the state in oppression [rem p. oppressam teneret], . . . all the senators demanded that Scaevola the consul should protect the Republic by force of arms. When he refused to use force, Scipio Nasica said: 'Since the consul, in sticking to the letter of the law, is causing the authority of Rome to collapse along with all its laws [ut *cum omnibus legibus* Romanum imperium corruat], . . . let all who wish the Republic safe follow me.'

---

8. Drusus: Tac. *Ann.* I 33.2, Suet. *Tib.* 50.1, *Claud.* 1.4. Germanicus: Tac. *Ann.* I 4.2, II 82.2.
9. Suet. *Tib.* 24.2, Tac. *Ann.* IV 9.1.

Fifty years later L. Cinna, whose four successive consulships were described by Cicero as *regnum* and *dominatus*, was similarly assassinated by
his frustrated political opponents. The centurion who killed him did so
with the words 'I am here to punish a wicked and *lawless* tyrant'.[10]

The idea of tyranny was much in the Romans' minds in the late second
and early first centuries BC. The classic tyrant's motto 'let them hate, so
long as they fear' (*oderint dum metuant*) comes from the *Atreus* of
L. Accius. As Seneca commented later (*de ira* I 19.4), 'you might know it
was written in Sulla's times'. The first-century annalists applied the idea
of tyranny and tyrannicide to early Roman history. One of them
attributed to P. Valerius Poblicola, in the first year of the Republic, a law
stating that 'anyone who sought to make himself tyrant might be slain
without trial, and the slayer be free from blood-guiltiness if he produced
proofs of the crime'. Another re-wrote the death of Romulus as the
assassination of a tyrant by a conspiracy of senators. The first known
reference to this version, in 67 BC, vividly illustrates its contemporary
political relevance. In the context of Gabinius' proposal for a special
command against the pirates, which the optimates thought would give
Pompey dangerously unlimited powers, one of the consuls—no doubt
C. Piso—told Pompey that if he emulated Romulus he would not escape
Romulus' fate.[11]

Eight years later, his words nearly came true. The suppression of
optimate opposition to Caesar in 59 is repeatedly described in Cicero's
letters as *regnum*, *dominatio* and *tyrannis*.[12] Pompey got most of the
blame, and was attacked from the stage in July in terms which made his
'tyrannical' status absolutely clear. As Cicero told Atticus,

> the lines might have been written for the occasion by an enemy of
> Pompey. 'If neither law nor custom can constrain', etc. [si neque *leges*
> neque mores cogunt] was recited to a loud accompaniment of shouting
> and clapping.

And sure enough, a month or so later a conspiracy of young senators to
assassinate Pompey was reported to the Senate. Cicero himself, the
informer alleged, had said that what was needed now was a Servilius

---

10. Plut. *Pomp.* 5.1; Cic. *Phil.* I 34, *de nat. deorum* III 81.
11. Plut. *Pobl.* 12.1, *Pomp.* 25.4.
12. Cic. *ad Att.* II 12.1, 13.2, 14.1, 17.1, 18.2, 21.1, etc.

Ahala, or a L. Brutus. Ahala, of course, had killed the would-be tyrant
Sp. Maelius in 440 BC; Brutus had achieved *libertas* by driving out the
Tarquins.[13]

The theme continues throughout the fifties. Caesar's enemies plotted
to have him killed, either by Ariovistus in Gaul or by one of his own
slaves.[14] M. Brutus in 54 BC minted coins showing his famous ancestor,
and Servilius Ahala too, at a time when his father-in-law Cato was
describing the opposition to Pompey and Crassus as a struggle with
tyrants for liberty.[15] In March 49, distraught at the progress of the civil
war, Cicero reflected that at least Caesar was mortal, and might be
'extinguished' in various ways. Once Caesar had installed himself as an
acknowledged autocrat, the assassination plots multiplied, in rumour if
not in fact: C. Cassius in 47, anonymous conspirators in 46, M. Antonius
in 45, and then finally Brutus and Cassius in 44.[16]

Assassination could not touch the multiple tyranny of the Triumvirs,
but it was a different matter when all power was again in the hands of a
single man. The conspiracy led by Fannius Caepio in 22 BC was clearly
no different in kind from those led by the younger Curio in 59 and by
M. Brutus in 44; it was provoked by Augustus' unrepublican behaviour,
and one at least of the conspirators was noted for his freedom of speech
(*parrhesia*)—the characteristic virtue of a free citizen as opposed to the
subject of a tyranny. Twenty years later, when Augustus' dynastic plans
and the promotion of his adopted sons had made explicit the
monarchical nature of his rule, we find another group of disaffected
senators executed for treason.[17] Although they were disgraced as the
lovers of Augustus' daughter, their plot had been to assassinate him. It is
not clear what they hoped for after that, but the fact that they crowned
Marsyas' statue in the Forum shows that they observed at least the
rhetoric of the tyrannicide tradition. For Marsyas, the companion of
Liber Pater, was for the Romans the symbol of *liberty*.[18]

13. Ibid. 19.3, 24.3.
14. Caes. *Bell. Gall.* I 44.12; Suet. *Jul.* 74.1.
15. Plut. *Pomp.* 42.1; see C.T.H.R. Ehrhardt, 'Roman Coin Types and the Roman
Republic', *Jahrbuch für Numismatik und Geldgeschichte* 34 (1984) 41–53.
16. Cic. *ad Att.* IX 10.3 (49 BC); *Phil.* II 26, 34 (47 and 45 BC); *Marc.* 21–23
(46 BC).
17. Dio LIV 3.3–4 (22 BC); LV 10.15, Velleius II 100.3–5 (2 BC).
18. Pliny *Nat. Hist.* VII 149, XXI 9; Servius on *Aeneid* IV 58.

The continuity of Roman ideas on tyranny is interestingly illustrated by the popularity of Atreus and Thyestes as a theme for drama. Accius' famous 'oderint dum metuant', which Seneca saw as a motto for the Sullan age, was quoted by Cicero as an awful warning in political speeches in 56 and 44 BC.[19] One of the assassins of Caesar, Cassius of Parma, was supposed to have written a *Thyestes*. The story was that Q. Varius, sent by Octavian to kill Cassius, took away the books in his desk after the murder, and produced the *Thyestes* as his own work.[20] Whether true or not, it shows that some people, at least, thought Thyestes a fitter subject for a tyrannicide than for a tyrant's accomplice. According to Ovid a certain Gracchus wrote a play on the same theme— and a Sempronius Gracchus was one of the senators executed in 2 BC. Mamercus Scaurus under Tiberius—like Curiatius Maternus under Vespasian—caused great offence to the ruler by writing a tragedy on Atreus and Thyestes.[21] We happen to know of an *Atreus* written by P. Pomponius Secundus, whose brother was one of the consuls in the fateful year AD 41. And one of Gaius' favourite quotations was 'oderint dum metuant'.[22]

Let's return to Josephus' narrative. It is AD 41, and the last day of the *ludi Palatini* in honour of the deified Augustus—probably 22 January. The shows are being held in an *ad hoc* temporary theatre close to the imperial property on the Palatine. About mid-afternoon (the ninth hour), Gaius leaves the theatre to bathe and lunch. He and his entourage enter the imperial complex, which consists of several adjacent houses with streets and passages in between. Leaving the rest of the party to go along the main route, lined with servants, Gaius turns off down a narrow passage, either to get to the baths more quickly or else to inspect the dancing boys from Asia who are to perform later in the programme.

Chaerea, present on duty, catches him up to ask for the watchword of the day. Gaius gives him one of his usual facetious obscenities. Chaerea answers him back with abuse, draws his sword and strikes for the neck.

---

19. Cic. *Sest.* 102, *Phil.* I 34.
20. Scholiasts on Hor. *Epist.* I 4.3.
21. Ovid *ex Ponto* IV 16.31 (Gracchus); Dio LVIII 24.4, Tac. *Dial.* 2–3.
22. Nonius 210L; Suet. *Gaius* 30.1. On Augustan and early-imperial tragedy, see Michael Coffey in *Studies in honour of T.B.L. Webster* I (Bristol 1986) 46–52.

Groaning in agony, the wounded Gaius makes off down the passage, but Cornelius Sabinus and several others are waiting for him. They kill him, and the assassins escape before the alarm is raised.

News of the emperor's death caused stunned terror in the theatre, and murderous rage among Gaius' German bodyguard. A general massacre of the theatre audience was only narrowly averted, as their officers managed to bring the Germans back under control with the threat of punishment for indiscipline 'either by the Senate, if power reverted to it, or by the ruler who succeeded' (151).

That summed up the situation exactly, and in the correct order. If the *princeps* died without an heir, then either the Senate resumed responsibility ('the Republic was restored'), as happened in 44 BC, nearly happened in 23 BC, and remained a theoretical possibility throughout the lifetime of Augustus and Tiberius; or else some powerful individual might succeed in establishing himself, whether by bloodless coup or by civil war, in the autocratic position left vacant by the defunct. Who, if anyone, might succeed in that, only time would show. But the first alternative—the Republic—was not only constitutionally proper, it was also immediate and automatic.

The Senate was called into session straight away, by the consul Q. Pomponius Secundus, brother of the playwright. The meeting started uncertainly, with a half-hearted enquiry into the murder. But as more senators turned up, including members of the conspiracy and senior figures, like Valerius Asiaticus, who openly approved of it, a mood of self-confidence quickly developed. The other consul, Cn. Sentius Saturninus, gave the necessary lead. 'Romans,' he began:

'it seems incredible, since it comes upon us unexpectedly after so long a time, yet we really do possess the honour of liberty. How long it will last we do not know; that lies with the will of the gods, who have bestowed it. But it is enough to make us glad, and to bring us together in joy, even if we are to be deprived of it. For men with a sense of honour and independent judgement, it is enough to live even one hour in a country that governs itself, controlled by the laws which made it great . . . What happened in the old days I know only from report, but I have seen with my own eyes the evils with which tyrannies fill the state. They discourage all excellence, deprive generosity of its freedom, set up schools of flattery and fear—and all because they leave public affairs not to the wisdom of the laws but to the caprice of the rulers. Ever since Julius Caesar decided to destroy the Republic, and

threw the state into confusion by doing violence to the rule of law,
making himself the master of justice but the slave of whatever brought
him personal satisfaction, there is no evil that the city has not suffered.'

His proposal of public honours for Chaerea and the other liberators was
enthusiastically endorsed.

By now it was late in the evening. Chaerea asked the consuls for the
watchword. 'Liberty', they said, and he went to pass it on to the urban
cohorts. The consuls themselves could hardly believe it:

> In the hundredth year since they had first been deprived of the
> Republic, the consuls were giving the watchword. For it was they who
> commanded the soldiers before the city was subject to tyranny.

Evidently Josephus, or his source, dated the effective end of the Republic
to Caesar's first consulship in 59 BC—appropriately, since it was Caesar's
dynasty that had come to an end.

The Senate knew by now that Gaius' uncle, Claudius, had been seized
by the Praetorian Guards and taken off to their barracks. The consuls
therefore sent for a friend of the imperial house, the Jewish client-king
Agrippa, who happened to be in Rome that winter. Agrippa obeyed the
summons as if from a late-night party, but that was a ruse. In fact, he had
already been to the barracks in secret, and urged the terrified Claudius to
keep his nerve. Now, disingenuously, he offered to go with a senatorial
deputation to persuade Claudius to lay down his authority.

At the barracks, all too aware of the Praetorians' overwhelming
military superiority, two of the tribunes delivered the message that
Claudius should yield to the Senate and the laws, while Agrippa privately
prompted his reply. It was conciliatory to this extent, that he promised
to rule in the interests of all; but it was clear that he did intend to rule.

The consuls now summoned the Senate again, this time not to the
Curia Iulia, a symbol of the Caesars' rule, but to the Capitoline temple of
Jupiter which had been dedicated in the first year of the Republic. Jupiter
was the god of the triumph—the bringer of victory, as Josephus puts it—
and the consuls knew by now that the Republic would have to fight for
its survival. But its own forces no longer believed in it. The urban
cohorts insisted that the Senate choose a worthy *princeps* from within its
own ranks. The meeting broke up in confusion, and at dawn, ignoring an
indignant appeal from Chaerea, the cohorts marched off to join the
Praetorians.

The next time the Senate met, it was on the Palatine with Claudius presiding. Chaerea was sentenced to execution. So were the other officers involved, with the exception of Cornelius Sabinus. But he kept faith with them, and fell on his sword.

It is a tragic tale, a story of heroism and blighted hope. To think of it, as we tend to do, merely as an irregular transfer of power within the 'Julio–Claudian' dynasty is both to trivialise it and to ignore its historical significance. What happened in January AD 41 was the resumption of constitutional government, and its subversion by a military coup.

We may sympathise with the Praetorians' view of the arrogance of powerful senators (224), and with the preference of the urban populace for an emperor to protect them against it and prevent exploitation and civil strife (228). No doubt the restored Republic would have been as unstable and corrupt as it had been in Cicero's day. But brave and honourable men thought it preferable to the alternative, and continued to think so even when the alternative was forced on them.

They staged their counter-coup the following year, while the Praetorians' puppet emperor was still unsure of his power. The leader was Chaerea's friend the senator Annius Vinicianus. With him were Pomponius Secundus the ex-consul, and a substantial number of senators and *equites*. The military force was supplied by L. Camillus Scribonianus, legate of Dalmatia and commander of the nearest legionary army to Italy. Camillus sent Claudius a peremptory order to resign, and mobilised his forces in the name of liberty and the Republic.[23]

But the Seventh and Eleventh legions were no more willing to fight for the Republic than the urban cohorts had been. The attempt collapsed, and an ugly witch-hunt followed. Informers, treason-trials, torture, executions, the corpses and severed heads of men and women exposed on the Scalae Gemoniae—all the horror of tyranny returned. It was a time of despair. As Cassius Dio puts it, the long succession of evils had brought matters to such a pass that to die well was the only virtue left.

Those of us who get our idea of Claudius from Robert Graves and Derek Jacobi would do well to remember that his ancient biographer emphasised *saevitia*, bloodthirstiness, among his characteristics. However, he did succeed in establishing himself as a moderately successful

---

23. Dio LX 15.1–3, Suet. *Claud.* 35.2.

ruler. Even more important, he made sure he had an acceptable and
legitimate successor. For more than twenty years, therefore, tyrannicide
was not a realistic political option.

It came back after the great fire of AD 64, when Nero had lost his
popularity and become suspicious and afraid; and with it came a renewed
longing for 'liberty and the laws'. It is true that the conspirators of AD 65
were not interested in the Republic. But others were, including M. Julius
Vestinus, one of the consuls of that year, whom they excluded from the
plot for that very reason. As it turned out, Piso's conspiracy collapsed,
and it was the republicans who got what they wanted. For in 68 Galba in
Spain succeeded where Scribonianus in Dalmatia had failed in 42. He
declared himself legate of the Senate and People of Rome, and hastily
organised a mint issuing coinage in the name of the Roman People. One
of his issues, with the legend *Libertas p. R. restituta*, imitates Brutus'
'Ides of March' type, with daggers and cap of liberty.[24] In the end, there
was no need for that: this tyrant turned the dagger on himself.

When Nero fled his palace, the Senate declared him a public enemy,
and the people danced in the streets. Bliss was it in that dawn to be
alive—and that dawn, that summer of 68, must be the context of another
strangely neglected historical document, the play *Octavia* falsely
attributed to Seneca.[25] The very fact of a play about contemporary
politics is eloquent of a sense of freedom. So too is the plot, a popular
rising against Nero, and the way the chorus dwells on the ancient virtue
of the Roman people, which drove out haughty kings (291–6) and gave
laws to Rome (676–9).

So why was the Republic not restored in June 68? Because the
Praetorian Guard hailed Galba as emperor; and the Senate and People
used their liberty to do the same. Galba too had a wolf by the ears. As
Tacitus makes him say, if it were possible to inaugurate constitutional
government again, he was the man to do it.[26] But it couldn't be done.

The year the Republic died, even as an idea, was AD 69, the year of the
civil wars. Galba's heir, addressing the Praetorians in January, had to
assume that for them 'republic' and 'senate and people' were just empty

---

24. Vestinus: Tac. *Ann.* XV 52. Galba: Suet. *Galba* 10.1; C.H.V. Sutherland,
    Roman History and Coinage 44 BC–AD 69 (Oxford 1987) 103–114.
25. See Patrick Kragelund, *Prophecy, Populism and Propaganda in the
    'Octavia'* (Copenhagen 1982).
26. Dio LXIII 29.1; Tac. *Hist.* I 16.1.

names, *vacua nomina*. Even academic theorists had to agree. When Vespasian was in Alexandria, preparing his victorious progress to Rome, the philosopher Euphrates urged him to 'put an end to autocracy; grant the Romans the favour of popular rule, and yourself the favour of inaugurating their liberty.' Apollonius of Tyana was also present. 'This is puerile babble,' he said, 'when the times demand something more practical.'[27]

So the great hope of Cassius Chaerea and his friends was finally snuffed out. They had killed Caligula; but thanks to the soldiers he would rise again, generation after generation. Say no to liberty and the laws, and what you get is Nero, Domitian, Commodus, and Caracalla.

---

27. Tac. *Hist.* I 30; Philostratus *vita Apol.* V 33–35.

2

THE GIANTS' REVENGE

It was early in the eighth century BC that the Greeks came to the bay of Naples, first as prospectors and traders, and finally as colonists. The earliest and most important of their settlements was Cumae, which in its turn founded daughter-colonies at Dikaiarchia (the modern Puteoli or Pozzuoli) and Nea Polis, 'new city', now Naples. Further round the bay, under Vesuvius itself, were Herakleion, 'the shrine of Herakles', whose name suggests a Greek foundation, and Pompeia, sited at the mouth of the river Sarno in a favourable position for contact with the hinterland. These were the Herculaneum and Pompeii of Roman times, destroyed in the great eruption of just nineteen centuries ago. The lowest levels at Herculaneum have not been explored, but at Pompeii it is known that the temple of Apollo and the Doric temple in the so-called 'triangular forum' date back to the sixth century BC.[1]

Wherever the Greeks went, they linked their new-found lands with the history of their own people—that is, in our terms, the legendary world of pan-Hellenic epic tradition.[2] The most striking feature of the bay of Naples, its volcanic geology, made them think not only of the fire-god Hephaistos—the Solfatara near Pozzuoli was known as 'Hephaistos' Market-Place'—but also of the Giants, those unruly sons of the Earth who dared to make war on the gods of Olympus, and would have vanquished them but for the hero Herakles.

---

1. See A.J. Graham, in *The Cambridge Ancient History* (second edition) III.3 (1982) 94–113, 163–95.
2. For the west, see Lionel Pearson, *The Greek Historians of the West: Timaeus and his Predecessors* (Atlanta 1987).

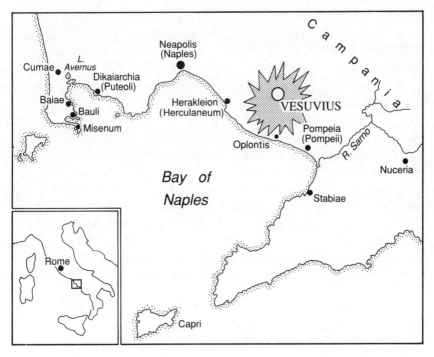

Figure 1
The Bay of Naples in antiquity.

Much of our information about these western legends comes from the geographer Strabo, a Greek writing at the time of the emperor Augustus. The sources he used were much older, and probably included the sixth-century poet Stesichorus and the fifth-century historians Hecataeus and Hellanicus, whose mythographies he rationalised for his own more scientific purpose.

For Strabo, Vesuvius was extinct. What struck him was the fertility of the land all round it, a phenomenon which he rightly attributed to earlier eruptions. 'The summit is mostly flat,' he writes, 'and totally sterile, ash-coloured in appearance, with porous cavities of blackened rock looking as if fire had eaten it away; from which we may infer that the place was once on fire, with live craters, until the fuel gave out. Perhaps this is why the surrounding country is so fertile . . . .'

The whole area was called Phlegra, the blazing land. It was a country 'full of sulphur and fire and hot springs', as Strabo puts it: 'some believe it is the thunderbolt-wounds of the fallen Giants that give out such streams of fire and water.' But Strabo is sceptical: the battle of the gods and Giants was located on the Plain of Phlegra 'for no other reason, it seems, than that the land is so fertile it was worth fighting over.'[3]

Herakles, as we have seen, was involved in this primeval battle; it was due to him that the Giants were worsted and imprisoned in the uneasy earth. The mythographers accounted for his presence in Italy by elaborating on his tenth Labour, the theft of the cattle of Geryon. At least as early as the fifth century BC, they had him driving the herd back from Spain through Provence to Italy and Sicily. That was not the quickest way back to Argos, but he made the mistake of following the coast round the Italian *riviera*—building as he went, so it was said, the first coast-road from Nice to Genoa, distant ancestor of the European *autoroute*. Many other local legends were attached to his journey, some, like the story of Cacus and Evander in Book VIII of Virgil's *Aeneid*, destined to attain the status of classics.

From Evander's town at the site of future Rome, he went south, still driving the cattle. Diodorus of Sicily takes up the story:[4]

> Hercules marching from Mount Palatine, passed through the maritime coasts of Italy, as they are now called, and came into the champaign country of Cumae, where (it is said) there were men infamous for their outrages and cruelties, called giants. This place is also called the Phlegraean plain, from a hill which antiently vomited out fire, like unto Aetna in Sicily, now called Vesuvius, which retains many signs and marks of its ancient irruptions.
>
> These giants, hearing of Hercules's approach, met him in battle array, and, fighting with the force and cruelty of giants, Hercules (with the assistance of the gods) overcame them, and cutting off most of them, quieted that country. These giants were called sons of the earth, by reason of the vast bulk of their bodies. These are the things that some report (whom Timaeus follows) concerning the destruction of the giants of Phlegraea.
>
> Leaving the plains of Phlegraea, he came to the sea, where he performed some remarkable works about the lake Avernus, (as it is called), which is consecrated to Proserpine. . . . Whereas this lake extended as far as the sea, it is said Hercules, by casting up of earth, so stopped up its current, that he made the way near the sea, now called the Herculean way.

---

3. Strabo V 4.8 (247), 4.6 (245), 4.4 (243).
4. IV 21.5–22.2: translation by G. Booth (1700).

While he fought the Giants, Herakles penned up the cattle near Baiae, at a place which ever after was known as Bauli (the modern Bacoli), after the Greek word *boaulos*, a cattle-pen. That characteristic etymology comes from Servius' commentary on the *Aeneid*, which also reports Herakles' triumphal procession—*pompe* in Greek—from which the town of Pompeia/Pompeii took its name.[5]

These legends were interpreted at various levels of sophistication in the Greco-Roman world. The normal way for an historian to treat them was to leave out the obviously 'mythic' elements and rationalise the rest. So Dionysius of Halicarnassus turns the story of Herakles in Italy into a full-scale invasion, leaving out the cattle and the Giants and making the hero the commander of an army and a fleet:[6]

> After Hercules had settled everything in Italy according to his desire, and his naval forces were arrived in safety from Spain, he offered up to the gods the tenths of his booty, and built a small town of the same name with himself, in the place where his fleet lay anchor (which, being now inhabited by the Romans, and lying in the midway between Pompeii, and Naples, has, at all times, secure havens) and having gained glory, worthy of emulation, and received divine honors from all the inhabitants of Italy, he set sail for Sicily.

When was all this conceived of as happening? Herakles was normally put in the generation before the Trojan War, which orthodox Greek chronology placed in what we would call 1194–1184 BC. Thus Aeneas, coming to Italy after the fall of Troy, is able to hear the story of Hercules (to adopt Virgil's Latin spelling) at first hand from the aged Evander. Moreover, the wanderings of Aeneas and Odysseus in their turn became part of the pseudo-history of the bay of Naples: Capri was the island of the Sirens, one of whom—Parthenope—had her tomb at Naples; Baiae was named after Baios, a member of Odysseus' crew, and Misenum after Aeneas' trumpeter Misenus; the entrance to hell was placed at lake Avernus, where there was supposed to be an oracle of the dead, consulted by both heroes.

All these are fairy-tales by our criteria; but the extension of Greek mythology into the western Mediterranean is historically important as

---

5. Serv. *ad Aen.* VII 662.
6. I 44.1: translation by Edward Spelman (1758).

having originally provided a kind of legendary 'charter' to justify the existence of the Greek cities that were founded along the coasts of Sicily, Italy and southern France.[7]

What of the *real* history of the cities round the bay? Strabo tells us that Pompeii and Herculaneum were first occupied by 'Oscans', that is, indigenous Italic peoples speaking the Oscan language, then by Etruscans and then by Samnites. The Etruscans controlled Campania from the sixth century until 474 BC, when they were defeated by Hieron of Syracuse at Cumae. But two generations later Sabellic peoples from the high inland plateaux of the Apennines occupied the fertile plain. They took Cumae about 420 BC, and *a fortiori* the other Greek centres must have fallen to them as well. Not that these Samnites were mere barbarians. Their own territory was tribal, but under Greek influence their new Campanian centres remained cities, unlike the villages of their mountain homeland. So Pompeii and Herculaneum became, as it were, bicultural—Oscan-speaking but still strongly Hellenised.

A century later they were under Roman control. After the Samnite Wars, Pompeii and Herculaneum, like Naples, became allies of Rome, and for two hundred years they benefited from the expansion of Roman power. Dikaiarchia, now renamed Puteoli, became the main west-coast port of Italy; Roman roads improved the communications, Roman coastal villas began to spring up round the bay, and by the late second century BC the archaeological record shows that Pompeii was a flourishing place.

But if Rome's allies were prosperous, they were not therefore contented. They did not get enough out of the expansion of the Roman empire, and they were subject to the increasing arrogance of Roman magistrates and commanders, against which they had no redress since they were not citizens of Rome. In the winter of 91–90 BC, the allies rose in rebellion. Pompeii and Herculaneum were among the insurgents. Though the allies had some success in the first year of the war, both towns fell to the Romans in 89 BC—after a siege in the case of Pompeii, which was captured by the Roman commander L. Cornelius Sulla. The allies got the citizenship they fought for, but their rebellion was punished.

Sulla was consul the following year, and then, after the civil war and his campaign against Mithridates in Greece, he became dictator. As sole

---

7. See Lionel Pearson, *Yale Classical Studies* 24 (1975) 171–95.

ruler of Rome in 81BC, he had to deal with centres of resistance still hostile to his authority, and he had to reward the veterans of three major wars. He solved both problems at once by settling his ex-servicemen in colonies all over Italy. Pompeii was one of them. 'Enemy' land was confiscated, and the ruling families of the allied city were replaced by reliable Romans.

The Greco-Oscan town now became Colonia Cornelia Veneria Pompeianorum. Its new titles commemorated the founder, Cornelius Sulla, and his tutelary deity, Venus. Not that the love-goddess was a suitable patron for a community at war within itself; the old inhabitants were effectively disfranchised, and the splendid new buildings that were now put up, the amphitheatre and the great square colonnade, were for the use and enjoyment of the new colonists only.[8]

A new covered theatre was also built, by the same two local oligarchs who were responsible for the amphitheatre. One of them, C. Quinctius Valgus, is known from Cicero, and from inscriptions found at other sites, as a great landowner with estates all over southern Italy that he had picked up cheap in Sulla's proscriptions. The other, M. Porcius, was a wine exporter; amphoras with his stamp have been found in several places in southern France, and the wine that filled them no doubt came from vineyards on the fertile slopes of Vesuvius.

Eventually the wounds healed, and a *modus vivendi* evolved. There seem to have been no equivalent traumas at the next great upheaval in Roman history, the civil wars which eventually brought Augustus to sole power; but a generation after that, local politics were once more fraught with discord. We do not know why, but from AD 41 to 52 no municipal magistrates were elected at Pompeii, and it seems that the city had an 'emergency' government of men appointed from outside by the emperor.[9] Even when things got back to normal, local rivalry with the neighbouring town of Nuceria broke out violently in the notorious amphitheatre riot of AD 59, when many visiting Nucerians were killed or injured. Tacitus, who reports the fracas, calls it a characteristic example of small-town disorder (*oppidana lascivia*).[10] It may have been because

---

8. Cic. *Sull.* 60–1, with my note in *Liverpool Classical Monthly* 2 (1977) 21–22.

9. See Paavo Castrén, *Ordo Populusque Pompeianus: Polity and Society in Roman Pompeii* (Rome 1975).

10. Tac. *Ann.* XIV 17.

of imperial disapproval that little help was given from Rome when the towns were seriously damaged by an earthquake in AD 62. Reconstruction was slow, and much remained to be done seventeen years later when the final disaster struck.

Vesuvius erupted on August 24th, AD 79. Here is Martial's urbane reaction:[11]

> *Vesuvio*, cover'd with the fruitful vine,
> Here flourish'd once, and ran with floods of wine.
> Here *Bacchus* oft to the cool shades retir'd,
> And his own native *Nisa* less admir'd;
> Oft to the mountain's airy tops advanc'd,
> The frisking satyrs on the summets danc'd;
> *Alcides* here, here *Venus* grac'd the shore,
> Nor lov'd her fav'rite *Lacedaemon* more:
> Now piles of ashes, spreading all around,
> In undistinguish'd heaps deform the ground,
> The Gods themselves the ruin'd seats bemoan,
> And blame the mischiefs that themselves have done.

Bacchus and the fruitful vine remind us of the fertility of the area, which impressed Strabo, and the vineyards of M. Porcius, the Sullan magistrate. But Venus and Hercules ('Alcides') are also there: the poet alludes not only to the patron goddess of Sulla's colony, but also to the legendary founder of the doomed towns. Legend and history are not differentiated. Nor are they even in the pages of the sober historian Cassius Dio:

> Numbers of huge men appeared of superhuman size, such as the Giants are represented; on the mountain, and in the countryside and cities around it, by day and night they were seen roaming the earth and wandering through the air . . . Then there was a sudden, portentous crash, as if the mountains were collapsing. Huge rocks bounced up as high as the very summits; there was fire everywhere and endless smoke, darkening the whole sky and blotting out the sun as if it were eclipsed. Light became darkness, day became night. People thought the Giants were rising in revolt, for now too their numerous phantom shapes appeared in the smoke, and a sound as of war-trumpets could be heard.

---

11. IV 44: translation by Joseph Addison (1705).

Though Dio was writing more than a century after the event, his account may still have some psychological validity. An eye-witness, the younger Pliny, describes the flames, the reek of sulphur, the black and dreadful cloud that descended to blot out everything in utter darkness, and the terrified refugees who believed that the gods were no more.[12]

Old legends can sometimes seem appallingly real. In the din and dark and terror of that day, the people of Pompeii and Herculaneum might well believe that the once-defeated Giants had broken out of their prison in the earth and were taking their terrible vengeance upon gods and men.

---

12. Dio LXVI 22.2–23.1; Pliny *Ep.* VI 20.14f.

3

JULIUS CAESAR AND THE
MAPPA MUNDI

Three medieval world maps

In 1988 the Dean and Chapter of Hereford proposed to fund the upkeep of their Cathedral by selling one of its treasures—a masterpiece of medieval cartography, Richard of Haldingham's *mappa mundi* (world map) which hung in the north aisle of the choir (Plate I). There was an outcry of public indignation, and eventually, with the help of the National Heritage Memorial Fund and Mr John Paul Getty, it was agreed that the *mappa mundi* should be in the hands of a trust, and exhibited in a purpose-built museum attached to the Cathedral.

Haldingham was a manor belonging to the prebendal church of Sleaford in Lincolnshire, and it may have been while he was a canon of Lincoln in the 1270s that Richard of Haldingham started work on his map. By 1290, however, he was in the household of Bishop Swinfield of Hereford, and so the completed work was presented to his new diocese, which treasured it for seven hundred years.[1]

Abbreviations

GLM: A. Riese (ed.), *Geographi Latini Minores* (Heilbronn 1878, repr. Hildesheim 1964).

LQS: C. Nicolet and P. Gautier Dalché, 'Les "quatre sages" de Jules César et la mesure du monde selon Julius Honorius: réalité antique et tradition médiéval', *Journal des Savants* (1987) 157–218.

1. W.N. Yates, 'The Authorship of the Hereford Mappa Mundi and the Career of Richard De Bello', *Trans. Woolhope Naturalists' Field Club* 41 (1973) 165–72.

It is painted on a single skin of vellum about 137 cm × 163 cm (54″ × 65″). In form, it is a sophisticated version of the medieval 'T-O' map, in which the three continents were schematically divided by a T within an O, the upper segment representing Asia, the lower left Europe, the lower right Africa.[2] Jerusalem is in the centre, and at the top, below a scene of the Last Judgement, the Earthly Paradise is represented in the far East. In the decorative border round the edge of the vellum runs the following legend, in bold and handsome script:

> A Iulio Cesare orbis terrarum metiri cepit: a Nicodoxo omnis oriens dimensus est: a Teodoco septemtrion et occidens dimensus est: a Policlito meridiana pars dimensus est.

> The world was first measured by Julius Caesar; the whole of the east was measured out by Nicodoxus, the north and west by Teodocus, the southern part by Policlitus.

In the bottom left-hand corner (Plate IIa), Nicodoxus, Theodocus (as he is now called) and Policlitus are portrayed receiving their commission from the emperor. The document reads:

> Ite in orbem universum: et de omni eius continentia referte ad senatum: et ad istam confirmandam huic scripto sigillum meum apposui.

> Go forth into the whole world, and report to the Senate on all its extent. And in confirmation thereof I have placed my seal on this ordinance.

The seal duly hangs from the document, bearing the inscription 's[igillum] Augusti Cesaris imperatoris'. Above the emperor—who is now Augustus, not Julius Caesar at all—is a text from scripture, the first verse of the second chapter of St Luke's Gospel, in the Latin of the Vulgate: 'Exiit edictum ab Augusto Cesare ut describeretur universus orbis.'

---

2. For all matters relating to ancient and medieval cartography, see the magnificent first volume of *The History of Cartography*, ed. J.B. Hartley and D. Woodward (Chicago 1987), esp. pp. 201–79 (by O.A.W. Dilke) and 286–370 (by David Woodward). Also O.A.W. Dilke, *Greek and Roman Maps* (London 1985), and C. Nicolet, *L'inventaire du monde* (Paris 1988).

The verb in St Luke's original Greek was *apographein*, to register or enrol, as in a census. King James' translators later rendered the verse 'There went out a decree from Caesar Augustus that all the world should be *taxed'*—and rightly, since the Roman census was mainly for the purpose of taxation. However, since *graphein* in Greek is the same as *scribere* in Latin (both mean to write or draw), St Jerome understandably translated *apo-graphein* as *de-scribere*, with the result that the Vulgate attributes to Augustus not an enrolment or registration, but a 'description' of the whole world, which a medieval reader would naturally understand as a mapping survey.

A very recent discovery in the archives of the Duchy of Cornwall has revealed part of a *mappa mundi* very close in date to the Hereford one. It is thought to have been commissioned by Edmund, Earl of Cornwall, for the newly-founded Ashridge College, Buckinghamshire, in about 1285.[3] The bottom right-hand corner survives, with an extensive inscription which may be translated as follows:[4]

> The eastern tract, measured out by Nicodoxus[?], has seven seas, nine islands, thirty-one mountains, ten provinces, sixty-six towns, twenty-two rivers, and fifty-one peoples. The southern part, measured out by Polliclitus, has two seas, seventeen islands, six mountains, twelve provinces, sixty-four towns, two rivers, and very many peoples. The northern and western part, measured out by Theodotus, has eleven seas, forty islands, twenty-two mountains, twenty-four provinces, one hundred and twenty-five towns, twenty-one rivers, and many peoples.
>
> In this true book, as if on some small notice-board, we have marked down certain causes of the sky, situations of lands and spaces of the sea, so that the reader may peruse them in a short space and discover in a brief compendium the etymologies [and] causes of them.

It is likely that both the Cornwall and the Hereford maps derive from the lost world map made in 1235 for Henry III's audience-chamber at Westminster, which is known today only from a tiny illustration in a psalter of about 1260 in the British Library.[5]

---

3. G. Haslam, 'The Duchy of Cornwall Map Fragment', in *Géographie du monde au moyen âge et à la Renaissance*, ed. M. Pellekiev (Paris 1989) 33–44.

4. Text at p. 227 below.

5. See Harley and Woodward (n. 2 above) 350.

A third *mappa mundi*, dating from about the same time as Henry III's, was painted under the guidance of Gervase of Tilbury for a North German ruler. It hung behind the high altar of the convent of Ebstorf in Lower Saxony until 1845, when it was transferred to the Historical Museum at Hannover; in 1943 it was destroyed by allied bombing. The Ebstorf map was similar to the Hereford and Cornwall examples but on a much larger scale (8 m × 7.5 m). It had a short Latin inscription written inconspicuously at the upper right:[6]

> *Mappa* means 'plan', whence *mappa mundi*, i.e. 'plan of the world'. This Julius Caesar first instituted, by sending out commissioners throughout the length and breadth of the whole world. He brought together, as it were beneath the glance of a single page, territories, provinces, islands, states, shallows, marshes, seas, mountains and rivers. This indeed provides no small advantage to readers and direction to travellers, and the [. . .] of pleasant sightseeing of [. . .] things.

It is clear that the annotators of all three maps were selecting items from a common source. Ebstorf and Hereford have Julius Caesar; Hereford and Cornwall have the three names of surveyors; Ebstorf and Cornwall refer to the convenience of consultation. Cornwall implies that the common source gave detailed numbers and categories of geographical features; Hereford implies that it referred to Augustus and the passage in St Luke's gospel. It is an obvious guess that this 'base text' was the inscription of the lost Westminster map. But where did the king's cartographer get his information from? And how much of it makes genuine historical sense?

The survey of the world

Two texts from late antiquity, both probably written in the late fourth or the fifth century AD, provide the earliest extant account of Julius Caesar's survey of the world. The first is in the geographical treatise of 'Julius

---

6. W. Rosien, *Die Ebstorfer Weltkarte* (Hannover 1952); Harley and Woodward 307–9; A. Wolf in *Géographie du monde* (n. 3 above) 51–68. Text at p. 227 below.

Honorius the orator';[7] the second, rather longer, is in the *Cosmography* of an author conventionally known as 'Aethicus' but in fact anonymous.[8]

The short version runs as follows:

> In the consulship of Julius Caesar and M. Antonius [44 BC], the whole world was traversed by four wise and chosen men: the east by Nicodoxus, the west by Didymus, the north by Theodotus, the south by Polyclitus. The east was measured in 21 years 5 months and 9 days, from the above consulship to that of Augustus (for the fourth time) and Crassus [30 BC]. The western part was measured in 26 years 3 months and 17 days, from the above consulship to that of Augustus (for the seventh time) and Agrippa [27 BC]. The northern part was measured in 29 years 8 months, from the above consulship to the tenth consulship of Augustus [24 BC]. The southern part was measured in 32 years 1 month and 20 days, from the above consulship to that of Saturninus and Cinna [garbled form of 19 BC].

The version in 'Aethicus' is rather more flowery:

> I have discovered, by careful and vigilant reading, that the Senate and People of Rome, the masters of the whole world, conquerors and rulers of the globe, at the time when their triumphs reached everything that lies under heaven, discovered that the whole earth is surrounded by a border of ocean; and in order not to leave it unknown to posterity, having subjugated the world by their prowess, they marked everything with their own boundary, wherever the earth extends. And lest anything should escape their godlike mind, which is the mistress of all things, they traced out what they had conquered[?] according to the four cardinal points of the sky, and by their celestial wisdom announced that everything that is surrounded by the ocean consists of three parts, meaning Asia, Europe and Africa . . .

There follows a discussion, expanded from Orosius' *Historia adversus paganos*, on whether Africa is fit to be considered as a separate continent. 'Aethicus' continues:

---

7. *GLM* 21–55; *LQS* 184–92, with earlier bibliography. The earliest MS of Julius Honorius (the 'first recension') does *not* contain it.
8. *GLM* 71–103; *LQS* 192–4. Texts at pp. 227–8 below.

> And so Julius Caesar, the inventor of the intercalary-day system, a man
> uniquely well-versed in divine and human matters, while he held the
> *fasces* of his own consulship, resolved by decree of the Senate that the
> whole world, now Roman in name, should be measured, through the
> agency of men of great wisdom endowed with all the virtues of
> philosophy. Therefore, in the consulship of Julius Caesar and M.
> Antonius . . .

He goes on to repeat, with only a few extra flourishes, the account of the
four surveys, and the lengths of time they took, as in the version quoted
above.[9] But he adds this final sentence:

> So the whole world was traversed by surveyors within 32 years, and a
> report on all its extent was made to the Senate.

Both versions go on to enumerate the seas, islands, mountains,
provinces, towns, rivers and peoples in the four parts of the world (in the
order east, west, north, south). The numerals vary somewhat between
the versions, and between the individual manuscripts of each version,
but even so there are clear correspondences with those given on the
Cornwall map. Hereford and Cornwall, however, have only three
surveyors. Honorius and 'Aethicus' give us four, one for each of the
cardinal points; in fact, their cosmography is relentlessly quadripartite,
though 'Aethicus' goes on to add an inconsistent tripartite description
drawn from Orosius.[10]

We can glimpse some of the ways in which the two versions of
Caesar's world survey were transmitted through the Middle Ages. In the
sixth century, the scholar-statesman Cassiodorus prescribed Julius
Honorius' *Cosmography* as required reading for the monks at Vivarium,
his monastery in Calabria; perhaps for that reason among others, the text
is known to have been read and copied in Italy in the seventh, eighth and
ninth centuries.[11] It also circulated in Spain, where after the Arab
conquest of 711 it was known and used by the country's new masters.
(An Arab chronicle of Spain, re-translated into Latin, preserves the names

---

9. He gives the period for the northern survey (incomplete in the shorter
   version) as 29 years, 8 months and 10 days.
10. *GLM* 56–70 (Orosius), 90–103 ('Aethicus').
11. Cassiod. *Inst. div. litt.* 25; *LQS* 162–3, 187–90.

of the four surveyors in a garbled but recognisable form.[12]) And at the
other end of western Europe, at the court of Charlemagne in 825, a
learned Irish monk called Dicuil, compiling a book on *The Measurement
of the World*, announced with pleasure that 'the cosmography that was
made in the consulship of Julius Caesar and Marcus Antonius' had just
come into his hands.[13]

That, presumably, was Julius Honorius. But from the eighth century
onwards it was the 'Aethicus' version that circulated much more widely,
in composite volumes containing the *Antonine Itinerary* and other
geographical and technical works. No up-to-date list of manuscripts
exists, but it was pointed out as long ago as 1853 that one group,
descended from a ninth-century codex now in Paris, has a defective text
of the 'survey of the world' passage: a scribe's eye has jumped (it is very
easy to do) from one consular date to the next.[14] As a result, Didymus
and his western survey disappear completely.

There was in any case a long tradition, going back originally at least as
far as Herodotus in the fifth century BC, that the world was divided into
three parts, namely Europe, Asia and Africa. That tripartite division was
very familiar to the medieval west through the works of Sallust, Orosius
and Isidore of Seville.[15] (Easily adapted to the biblical vision of a world
centred on Jerusalem, it was expressed in the 'T-O' maps referred to at
p. 23 above.) The accident that one of Caesar's four surveyors had
dropped out of the text of 'Aethicus' might now give rise to the illusory
idea that his quadripartite world was really the familiar tripartite one.

The confusion is first apparent in the encyclopaedia of Lambert of
St Omer, the *Liber Floridus*, written between 1112 and 1121. Lambert
incorporates the survey into a short biography of Julius Caesar:

> After this, returning to Rome in triumph, he was received with honour
> by the Senate. Then he ordered that the kingdoms of the east, south,

---

12. T. Mommsen (ed.), *Chronica minora* II (MGH auctores antiquissimi XI,
    Berlin 1894) 380; text at p. 228f. below.
13. Dicuil *De mensura orbis terrae* 6.20, 6.37; text and commentary in
    J.J. Tierney (ed.), *Scriptores Latini Hiberniae* V (Dublin 1967).
14. K.A.F. Pertz, *De cosmographia Ethici libri tres* (Berlin 1853) 57, 63;
    cf. *LQS* 204.
15. Herodotus II 16.1, IV 42.1; Sallust *Bellum Iugurthinum* 17.3; Orosius *Hist.*
    I 2; Isidore *De natura rerum* 48, *Etymologiae* XIV 2.

north and west, and the provinces and islands, should be measured by
three men of great wisdom, namely Nicodoxus and Pollyclito [*sic*] and
Theodotus . . .

Immediately below this passage is a painting of the emperor Augustus
holding a tripartite 'T-O' globe, with the verse from St Luke (*Exiit
edictum*, etc.) inscribed round the image.[16] In an earlier passage, headed
'On the three parts of the world', Lambert had referred to the rivers of
the east, west, north and south. Later, however, he announces 'Europe
the fourth part of the world':[17]

It was measured by Theodotus when Julius Caesar was emperor. It is
called the third part but it is really the fourth, since Asia contains two
parts, Africa a third and Europe a fourth. Europe has 11 seas, 40 islands,
20 provinces, 21 mountains. It also has 120 towns, 21 rivers, and
various peoples 33 in number.

We are very close here to the common source of the Ebstorf, Hereford
and Cornwall map-makers.

Their intellectual world is best illustrated by the voluminous works of
Albertus Magnus (1193–1280), which have been described as 'the
greatest repository of Aristotelian science of the Christian Middle Ages'.
At the beginning of the third book of his *De natura locorum*, written at
Cologne between 1251 and 1254, Albert too combines St Luke with the
defective text of 'Aethicus'. He slides rather evasively over the
inconsistency between Augustus and Julius Caesar, and hazards his own
explanation for the absence of a surveyor of the west:[18]

My main purpose in this description [of the world] is to imitate that
made under Augustus Caesar. He was the first to order 'that the whole
world should be described'; true, certain emperors before him had also
made the attempt, but it was he who brought about the completion of

16. A. Derolez (ed.), *Lamberti S. Audomeri canonici Liber Floridus* . . . (Gent
    1968) 280; text at p. 229 below.
17. Ibid. 106, 481.
18. P. Hossfeld (ed.), *Alberti Magni ordinis fratrum praedicatorum De natura
    loci* . . . (Munster 1980) 29; text at p. 229 below. The quotation is from
    J.K. Wright, *Geographical Lore of the Time of the Crusades* (New York 1925)
    406f.

it throughout the four habitable parts, by sending out commissioners to measure and describe the world. The eastern parts were described by a certain Nocodoxus, a philosopher; the northern by Theodotus, another philosopher; the wise Polyclitus described the southern parts; the Romans already knew the western parts through their own journeyings, since their domains and their roads were predominantly in the west. And so the description of the whole world was completed in 32 years, and all its extent, as it then was, was reported to the Senate.

The Hereford map-maker needed no such stratagem: he (or his source) simply added the western survey to Theodotus' northern one. The inscription is so laid out that the name of Nicodoxus (east) is next to Asia on the map, that of 'Policlitus' (south) next to Africa, and that of 'Teodocus' (north and west) next to Europe. Similarly, a north-Italian chronicler a century later, using 'Aethicus' and the *Antonine Itinerary* that was bound with it, remarks that the Senate ordered a survey of the world 'in Europe, Asia and Africa'.[19]

Our last witness brings us to the Renaissance and the age of the printed book. Felix Hemmerlein ('little hammer', Latinised as Malleolus) was a learned cleric of Zurich. About 1445 he dedicated to Duke Albrecht VI of Austria a dialogue *On Nobility and Rusticity*, 'packed full', the title-page assures us, 'with the sayings, histories and pleasantries of sacred Theology, the laws, the Philosophers and the poets.'[20] In chapter 104, he gives at length the account of Julius Caesar's survey that we know from 'Aethicus'. But then he goes on:

So in his time he began [the world survey] in a praiseworthy manner; and after his death Octavian Augustus brought it to a careful conclusion in this way: the whole world was traversed by two hundred surveyors over a period of 32 years, and all its extent was reported to the above-mentioned Octavian and the Senate.

The explicit reference to Augustus taking over Caesar's project is not in 'Aethicus'. (Nor are the two hundred surveyors, but they are probably

19. L.A. Muratori (ed.), *Scriptores rerum Italicarum* VIII (1726) 474b; *LQS* 207.
20. *Felicis malleoli. vulgo hemmerlein: Decretorum doctoris iure consultissimi. De Nobilitate et Rusticitate Dialogus. Sacre Theologie: iurium: Philosophorum et poetarum sententiis: hystoriis et facetiis refertissimus* (1490?) f. 104.

the result of a misreading.[21]) Like Lambert, Albert and the Hereford map-maker, Hemmerlein now brings in St Luke:

> As a result of the publication of the faithful report and description made by the said surveyors, Augustus sent out an edict that all the world should be described. And this description was first made by Cirinus as governor of Syria (Luke chapter 2), to preserve the memory of the results of so wonderful and inestimable an enterprise, from which those who wish to know [may discover] not only places but also the inhabitants of places. And according to the truthful word of the Evangelist, everybody went to make his declaration, each to his own city. As a result, thanks to the travelling surveyors mentioned above, in the three principal regions of the world, the following were written down by name: seas, 30 in number; islands, 72; prominent mountains, 40; provinces, 78 . . . [I omit a digression on ecclesiastical provinces]; civilised cities and towns, 370; major rivers, 57; races, 190, some of which are listed in the *Acts of the Apostles* chapter 2.

These categories are given, in the same order, in both 'Aethicus' and Julius Honorius. Now, however, Hemmerlein cites his source:[22]

> All these—seas, islands, mountains, provinces, cities, towns, rivers and races—are notably set out in the *Itinerary of the City of Rome*, individually and each with its individual name, as I have carefully seen and examined them, very properly drawn and even with leagues and miles for the distances between places.

The manuscript Hemmerlein had scrutinised evidently contained several works, the first of them, on the city of Rome, giving its title to the whole. One of them was clearly a description of the whole world, illustrated in detail with what sounds like a world map of some sort.

Such compendia of geographical and other useful works were characteristic of late antiquity. One such was the collection for which 'Aethicus' wrote his cosmography; it certainly contained a description of

---

21. 'Aethicus' has *a dimensoribus peragratus est*; Hemmerlein has *ducentis dimessoribus . . . peragratus est*. Professor Michael Reeve points out to me that in a manuscript that used the *cc* form of *a*, the preposition could be read as a numeral, for 200.
22. Text at p. 230 below.

the city of Rome (though that does not survive in the copies we have), and the copyist's introduction gives us an idea of the genre:

> Here begins the Cosmography with its itineraries and harbours; and consuls' names and diverse matters from the *fasti* of the Romans, without which nobody can be among the wise.

A better parallel is the lost Speyer manuscript, which contained not only 'Aethicus' and Dicuil and other geographical matter, but also illustrated texts of *De rebus bellicis* and the *Notitia dignitatum*.[23]

We happen to know, from a first-hand source preserved by Dicuil, that in 435 the emperor Theodosius commissioned two of his staff, a scribe and an artist, to reproduce a world survey and map.[24] What texts there were in Hemmerlein's manuscript, and how close its illustrated description of the world was to an ancient exemplar, we shall never know. It is just another reminder of how much survived even as late as the fifteenth century which is lost to us today. But it is certainly not impossible that the makers of the Ebstorf, Hereford and Cornwall maps had access, directly or indirectly, to material from the ancient world which we no longer possess.

World conquests

So much for the textual history. It takes us back no further than the fifth or late fourth century AD, half a millennium after the events described are supposed to have taken place. But are those events credible? Can we believe the testimony of Julius Honorius and 'Aethicus' on the world survey of Julius Caesar? I think there are three *prima facie* reasons to answer 'yes'.

First, the names of the surveyors. Nicodoxus, Didymus, Theodotus and Polyclitus do not sound like late-antique inventions, and learned geographers in the first century BC would naturally be men of Greek origin and culture. (A recently-discovered inscription reveals a 'land-measurer', *geometres*, making a dedication to Augustus at a town in

---

23. *GLM* xxviii, 71; for the Speyer MS, see M.D. Reeve in L.D. Reynolds (ed.), *Texts and Transmission: a Survey of the Latin Classics* (Oxford 1983) 253-7.
24. Dicuil 5.2; text at *GLM* 19-20.

Thessaly; unfortunately, the name is missing.) It is even possible that one of the four can be identified. A Didymus who wrote on measurements in Alexandria, the intellectual capital of the Hellenistic world, has been plausibly dated to the second half of the first century BC.[25]

Second, their four-fold division of the world, as reflected in Julius Honorius and the first part of 'Aethicus'. 'The north' is Greece, the Aegean and Asia Minor; 'the south' is the southern coast of the Mediterranean from Morocco to Egypt; 'the west' is Europe from Spain to Bulgaria; 'the east' is Asia from Syria to Sri Lanka.[26] It makes no sense on a modern map; it doesn't fit the tripartite world of the Middle Ages; but it is quite consistent with a Hellenistic world-picture, and perfectly credible for the first century BC.

Thirdly, if such an ambitious project was indeed undertaken, its successful completion after 32 years would certainly have deserved commemoration, and the circumstantial detail of the consular dates does not look like mere invention.

But a serious problem remains. The dates do not add up. The commission is dated to 44 BC, but those carefully specified periods of time taken by the commissioners imply that Didymus and Theodotus began in 54 or 53, and Nicodoxus and Polyclitus in 52 or 51.[27] To explain the inconsistency we must attack the problem from the other end.

There was a close connection in the ancient world between map-making and imperial conquest. The greatest of the Greek geographers, Eratosthenes in the third century BC, pointed out that the conquests of Alexander the Great had added substantially to the empirical knowledge of geography; and Strabo, who quotes him, adds that the same was true in his day of the Roman and Parthian empires. Significantly, it was in the generation after Alexander that the philosopher Theophrastus arranged in his will for 'the panels showing maps of the world' to be set up in the lower portico of the Peripatos at Athens.[28]

In Rome, one of the consuls of 268 BC celebrated the completion of the conquest of Italy by dedicating a temple to Tellus, the Earth; it was

---

25. *LQS* 177. Thessaly: *Archaeological Reports* 35 (1988–9) 50.
26. *GLM* 24–54, 73–90.
27. Attempted explanations (unconvincing) in *GLM* xxiii–iv and *LQS* 166–76.
28. Strabo I 14; Diogenes Laertius V 51.

probably he who decorated the temple with a map of Italy that was still admired two centuries later.[29] By then the Romans, like Alexander, were talking casually of the conquest of the world. Alexander's emulator, Pompey the Great, boasted that in his Asiatic war he had conquered from the Caspian to the Red Sea; his spectacular triumphal procession in 61 BC featured a huge trophy symbolising the submission of the whole inhabited world, and the great portico that was his triumphal monument contained a statue group of Pompey himself surrounded by the fourteen nations he had conquered. It is probably no accident that his cultured friend Cicero, in temporary retirement from politics, spent 59 BC trying to write a major geographical work, and finding the material very difficult.[30]

Pompey's astonishing campaigns had set a new standard of military glory for his rivals to aspire to. One of them was C. Iulius Caesar, who left for his province in 58 BC determined to do in the west what Pompey had done in the east. Within three years he had conquered the whole of Gaul, to the northern ocean and the Rhine. Again, the literary men responded: the poet Varro of Atax followed up his *Gallic War* epic with a geographical work (*Chorographia*), and we know also of prose geographies being written about this time by Nigidius Figulus, Terentius Varro and Cornelius Nepos.[31]

By 55 BC Caesar was ready for his next stage of conquest, beyond the Ocean and the Rhine to Britain and Germany. We know he was studying Eratosthenes and the Greek geographers, and interrogating captured Germans on the extent of the 'Hercynian forest', which allegedly stretched more than 60 days' journey eastwards from the Rhine to the land of the Dacians in modern Rumania. Meanwhile another rival of Pompey, Marcus Crassus, was planning a campaign against the Parthians, with hopes of extending Pompey's conquests to Babylon, Egypt, even

---

29. Florus I 19.2; Varro *De re rustica* I 2.1.
30. Dio Cassius XXXVII 21.2; Pliny *Natural History* XXXVI 41; Cicero *Ad Atticum* II 4–7 ('magnum opus est'). For the background, see Nicolet (n. 2 above) 45–55, and P.A. Brunt, *Roman Imperial Themes* (Oxford 1990) chs 5, 14, 18.
31. E. Rawson, *Intellectual Life in the Late Roman Republic* (London 1985) ch. 17, esp. pp. 263–6.

India.[32] A contemporary poem of Catullus reveals the heady atmosphere of anticipation:

> Furius and Aurelius, Catullus' companions
> whether he goes to furthest India
> where the shore is beaten by the far-resounding
>   Eastern Ocean,
>
> or to the Hyrcani and the effeminate Arabs
> or the Sacae or the arrow-carrying Parthians,
> or to the plains discoloured by the
>   sevenfold Nile,
>
> or whether he crosses the lofty Alps
> to visit the monuments of great Caesar,
> the Gallic Rhine and, furthest of all, the
>   horrible Britons . . .

In another poem Catullus describes Britain as 'the furthest island of the *west*'; so here his travelogue extends from one end of the world map to the other, *extremi Indi* to *ultimi Britanni*, all of them places where a young Roman might go with a conquering army.[33]

Another precious contemporary document is a letter of Cicero, written in July 54 BC, about Caesar's building programme in Rome. He was spending his booty on an ambitious extension of the Forum and grand new buildings in the Campus Martius, where one of his plans was for a great portico to surround the voting enclosures for the popular assembly.[34] This, I think, is the context in which we should place the commission of the four surveyors. A world map for a world conquest, and divided not in three parts (for the three continents) but in four, for a rectagular portico surrounding the Roman People in whose name the conquests were carried out.

---

32. Caesar *Gallic War* VI 25; Plutarch *Crassus* 16.2 and esp. *Comparison of Nicias and Crassus* 4 ('Caesar west to Britain, Crassus east to India').
33. Catullus 11.1–12, cf. 29.12. For conquest 'from Britain to India', see Nicolaus of Damascus *Life of Augustus* 95 (on Caesar); for conquest 'from the rising to the setting sun', Sallust *Catiline* 36.4, Ovid *Ex Ponto* I 29–30.
34. Cicero *Ad Atticum* IV 16.8. Fig. 2 (p. 39) shows the voting enclosures (Saepta Iulia) as they were completed by Augustus and restored by Hadrian.

We must forget the circular, Jerusalem-centred maps of the medieval world. How the Romans visualised *their* world can be inferred from the one ancient world map that survives, the so-called Peutinger Table.[35] This is a twelfth-century copy of a fourth-century map, but the fourth-century map in its turn was based on a much earlier model, since it includes the towns destroyed by Vesuvius in AD 79. What is important about it is its shape—immensely elongated on the east–west axis, it was originally 675 cm wide by 34 cm high. The world as conceived by the Greeks and Romans had been enormously extended eastwards (by Alexander) and westwards (by Rome), but to north and south it soon petered out into Scythian forest and Saharan sand. Catullus' poem confirms for the first century BC what the Peutinger Table attests for a later period, that the Romans measured the extent of the world not from north to south but from east to west—from India to Britain. So the long wall of a public portico was the ideal site for a world map, as it had been for Theophrastus in Athens.

I imagine that in 54 BC Caesar was hoping to collaborate with Crassus. His own projected conquest of Britain and Germany would provide the new data for the west; Crassus' Parthian campaign would do the same for the east. So Didymus and Theodotus were commissioned in 54 BC to plan the west and north sides of the colonnade. Who was to do the other two we do not know, for Crassus' expedition was wiped out at Carrhae in Syria in 53 BC; thirty thousand Romans died, and the conquest of the far east was abandoned. So too was that of the far west. Serious rebellions brought Caesar back from Britain, and for two very busy years he was fully extended reconquering his original conquests.

By 51 BC he had once more established control in Gaul. The more grandiose plans were put aside, and he made the most of what he *had* done. As one of his political supporters later wrote,[36]

> in the consulship of Servius Sulpicius and Marcus Marcellus [51 BC], with the whole of Gaul this side of the Rhine, from the Mediterranean to the Atlantic, wholly subjected except where marshes made it impossible to penetrate, the Roman state was at the peak of its imperial power.

---

35. E. Weber, *Tabula Peutingeriana: Codex Vindobonensis 324* (Graz 1976); Hartley and Woodward (n. 2 above) 238–42.
36. Sallust *Histories* fr. I 11M.

Caesar was now looking forward to a second consulship in 49, when his glorious triumph would eclipse even Pompey's. The great building programme was resumed. Now that Crassus was dead, there was no need to share the glory: if we may believe the late tradition, it was in 51 that Nicodoxus and Polyclitus were commissioned to complete the world survey to the east and south.

This reconstruction is inevitably speculative. But it is based on contemporary evidence, and it does at least provide an intelligible context for the implied starting dates of the four commissioners' work. However, there is still the internal inconsistency: the tradition alleges that they began work in 44 BC. That cannot be right if the times of completion are reliable; but *something* must have happened in 44 BC for that date to be so conspicuously repeated. We must take the story a little further.

Caesar had to fight to get his glory. The crossing of the Rubicon, the civil war, the dictatorship—all were necessary for his greatness to be given what he thought was its due. The triumph came at last in 46, then renewed civil war, then a far-reaching programme of administrative reforms which he hoped would be set in motion while he led a war of vengeance against the Parthians. But on 15 March 44 BC, he was murdered.

The plans he left unfinished were those of a ruler with an empire to govern, not those of an ambitious war-lord out to eclipse his rivals. Times had changed since 54 BC. In particular, it is likely that the world map project had by now been detached from the portico around the voting enclosures, which was eventually completed as a huge elongated rectangle. On the other hand, it was a time of grand public initiatives, like the dictator's projects to unify the whole body of Roman law, and to collect the complete texts of all Greek and Latin literature into a huge public library.[37] In that context, it is quite possible that Caesar made an announcement in 44 BC that his privately commissioned surveyors should 'report to the Senate' (as in 'Aethicus', and on the Hereford map), and that their findings should be available in the archive of an organised imperial administration. Some such document, at any rate, would account for the confusion of dates in our late tradition.

---

37. Suetonius *Divus Iulius* 44.2

Agrippa's map

After Caesar, the history of the Roman imperial world map is much better understood.

The Ides of March were followed by over twenty years of renewed civil war, until Caesar's adopted son defeated the last of his rivals, and conquered the hitherto independent kingdom of Egypt, in 30 BC. Two years later he held his triumph—another world conqueror's celebration, designed to outdo those of 61 and 46 BC—and in 27 the young Caesar took the name of Augustus, as 'first citizen' (*princeps*) to preside over a new era of peace, prosperity, and renewed imperial conquest. We know from contemporary writers that there were world-maps to be seen in Rome in the thirties and twenties BC,[38] but Augustus intended to make them obsolete. If Caesar's four commissioners did indeed report, as we are told, in 30, 27, 24 and 18 BC, it was just in time to see their data superseded by a new programme of glorious imperial expansion.

Augustus was expected to take up the unfinished business of Britain and Parthia. In fact, he was satisfied with diplomatic solutions on both those fronts. He preferred to turn his attention to territories his predecessors had never seen. His armies penetrated southern Arabia (26–25 BC) and Ethiopia (25–23), and conquered the whole of Germany and central Europe as far as the Elbe and Danube (16–8). A new world map was planned. Augustus' old friend, senior general and son-in-law Marcus Agrippa was entrusted with the project, which was carried on after Agrippa's death in 12 BC by his sister Vipsania Polla, and finally brought to a conclusion by Augustus himself.[39]

Most modern scholars assume that the Augustan project was the first of its kind.[40] But if the late tradition about Caesar's survey is indeed credible, it is clear that Agrippa's job was essentially one of up-dating the four commissioners' results. The clearest evidence that he had inherited the data provided by the Caesarian survey is the fact that he designed the Augustan map for a square portico. His Porticus Vipsania was, in fact, just opposite the voting-enclosure portico in the Campus Martius which I have suggested was the place Caesar originally meant to house it.[41]

---

38. Vitruvius *De architectura* VIII 2.6; Propertius IV 3.37.
39. Pliny *Natural History* III 17, VI 139; Nicolet (n. 2 above) 107, 266f.
40. Dilke and Nicolet (n. 2 above) are honourable exceptions.
41. Dio Cassius LV 8.4.

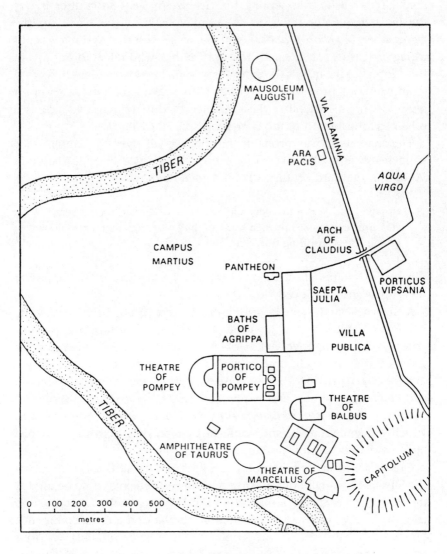

Figure 2
The Campus Martius area of Rome in the time of Augustus.

We have a great deal of information about what was on the Augustan map. Strabo, who was writing his *Geography* very soon after it was finished, frequently refers to it anonymously, as the work of 'the geographer' (*ho chorographos*), which may suggest that Agrippa was not thought of as its sole creator. The only author who refers to Agrippa in the context of the map is the elder Pliny, who knew of, and used, written 'commentaries' produced by Agrippa before the map itself was set up. It is important to remember the existence of this written evidence as a possible contribution to the later geographical tradition.[42]

The map itself was probably reproduced all over the empire. We happen to know of a map to be set up in a portico in Augustodunum (Autun) in the third century AD,[43] designed to show

> all lands and seas and every city, race or tribe that unconquerable
> emperors either assist by their sense of duty or conquer by their valour
> or control by inspiring fear.

Clearly the traditional connection between world maps and world power was still as strong as ever.

A map designed to fit in a long portico could not be to scale. The Peutinger Table gives us an idea of the sort of 'distortions' (by our criteria) that were involved. However, detailed measurements were given on the map itself, both road-distances between towns and overall dimensions of provinces and continents. Besides the references in Strabo and Pliny, most of our information about these figures comes from two late texts, the *Divisio orbis terrarum* and *Dimensuratio provinciarum*, which descend from a hand-book into which data from the map had been copied, no doubt for educational use.[44]

Once transcribed into book form, and thus detached, as it were, from the physical constraint of the portico, the measurements could be used as the basis for any shape of map. Both the *Divisio* and the *Dimensuratio* take for granted the traditional tripartite format of the three continents; on the other hand, the roughly contemporary treatise of Julius Honorius seems to preserve both Caesar's four-fold division and the Hellenistic world-picture of the Greek geographers he employed. It shows how

---

42. Strabo II 120 etc. (full citations in *GLM* 1–8); Pliny *Natural History* III 17.
43. *Panegyrici Latini* (ed. Mynors) IX 20.2.
44. *GLM* xvii–ix, 9–20.

complex was the geographical tradition in late antiquity, which we try to reconstruct from the haphazard survival of texts.

A striking example was pointed out more than twenty years ago by a Polish scholar investigating the Romans' knowledge of central Europe. King Alfred's Anglo-Saxon translation of Orosius' geographical description of the world incorporates some material not found in Orosius but almost certainly (from parallels in Pliny and the *Dimensuratio*) deriving somehow from the Augustan map or the commentaries of Agrippa.[45] Professor Linderski rightly drew attention to

> the persistence of classical tradition in the mediaeval geographical treatises, especially the persistence of data derived from the work of Agrippa. Classical elements are presumably still to be discovered in many places, in Alfred and elsewhere, where nobody suspects their presence.

Did Felix Hammerlein's Zurich manuscript (p. 31 above) include Agrippa's commentaries among its texts? A compilation from late antiquity, copied in the Carolingian age—no doubt with adjustments to fit the tripartite world of T-O maps and St Luke's Augustus in the Vulgate—might conceivably have preserved as late as the fifteenth century a not wholly garbled version of Agrippa's data.

At any rate, it was surely Agrippa who first recorded Caesar's great project, the commissioning of the four surveyors, and the Senate's decree (if such it was) of 44 BC. Who else but Agrippa would have given those careful dates and times for the completion, duly reported to the Senate, of the four surveys? It was to Nicodoxus, Didymus, Theodotus and Polyclitus that he owed the basic data for his map. And I think we can hear, in the phraseology of 'Aethicus', the authentic pomp and pride of the Augustan age:[46]

> Senatum populumque Romanum totius mundi dominos, domitores urbis et praesules, cum quidquid subiacet caelo penetrarent triumphis . . . subiugato virtute sua orbe totum qua terra protenditur proprio limite signavisse.

---

45. J. Linderski, 'Alfred the Great and the Tradition of Ancient Geography', *Speculum* 39 (1964) 434–9.
46. Translated at p. 26 above.

Those sentiments (if not those words) could well have come from the preface to the *Commentaries* of Augustus' son-in-law and leading general.

So I think we can give the map-makers of Hereford and Cornwall the credit for reporting, as best they could, what was ultimately a near-contemporary account of one of the most grandiose projects of Roman imperialism.[47] There is no comparison in either size or shape between the Hereford map and the one Caesar planned. What they had in common was the concept: a map was a message, to decorate a public place. In the portico, it showed the glory of empire; in the cathedral, the glory of God.

---

47. As briefly asserted by R. Uhden, 'Zur Überlieferung der Weltkarte des Agrippa', *Klio* 26 (1933) 267–78, at p. 271f.

4

MORTAL TRASH

Pegasus, in which this piece first appeared, generally comes out in the summer term, when most of its readers have examination papers much in mind. Let them spare a thought for Father G.M. Hopkins, SJ, Professor of Greek at University College, Dublin, from 1884 until his death in 1889. He was appointed at the age of 39, a man with a brilliant mind (double First at Balliol) but no experience of teaching beyond a seven-month stint as a schoolmaster immediately after taking his degree, and a year as 'professor of rhetoric' at a Jesuit seminary in 1873–4. He didn't mind the lecturing part of his duties—though what he gave his students was evidently far above their heads, and they paid him back for it with uproar in the classroom—but the examining was a constantly recurring nightmare.

'Several times a year', his biographer reports,[1] 'he had to mark batches of examination papers, up to five hundred at a time, sent in from the constituent colleges of the Royal University [of Ireland]. It seems to have been part of the professor's ordinary duties to carry this load single-handed . . .' That would be bad enough for anyone ('331 accounts of the First Punic War with trimmings', he groaned to his friend Robert Bridges)[2], but for one of Hopkins' temperament it was particularly demanding. He was obsessively punctilious, and his moral scrupulousness in making decisions was so acute that grading the papers practically paralysed him. 'While the Examining Board were crying for

---

1. Bernard Bergonzi, *Gerard Manley Hopkins* (London 1977) 126.
2. C.C. Abbott (ed.), *The Letters of Gerard Manley Hopkins to Robert Bridges* (ed. 2, London 1955) 236.

his returns, he would be found with a wet towel round his head agonising over the delivery of one mark.'[3]

In 1888, wet weather had added to his miseries. 'What a preposterous summer!' he wrote on 29 July: 'It is raining now: when is it not? However there was one windy bright day between floods last week: fearing for my eyes, with my other rain of papers, I put work aside and went out for the day, and conceived a sonnet.'[4] Though hardly recognisable as a sonnet in the normal meaning of the word, what he conceived became one of the great poems of the English language.

Clear light after the rain, bright cumulus driven by the wind—the weather that day was just the sort that appealed to Hopkins, as we know from many descriptions in his *Journals*, and brought out his most exact and imaginative observations. On this occasion he noticed how the wind was drying up the mud, and perhaps it was that that put him in mind of the Ionian philosopher Heraclitus, who had said, in his oracular way, 'Earth lives the death of water . . . to water, it is death to become earth.' (Had Hopkins been marking papers on the pre-Socratics?)

In Heraclitus' view, the elements earth, air and water were all mutations of the original element, fire:[5]

> this ordered universe . . . was not created by any one of the gods or of mankind, but it was for ever and is and shall be everlasting Fire, kindled in measure and quenched in measure.

The idea of the physical universe as a great consuming fire, ever re-fuelled and never failing, was very attractive to Hopkins, who adapted it without difficulty to Christian theology. 'Yet, for all this, nature is never spent,' he had written in *God's Grandeur* (1877); and the reason was the immanence of the Holy Spirit. In that poem, he had turned to the everlastingness of nature as a consolation for industrial man's corruption of the world; here, the contrast between man's 'footprint' and nature

---

3. Anon., *Dublin Review*, September 1920: quoted in M. Bottrall (ed.), *Gerard Manley Hopkins: a Casebook* (London 1975) 63.
4. C.C. Abbott (ed.), *The Correspondence of Gerard Manley Hopkins and Richard Watson Dixon* (ed. 2, London 1955) 157.
5. H. Diels (ed.), *Die Fragmente der Vorsokratiker* I (ed. 6, Berlin 1951) 168, 159, 157: fragments 76, 36, 30 (trans. Kathleen Freeman).

goes the opposite way. Nature is everlasting, man is mortal. He is the most wonderful of creatures, but doomed to oblivion.

Or at least, he would be but for Christ. Father Hopkins pulls himself up short, and exults in the *immortality* of man, as assured by the Resurrection. The tragedy becomes a triumph; the meditation on nature and the eternal flux of things becomes an affirmation of Christian belief. It is a beautiful illustration of the way Hopkins' poetic genius is inseparable from his life and his faith. Three weeks later, spending his vacation in Scotland, he used the same experience as the basis of a sermon: 'I am going to preach tomorrow', he wrote to Bridges from Fort William, 'and put plainly to a Highland congregation . . . what I am putting not at all plainly to the rest of the world, or rather to you and Canon Dixon, in a sonnet in sprung rhythm with two codas.'[6]

Here, at last, is the poem:

That Nature is a Heraclitean Fire, and of the Comfort of the Resurrection

Cloud-puffball, torn tufts, tossed pillows flaunt forth, they chevy on
    an air–
Built thoroughfare: heaven-roysterers, in gay-gangs they throng; they
    glitter in marches.
Down roughcast, down dazzling whitewash, wherever an elm arches,
Shivelights and shadowtackle in long lashes lace, lance, and pair.
Delightfully the bright wind boisterous ropes, wrestles, beats earth
    bare
Of yestertempest's creases; in pool and rutpeel parches
Squandering ooze to squeezed dough, crust, dust; stanches, starches
Squadroned masks and manmarks treadmire toil there
Footfretted in it. Million-fuelèd, nature's bonfire burns on.
But quench her bonniest, dearest to her, her clearest-selvèd spark
Man, how fast his firedint, his mark on mind, is gone!
Both are in an unfathomable, all is in an enormous dark
Drowned. O pity and indignation! Manshape, that shone
Sheer off, disseveral, a star, death blots black out; nor mark
        Is any of him at all so stark
But vastness blurs and time beats level. Enough! the Resurrection,

---

6. *Letters to Bridges*, 279. (In fact, there are three 'codas'.)

A heart's clarion! Away grief's gasping, joyless days, dejection.
     Across my foundering deck shone
A beacon, an eternal beam. Flesh fade, and mortal trash
Fall to the residuary worm; world's wildfire, leave but ash:
     In a flash, at a trumpet crash,
I am all at once what Christ is, since he was what I am, and
This Jack, joke, poor potsherd, patch, matchwood, immortal
     diamond,
          Is immortal diamond.

The collocation of Greek and Christian ideas in the title is entirely characteristic: as a Jesuit classicist, Hopkins was as familiar with the pagan authors as he was with scripture and the fathers of the Church. In September, though suffering from an affliction of the eyes which made reading difficult, he wrote to Bridges: 'I *must* read something of Greek and Latin letters, and lately I sent you a sonnet, on the Heraclitean Fire, in which a great deal of early Greek philosophical thought was distilled; but the liquor of the distillation did not taste very Greek, did it?'[7]

Well, yes and no. In the first part of the poem at least, the four elements of early Ionian philosophy make their appearance in turn: air, water, earth, fire.[8] On the other hand, the imagery is developed according to the Franciscans' scheme of stages towards the apprehension of the divine being: shadow, footprint, reflection, light.[9] The Greek ideas and the Christian application of them are hardly to be disentangled. With that in mind, we may, I think, detect a hitherto unnoticed classical allusion in the poem, which connects it with one of Hopkins' most cherished preoccupations.

At the end of his second year at Oxford, Hopkins wrote a lengthy piece entitled 'On the Origin of Beauty: a Platonic Dialogue'.[10] Both the subject and the manner remind us that among the influences on him in those formative years were Walter Pater, already a stimulating exponent

---

7. Ibid. 291.
8. W.H. Gardner, *Gerard Manley Hopkins* I (ed. 2, London 1948) 162.
9. A. Heuser, *The Shaping Vision of Gerard Manley Hopkins* (Oxford 1958) 94 and 117 n. 7 (quoting St Bonaventure on *umbra, vestigium, imago, lumen*).
10. H. House and G. Storey (eds), *The Journals and Papers of Gerard Manley Hopkins* (London 1959) 86–114.

of the theory of aesthetics,[11] and Benjamin Jowett, Hopkins' tutor as Classical Fellow of Balliol, whose deep knowledge of and love for Plato is reflected in that of his pupil.[12]

Of all Plato's works, there is none Hopkins is likely to have known and loved more than the *Symposium*. Socrates' speech at the banquet, in which he reports how Diotima, the wise woman of Mantinea, instructed him in the nature of love, culminates in a great passage on the apprehension of transcendental beauty which is very close to Hopkins' own preoccupations at the time he was both reading Greek philosophy for 'Greats' and making his resolve to enter the Roman Catholic Church.

In 1866, he copied into one of his Oxford notebooks a passage from St Bonaventure's *Life of St Francis*:[13]

> Everything incited him to the love of God, he exulted in all the works of the creator's hand and, by the beauty of His images, his spirit rose to their living origin and cause. He admired Supreme Beauty in all beautiful things, and by the traces impressed by God on all things he followed the Beloved. To him all creation was a stairway which led him up toward Him who is the goal of all desires . . .

It is easy to see how much this has in common with Diotima's instructions to Socrates, on the graduation of the true lover from desire of the physical beauty of an individual to that of physical beauty in general, and from there to moral beauty, to the beauty of knowledge, and finally to the contemplation of abstract Beauty itself. All that had to be added to the Platonic conception was the Christian God, and it was from Plato, via the Greek fathers of the Church, that the Franciscans derived their doctrine.

How much this idea meant to Hopkins throughout his life may be seen both in his preaching and in his poetry. His sermon at St Joseph's, Leigh,

---

11. See Bergonzi, op. cit. 18f.; *Journals and Papers*, 80–3 (an essay for him by Hopkins), etc.
12. See especially *Correspondence with Dixon*, 141 and 147 (on Plato and Wordsworth) in 1886; but references to Plato abound, from 1865 onwards (*Journals and Papers*, 53: Jowett's lectures on the *Republic*).
13. Quoted by Heuser, op. cit. 108 n. 5; ibid. 37 on the tradition—including Duns Scotus, who made such an impression on Hopkins when he read him in 1872 (Bergonzi, op. cit. 69f.).

on November 23rd, 1879, was on the beauty of Christ—and Plato (though in the *Republic*, not the *Symposium*) naturally suggested himself:[14]

> Far higher than beauty of the body, higher than genius and wisdom the beauty of the mind, comes the beauty of his character, his character as a man. For the most part his very enemies, those that do not believe in him, allow that a character so noble was never seen in human mould. Plato, the heathen, the greatest of the Greek philosophers, foretold of him: he drew by his wisdom a picture of the just man in his justice crucified and it was fulfilled by Christ.

Physical beauty as a stage towards the beauty of God appears most clearly in his 1885 sonnet *To What Serves Mortal Beauty?* (in which his answer to the question was 'it . . . keeps warm/Men's wits to the things that are'), and above all in the beautiful 'maidens' song' of 1882, *The Leaden Echo and the Golden Echo*. Despair at the inevitable loss of beauty in physical decay is countered by the promise that its sacrifice to God ensures its eternal preservation.

> Give beauty back, beauty, beauty, beauty, back to God, beauty's self
>   and beauty's giver.
> See; not a hair is, not an eyelash, not the last lash lost . . .

In that poem, Hopkins' marvellous cumulative rhetoric is deployed on the *mundus muliebris* (as he put it) of earthly beauty,[15] just as it is on the flaunting clouds in the 'Heraclitean fire' poem. Gay-gangs of clouds: gaygear for the girls; long lashes lace: loose locks, long locks . . . And the very 'flower of beauty' in a girl is described by comparison with nature and landscape:

> the wimpled-water-dimpled, not-by-morning-matchèd face . . .

For the beauty of nature, no less than the beauty of persons, provides an

---

14. C. Devlin, SJ (ed.), *The Sermons and Devotional Writings of Gerard Manley Hopkins* (London 1959) 37; the reference is to *Republic* II 361e–362a.
15. *Letters to Bridges*, 161 (November 1882).

insight into the beauty of God.[16] Another striking cloudscape, this time in Wales in 1877, had produced *Hurrahing in Harvest*, where the point is made explicitly:

> I walk, I lift up, I lift up heart, eyes,
> Down all that glory in the heavens to glean our Saviour . . .

The point of this argument is to suggest that the idea of a progression from transient visible beauty to the eternal beauty of the Divine is likely to be present, even if only subconsciously, in *That Nature is a Heraclitean Fire* . . .; that the physical beauty of nature was, for Hopkins, no different in this regard from the physical beauty of persons; and therefore that Socrates' speech in the *Symposium*, in which the apprehension of ultimate beauty begins with the desire of beautiful individuals, was part of the complex of the ideas in Hopkins' mind as he 'conceived' the poem on that day in July. The proof of it, I think, lies in the phrase he uses for the transition from mortal to immortal: 'flesh fade, and mortal trash . . .'

The culmination of Socrates' speech—supposedly repeating what Diotima had told him—is as follows:[17]

> 'This above all others, my dear Socrates,' the woman from Mantinea continued, 'is the region where a man's life should be spent, in the contemplation of absolute beauty. . . . What may we suppose to be the felicity of the man who sees absolute beauty in its essence, pure and unalloyed, who, instead of a beauty tainted by human *flesh* and colour and a mass of *perishable rubbish*, is able to apprehend divine beauty where it exists apart and alone? . . . He will have the privilege of being beloved of God, and becoming, if ever a man can, immortal himself.'

μὴ ἀνάπλεων σαρκῶν τε ἀνθρωπίνων καὶ χρωμάτων καὶ ἄλλης πολλῆς φλυαρίας θνητῆς, ἀλλ' αὐτὸ τὸ θεῖον καλόν . . . What the Penguin translator renders as 'perishable rubbish' is really just 'mortal trash'.

---

16. Cf. *Journals and Papers*, 254 (August 1874): 'As we drove home the stars came out thick: I leant back to look at them and my heart opening more than usual praised our Lord to and in whom all that beauty comes home'.
17. Plato *Symp.* 211d–e, 212a: trans. W. Hamilton. My italics.

You may object that even from a work so central to his ideas, Hopkins could hardly have remembered an unemphatic detail like that. But listen to his friend Bridges, who tried to spend one of Hopkins' visits to him in reading classical authors together: 'He was so punctilious about the text, and so enjoyed loitering over the difficulties, that I foresaw we should never get through, and broke off from him to go my own way.'[18] It was just the same disproportionate obsession with detail that made him so hopeless an examination marker.

It is just over 100 years since Hopkins wrote *That Nature is a Heraclitean Fire* . . .; and already more than thirty since the author of this piece first noticed 'mortal trash' while reading the *Symposium* as a set book, in Hopkins' old college.

---

18. R. Bridges (ed.), *The Poems of Digby Mackworth Dolben* (London 1915) ci, quoted by Bergonzi, op. cit. 39 (cf. ibid. 129, quoting Canon Dixon: 'he dwelt on the niceties of the language').

5

THE CENTAUR'S HOOF

At the point in his memoirs where he deals with the genesis of *A Dance to the Music of Time*, Anthony Powell describes himself as 'well disposed in the arts towards discipline in structure.'[1] The great novel sequence itself provides a conspicuous example.[2] The first volume, *A Question of Upbringing*, opens on a gang of workmen digging up the road. There is an acrid smell. Snowflakes from the grey sky hiss on the hot coals of their fire-bucket. The narrator, Jenkins, reflects:

> For some reason, the sight of snow descending on fire always makes me think of the ancient world—legionaries in sheepskin warming themselves at a brazier: mountain altars where offerings glow between

---

1. *Faces in My Time*, Vol. III of *To Keep the Ball Rolling: The Memoirs of Anthony Powell* (London: Heinemann 1980) 212; Vol. I, *Infants of the Spring* (1976); Vol. II, *Messengers of Day* (1978).
2.   I *A Question of Upbringing* (1951)
   II *A Buyer's Market* (1952)
   III *The Acceptance World* (1955)
   IV *At Lady Molly's* (1957)
   V *Casanova's Chinese Restaurant* (1960)
   VI *The Kindly Ones* (1962)
   VII *The Valley of Bones* (1964)
   VIII *The Soldier's Art* (1966)
   IX *The Military Philosophers* (1968)
   X *Books Do Furnish a Room* (1971)
   XI *Temporary Kings* (1973)
   XII *Hearing Secret Harmonies* (1975)
   Page references are according to the pagination of the original editions (Heinemann).

wintry pillars; centaurs with torches cantering beside a frozen sea—
scattered, unco-ordinated shapes from a fabulous past, infinitely
removed from life; and yet bringing with them memories of things real
and imagined. These classical projections, and something in the
physical attitudes of the men themselves as they turned from the fire,
suddenly suggested Poussin's scene in which the Seasons, hand in hand
and facing outward, tread in rhythm to the notes of the lyre that the
winged and naked greybeard plays. The image of Time brought
thoughts of mortality: of human beings, facing outward like the
Seasons, moving hand in hand in intricate measure: stepping slowly,
methodically, sometimes a trifle awkwardly, in evolutions that take
recognisable shape: or breaking into seemingly meaningless gyrations,
while partners disappear only to reappear again, once more giving
pattern to the spectacle: unable to control the melody, unable,
perhaps, to control the steps of the dance. Classical associations made
me think, too, of days at school, where so many forces, hitherto
unfamiliar, had become in due course uncompromisingly clear.
(I, 1–2)

Twelve volumes later, in the final chapter of *Hearing Secret
Harmonies*, Jenkins is making an autumn bonfire at his house in the
country, within earshot of a nearby quarry. An old newspaper reminds
him of the Bosworth Deacon Centenary exhibition at the Barnabas
Henderson Gallery: it was there that he had heard from Bithel of the
death of Widmerpool. Outside the gallery, he had seen the men digging
up the road.

The smell from my bonfire, its smoke perhaps fusing with one of the
quarry's metallic odours drifting down through the silvery fog, now
brought back that of the workmen's bucket of glowing coke, burning
outside their shelter. . . . The thudding sound from the quarry had
declined now to no more than a gentle reverberation, infinitely
remote. It ceased altogether at the long drawn wail of a hooter—the
distant pounding of centaurs' hoofs dying away, as the last note of their
conch trumpeted out over hyperborean seas. Even the formal measure
of the Seasons seemed suspended in the wintry silence. (XII, 271, 272)

Throughout *A Dance to the Music of Time*, reverberations from
antiquity are heard continually, giving added resonance to more than
one of Mr Powell's recurring themes. Those fabulous centaurs and their
world are, I think, hardly less significant for the understanding of his
work than even the eponymous Poussin itself.

Initiations

Bilious from the heat and the journey, the seventeen-year-old Nicholas Jenkins arrives at Mme Leroy's establishment, La Grenadière:

> Madame Leroy led the way through the door in the wall in the manner of a sorceress introducing a neophyte into the land of fäerie . . . Madame Leroy, like Circe, moved forward through this enchanted garden, ignoring the inhabitants of her kingdom as if they were invisible, and we passed into the house, through a glass-panelled door. (I, 110,111)

At the end of his stay, as he becomes aware of moving into a new stage of his life, the same idea recurs: 'Life at La Grenadière was not altogether like life in the outer world. Its usage suggested a stage in some clandestine order's ritual of initiation' (I, 162). With each new area of experience, each new circle of acquaintance, magic and mystery mark the transition.

Take the visit to the Templers' earlier in the first volume. The house is presented as a place of mystery, a sea-palace where any adventure might be expected (I, 73)—and there Nicholas not only meets Jean for the first time but learns from the unwitting Lady McReith of the power of physical contact. Nearly ten years later, his affair with Jean begins on the way from dinner at the Ritz to Templer's house at Maidenhead. Not the same house (though it seems so to Jenkins), it is described in similar terms: a 'mysterious snowy world of unreality, where all miracles could occur' (III, 66). The wintry scene recalls the 'frame' of the whole work, even to the muffled thuds (not a quarry, but snow falling from the trees), and just as the workmen with their tripods seem to be performing some arcane rite (I, 1), so too this initiation is introduced by the appropriate observances:

> Afterwards, that dinner in the Grill seemed to partake of the nature of a ritual feast, a rite from which the four of us emerged to take up new positions in the formal dance with which human life is concerned. (III, 63)

Shepherd's Market, where Nicholas has his London flat, is an enchanted precinct (II, 153). So is Stourwater—at least the first time,

when he meets Jean there, though the impression of a magician's castle
does not survive his later visit with Isobel (II, 186; VI, 107). Nicholas'
perceptions become progressively more subtle. It is not magic or ritual,
but curiosity, that brings him to Thrubworth when he first meets Isobel;
but enchantment is implied, as Quiggin quotes Coleridge and the old
champagne flows like wine in a fairy story (IV, 137, 146). The Mortimer
is the scene and symbol of Nicholas' friendship with Moreland and his
musical cronies, but it is only its bombed ruins, in one of Mr Powell's
most artful flashbacks, that appear as 'a triumphal arch erected
laboriously by dwarfs, or the gateway to some unknown, forbidden
domain, the lair of sorcerers' (V, 1). As for the greatest initiation of all,
into the army and the war, it is only revealed as such—though
Pennistone does call himself a neophyte (VII, 109)—when the 'arcane
processes' are enacted in reverse with the collection of demob suits at
Olympia (IX, 241).

Now, all this is conceived in surprisingly classical terms. Mme Leroy is
not merely a sorceress, she is Circe; Sillery at Oxford is not just a wizard
or shaman, he is Tiresias (I, 208, 214f.). Lady Warminster, stepmother to
Nicholas' new in-laws, has a witch-like quality later defined as that of
Cassandra or 'a very patrician sibyl' (IV, 206, 208; V, 73). And when we
come to the three *real* sorcerers in Nick Jenkins' experience, the ancient
world is omnipresent.

First, Mrs Erdleigh, encountered in the Ufford, where the corridors are
like the catacombs of hell (III, 1): she moves like a being from another
world, 'as if [she] had existed long before the gods we knew' (III, 6, 12).
For her, as an astrologer, the gods are planetary powers: Uncle Giles has
Saturn in the Twelfth House (III, 13), Odo Stevens is favoured by Mars
(IX, 131), and Isobel is ruled by Jupiter ('give no credence to Neptune':
XI, 243). Nick himself was born under Sagittarius: 'I can see at once from
your face that you are well situated. The Centaur is friend to strangers
and exiles. His arrow defends them' (IX, 131). When Pamela
Widmerpool meets Russell Gwinnett at the Bragadin *palazzo*, 'Pluto
disports himself in the Eighth House' with dire results, and Mrs
Erdleigh's last vain warning to Pamela is that 'the vessels of Saturn must
not be shed to their dregs' (IX, 246, 260). Her art comes from the revelation of Hermes Trismegistus (XI, 246): a mere layman might consult
her like the Delphic oracle (Odo Stevens, IX, 138), but to a fellow-
magician she is more appropriately a priestess of Isis (VI, 196).

It is Dr Trelawney who gives her that salutation. First seen as a utopian
simple-lifer 'with classical Greek overtones' (VI, 83), the Doctor has

moved on to more potent theurgy by the time he prophesies the Second World War:

> 'The sword of Mithras, who each year immolates the sacred bull, will ere long now flash from its scabbard. . . . The Slayer of Osiris once again demands his grievous tribute of blood. . . . The god, Mars, approaches the earth to lay waste.' (VI, 192)

Mrs Spurling, in her splendid *Handbook* to the *Music of Time*, suggests that the narrator himself uses the same sort of language of the First World War. But Jenkins' phrase—'No one yet realised that the Mute with the Bowstring stood at the threshold of the door' (VI, 71)—alludes not to supernatural powers but to the Sultan of Turkey's executioner, familiar from the canto of *Don Juan* that he later quotes to describe Castlemallock.[3] Trelawney's vocabulary, like Mrs Erdleigh's, comes from remoter sources than Byron.

One such source—Eugenius Philalethes, alias Thomas Vaughan—provides the title for the last volume of the series, dominated by the sinister figure of Scorpio Murtlock. With him, the theme of magic becomes identified with that pursuit of power through the will which is set throughout the work against the arts and the imagination. Murtlock is very much a figure of the sixties, but the first hint Jenkins gets of his capacities is a classical one, as Murtlock reads his thoughts about Roman augury and the flight of birds (XII, 20). (He is wrong about inspecting the entrails, though—that was the *haruspices*.) Isis, Osiris, and Mithras recur, mentioned by Canon Fenneau rather than Murtlock himself (XII, 134, 242), but the most startling manifestation involves the greatest of the gods of the irrational, Dionysus.

Widmerpool is in thrall to Murtlock and his cult, along with Bithel, whom he had had thrown out of the army after an incident reported to Nick by Private Stringham:

---

3. Hilary Spurling, *Handbook to Anthony Powell's Music of Time* (London: Heinemann 1977) xiv–xv. Byron, *Don Juan* canto 5 stanza 58 ('I pass my evenings in long galleries solely', VII, 168) and stanza 89 (mutes, bowstring). Erridge's butler, Smith, asked to bring sherry, 'bowed his head as one who, having received the order of the bowstring, makes for the Bosphorus' (IV, 132).

'Bithel's drunk?'
'Got it in one. Rather overdone the Dionysian rites.'
(VII, 176)

For that, Murtlock has made Widmerpool do unspeakable penance. Now ('never knew such a man for penances', says Bithel: XII, 268), he is eager to make amends to Sir Bertram Akworth, of whose homosexual invitation to Templer he had informed the school authorities fifty years before.

'I was only a boy—a simple boy at that—who knew nothing of such experiences as cohabiting with the Elements, as a means of training the will. . . . In those days I knew nothing of the Dionysiac necessities.'
(XII, 223, 225)

The tables are turned—and by this stage, the Dionysian rites have a new dimension. 'Cohabiting with the elements' makes us think not only of the ritual orgy on Midsummer Night, when Murtlock's group tries to summon Trelawney from the dead, but also of Mrs Erdleigh's ever-memorable last words, denouncing Pamela Widmerpool's necrophily: 'Court at your peril those spirits that dabble lasciviously with primeval matter, horrid substances, sperm of the world, producing monsters and fantastic things . . .' (XI, 261).

Nymphs and tritons

It is clear that both heredity and environment gave Jenkins this determinedly supernatural way of looking at the world. His mother had a taste for psychical investigation (VI, 5), and he grew up in a haunted house, an only child with an unrestricted imagination.[4] 'In such a place, after nightfall, the bravest might give way to nameless dread of the occult world' (VI, 4). The classical overtones come partly from his nervous fascination with Dr Trelawney's young followers in their Grecian tunics (VI, 66), but above all from Miss Orchard, the visiting governess, and her lessons on mythology and the gods of Olympus. The Furies, who give

---

4. In *Infants of the Spring* (above, n. 1) 57, Anthony Powell writes of his own childhood that 'life seemed all at once geared to forces implacable and capricious, their peril not to be foretold.'

their euphemistic name to the sixth volume (and drive Pamela into marriage with Widmerpool in the tenth), are only the most conspicuous members of the mythological population she put into his receptive mind.

At a structurally critical point in the story, just before the 'ritual feast' which leads to the affair with Jean Duport, Jenkins is sitting in the Ritz Grill, brooding on the difficulties of novel-writing. Those South Americans over there—how could one convey to them, for instance, the true complexity of English life? The South Americans—later revealed (IX, 232) as including Carlos Flores, who marries Jean after her divorce from Duport—are sitting grouped underneath the bronze nymph in her grotto of artificial rocks:

> Away on her pinnacle, the nymph seemed at once a member of this Latin family party, and yet at the same time morally separate from them: an English girl, perhaps, staying with relations possessing business interests in South America, herself in love for the first time after a visit to some neighbouring estancia. Now she had strayed away from her hosts to enjoy delicious private thoughts in peace while she examined the grimacing face of the river-god carved in stone on the short surface of wall by the grotto. Pensive, quite unaware of the young tritons violently attempting to waft her away from the fountain by sounding their conches at full blast, she gazed full of wonder that no crystal stream gushed from the water-god's contorted jaws. Perhaps in such a place she expected a torrent of champagne. Although stark naked, the nymph looked immensely respectable; less provocative, indeed, than some of the fully dressed young women seated below her, whose olive skins and silk stockings helped to complete this most unwintry scene. (III, 31–32)

Since love and sexual adventure form such a large part of his subject matter, it is not surprising that nymphs and satyrs should occur so regularly in Jenkins' narrative. His own first recorded sexual experience was with a nymph in a grotto, for so he describes the back room of Mr Deacon's shop in which, 'like a grubby naiad,' Gypsy Jones was accustomed to recline (II, 164; IV, 46). At the Ritz that very day is Bijou Ardglass, mistress of Jean's husband and one of the 'well-known nymphs' identified by Sillery at Mrs Andriadis' party (II,125). Pamela Widmerpool—herself stark naked—was the 'midnight nymph' on Bagshaw's landing (XI, 193); earlier, when she left Widmerpool for Trapnel, and the hot tap running, Jenkins had thought 'it was like a mythological story: a nymph for ever running a bath that never filled, while her husband or lover waited for her to emerge' (X, 178).

Young Nicholas' introduction to the erotic world is vicarious—through 'Templer's unfortunate experience', of which he and Stringham demand the details on the return of their friend from London. Templer himself is described as he arrives:

> His large pointed ears were like those attributed to satyrs, 'a race amongst whom Templer would have found some interests in common,' as Stringham had said, when Templer's ears had been dignified by someone with this classical comparison. (I, 29)

The most potent symbol of erotic experience for Nick Jenkins is the *Luxuria* panel on the tapestries of the Seven Deadly Sins at Stourwater. Jean points out to him a satyr, or at least a satyr-like devil, superintending the couple 'clenched in a priapic grapple' on a four-poster bed in the house on the hill in the background (II, 190, 191). Meeting her again years later as Mme Flores, Jenkins reflects:

> How could this chic South American lady have shared with me embraces, passionate and polymorphous as those depicted on the tapestry of Luxuria that we had discussed together when we had met at Stourwater? (IX, 235)

Priapic, polymorphous . . . and never 'Lust', always *Luxuria*. One is reminded of the 'reveries of concupiscence' tormenting Nick in his camp bed at Castlemallock (VIII, 16; VII, 193). Classical vocabulary, as well as mythology, helps him to describe the sexual life, to express his meaning, like Trapnel (X, 133), 'in an oblique manner'.

The second visit to Stourwater and its tapestries produces a most elegant piece of obliquity in Moreland's suggestion of Andromeda or Marsyas as a subject for their host's camera, in malicious allusion to Sir Magnus' sado-masochistic tastes (VI, 123). Andromeda, as it happens, or her medieval analogue, occurs to Jenkins in very different circumstances, fire-watching on the War Office roof as the V-1's come over: 'All three swooped to the ground, their flaming tails pointing upwards, certainly dragons now, darting earthward to consume their prey of maidens chained to rocks' (IX, 148). There is death as well as love. All the same, for a man who had been reading Ariosto, maidens chained to rocks could hardly fail to recall the farcical scene of Ruggiero, the rescuer of Angelica, struggling out of his armour to take advantage of her.[5]

More often, the war evokes infernal images: 'All the world was dipped in a livid, unearthly refulgence, theatrical yet sinister, a light neither of night nor day, the penumbra of Pluto's frontiers' (VIII, 12). That was an early air raid on Belfast, witnessed by Jenkins when in charge of the Defence Platoon at Division HQ. Pluto's frontiers had been crossed when the regiment sailed for Northern Ireland, in stygian darkness on a pitchy, infernal lake, with an appropriately ominous comment from Bithel (VII, 41: 'She's gone to a Better Place, now, you know'). When Jenkins manages to get to London during his leave, 'I knew how Persephone must have felt on the first day of her annual release from the underworld' (VII, 110). Later, in his War Office days, he finds Pluto in a less malignant aspect—as the acronym of Pipe Line Under The Ocean, 'appropriately recalling the Lord of the Underworld', a secret installation not to be shown to the allied attachés on their post-D Day tour (IX, 156). The ascent from his realm is now merely the return from Q (Ops.) in the basement, where

> the unsleeping sages of Movement Control spun out their lives, sightless magicians deprived eternally of the light of the sun, while, by their powerful arts, they projected armies or individuals over land and sea or through the illimitable wastes of the air. . . . Like Orpheus or Herakles returning from the silent shades of Tartarus, I set off upstairs again, the objective now Finn's room on the second floor. (IX, 35, 37)

This last allusion has tempted one critic into interpreting *A Dance to the Music of Time* in terms of a mythic opposition between Orpheus and Mars; other 'mythical patterns' are then derived from Jenkins' casual reflection that Albert, landlord of the Bellevue Hotel, is like Sisyphus (in

---

5. *Orlando Furioso* 10.91–11.9. 'Twenty years before, writing a book about Robert Burton and his *Anatomy of Melancholy*, I had need to glance at Ariosto's epic, Burton being something of an Ariosto fan' (XII, 30). Strictly speaking, that takes us back only to 1948, according to Mrs Spurling's chronology; but *Borage and Hellebore* was evidently published in 1947, and it is reasonable to assume that Jenkins was already working on Burton during the war, just as Mr Powell was working on Aubrey (see the preface to *John Aubrey and his Friends*, London: Heinemann 1963).

fact, more like Charon, in that he has just ferried Uncle Giles over the Styx), or from figures not mentioned in the work at all, like Apollo, Odysseus, or Proteus.[6] That seems to me an unsatisfactory reading, appropriate to a theorist for whom 'myth' is a critical tool rather than an author in whose mind mythological characters, like historical ones, are simply part of the furniture.

If an exemplary illustration is needed of how mythology 'works' in the novel, consider the great Tiepolo ceiling in the Bragadin palace in Venice. Its subject is Candaules King of Lydia, his Queen, and his friend Gyges.

> These persons stood in a pillared room, spacious, though apparently no more than a bedchamber, which had unexpectedly managed to float out of whatever building it was normally part—some palace, one imagined—to remain suspended, a kind of celestial 'Mulberry' set for action in the upper reaches of the sky. . . . Meanwhile, an attendant team of intermediate beings—cupids, tritons, sphinxes, chimaeras, the passing harpy, loitering gorgon—negligently assisted stratospheric support of the whole giddy structure and its occupants. (XI, 83)

The main scene is a drama of love and power. The description evokes the war—not only the Mulberry, 'vast floating harbour designed for invasion, soon to be dismantled and forgotten, like the Colossus of Rhodes or Hanging Gardens of Babylon' (IX, 169), but also the very colours of the painting, grey and saffron, pink and gold, like the searchlit clouds on the night of the Belfast blitz (VIII, 11). And the mythological figures, picturesque and essentially casual, are little more than a frame, holding the composition together but not part of it. What the passing harpy does for the picture, the cantering centaur does for the novel as a whole.

---

6. Frederick R. Karl, 'Sisyphus Descending: Mythical Patterns in the Novels of Anthony Powell', *Mosaic* 4 (1971) 13–22 (p. 19 for the Tartarus reference, which becomes 'Tartary' in the next line; Sisyphus [VI, 148]: p. 17f., 22; Apollo: p. 15, 16; Odysseus, Proteus: p. 14, 22). Bernard Bergonzi has a much sounder instinct, I think: 'Unlike Evelyn Waugh, Powell is not a mythologizer' (*Anthony Powell*, 2nd ed., Writers and their Work, No. 221 [Harlow: Longman for the British Council, 1971] 21).

Classical subjects

As a narrator, Nick Jenkins is not at all confessional. One of the few personal declarations he lets fall comes at the beginning of the fifth volume, where he first meets Moreland and his musical friends: 'music holds for me none of that hard, cold-blooded, almost mathematical pleasure I take in writing and painting' (V, 15). Later, he admits to a classical taste (IX, 224: reservations, therefore, about Blake) and a prejudice in favour of symmetry (X, 207: despite an obsession with Burton). In the final volume, among the minor advantages of getting old, he includes 'a keener perception for the authenticities of mythology', including 'the latterday mythologies of poetry and the novel' (XII, 30). What these tastes add up to is a notable sense of the continuity of Western European culture.

Jenkins' position in the world of art and letters is indicated in the final volume, where we find him at a Royal Academy dinner, and on the panel of judges for a literary prize. He makes constant reference to works of art and works of literature (invaluably catalogued in Mrs Spurling's *vade mecum*), several of which have a structural or even symbolic importance: the second volume is dominated by Mr Deacon's picture *The Boyhood of Cyrus*, the fifth by a copy of Bernini's *Truth Unveiled by Time*; Stringham leaves the stage to the accompaniment of a Browning poem in *The Soldier's Art*, while the retrospective mood of the last volume is evoked by Ariosto and the 'valley of lost things'. More particularly, art is often used as an aid to physical description, as of Moreland when first introduced:

> His short, dark, curly hair recalled a dissipated cherub, a less aggressive, more intellectual version of Folly in Bronzino's picture, rubicund and mischievous, as he threatens with a fusillade of rose petals the embrace of Venus and Cupid; while Time in the background, whiskered like the Emperor Franz-Joseph, looms behind a blue curtain as if evasively vacating the bathroom. (V, 16)

And literature provides an extra dimension to the description of places ('Pepys' on Dogdene in the fourth volume, 'Byron' on Castlemallock in the seventh), or to the narrator's reflections on his experience, serving the mature Jenkins in much the same way as the notions of initiation and magic served his younger self.

Classical works take their place naturally here. There is no shift of intellectual attitude when Mark Members, in Sillery's rooms in Oxford, changes his Boyhood of Raleigh pose for that of the Dying Gladiator (I, 181), nor any sense of the recherché when the newly-demobilized, post-war Jenkins finds the army as remote 'as the legionaries of Trajan's Column, exercising, sweating at their antique fatigues, silent files on eternal parade to soundless military music' (X, 1). As for literature, the modern novelist looks back to the Roman one. 'The court, as it were, of a military Trimalchio' is how Army Group Main HQ—in contrast with the lack of fuss at Montgomery's Tactical Headquarters—strikes Major Jenkins as he guides his allied attachés on their Normandy tour (IX, 170, 178). Later, the disquisitions of X. Trapnel on 'The Heresy of Naturalism' bring in Petronius' character as naturally as those of Disraeli, Balzac, and Dickens: 'Who cares which way Trimalchio voted, or that he was a bit temperamental towards his slaves?' (X, 216).

Similarly, Trapnel on biography and memoirs:

'Didn't Petronius serve as a magistrate in some distant part of the Roman Empire? Think if the case [of Jesus] had come up before him. Perhaps Petronius was a different period.'

The *Satyricon* was the only classical work ever freely quoted by Trapnel. He would often refer to it. (XII, 85–86)

The period evidently appealed to him: his idea of floating down the Maida Vale canal in a private barge waving to the tarts is, in fact, borrowed from Nero himself (X, 220: Suet. *Nero* 27.3). Nick Jenkins too knows his way around the Neronian age. At the Boadicea statue on the Embankment, 'the chariot horses recalled what a squalid part the philosopher, Seneca, with his shady horse-dealing, had played in that affair' (XI, 277). Perhaps that is why we hear of Petronius but never of Apuleius, though *The Golden Ass* is much concerned with sex and magic and has a narrator motivated, like Jenkins, by curiosity.

It is worth remembering that Trimalchio first appears indirectly, via a work of art. His name is given to one of the racehorses in Stringham's pair of eighteenth-century prints, which help to form the symmetry of the first trilogy (I, 9; III, 205). From the very beginning, art and the ancient world are inseparable. The first painting to be mentioned, after the introductory Poussin, is a Veronese in the National Gallery, invoked to describe Stringham as a younger version of Alexander receiving the children of Darius after the Battle of Issus (I, 8). Mr Deacon, meeting the thirteen-year-old Nicholas and his parents in front of Perugino's St Sebastian in the Louvre, points out that the saint must have been older and more rugged than his portrayal, since he held the rank of centurion (II, 11). Deacon's own paintings are ruthlessly summed up by Duport in the last volume as 'these naked Roman queers' (XII, 253); they include scenes of Olympic athletes, Spartan youth at exercise, a boy slave reproved by his master, *The Pupils of Socrates*, *By the Will of Diocletian*, and in general 'the rhythmic myths of the Greeks, and the strong legends of the Romans' (II, 3, 4; IV, 169; VI, 80; XII, 247). The 'Dogdene Veronese' and the 'Bragadin Tiepolo'—each of which has an important psychological bearing on the drama of Widmerpool, Pamela and Gwinnett in the penultimate volume—are both of classical subjects, respectively Iphigenia from Greek tragedy and Candaules and Gyges from Herodotus (XI, 21f., 76).

The classical perspective is just as clear in Jenkins' other 'cold-blooded pleasure', literature, from the Hellenizing Victorians favoured by his housemaster Le Bas—Cory's Callimachus, De Tabley's *Medea*, Andrew Lang on Theocritus (I, 39–41; IX, 62f.)—to Burton's citation of Ammianus, Philostratus and Galen on 'vegetal love',[7] which comes to Jenkins' mind, brooding under the school portico on Pamela Widmerpool's sex life, just before he meets the ancient Le Bas a generation later (X, 230). Even in *The Valley of Bones*, what small literary consolation Nick can find in his regimental wilderness is equally allusive. 'Byron', writing to Caroline Lamb about her host, Hercules Mallock:

'He to whose *Labours* you appear not insensible was once known to your humble servant by the chaste waters of the Cam. Moderate, therefore, your talent for novel writing, My dear Caro, or at least spare

---

7. Robert Burton, *Anatomy of Melancholy* 3.2.1.1, citing in the first instance the *Geoponica* attributed to Constantine Porphyrogenitus (10th century AD). Palm trees in love: Ammianus Marcellinus 24.3.13; Philostratus *Imag.* 1.10.6; Galen (ed. Kühn) 8.428. For Le Bas' tastes, and his sensitivity about them, cf. Richard Jenkyns, *The Victorians and Ancient Greece* (Oxford: Blackwell 1980) 290: 'Whenever the name Theocritus crops up in later Victorian literature, or any reference to Sicily, homosexuality is seldom far to seek.'

me an account of his protestations of affection & recollect that your
host's namesake preferred *Hylas* to the *Nymphs.*' (VII, 171)

It is in 'Lady Caro's Dingle' in the park at Castlemallock that Captain
Rowland Gwatkin sees his beloved Maureen in the arms of the dwarfish
Corporal Gwylt. And how does he recover from this traumatic
destruction of his romantic illusions? By remembering, with Nick's help,
a favourite piece of Kipling. It is the song that follows the Roman Wall
story in *Puck of Pook's Hill*: 'Mithras, also a soldier, keep us pure till the
dawn!' (VII, 90f., 230).

Moreland, quoting Ben Jonson: 'Fart upon Euclid, he is stale and
antick./Gi'e me the moderns' (X, 119). But for Jenkins, Sir Philip Sidney
leads back to the Muses on Mount Parthenius, and Shakespeare to
Pompey's galley, with Antony, Lepidus, and Enobarbus drunk (IX,
182, 170). *Antony and Cleopatra* comes in again as Nick tells Gwinnett
about Trapnel's last appearance:

'It was the god Hercules deserting Antony.'
'As a matter of fact the god Hercules returned in Trapnel's case. There
was music in the air again, though only briefly.'
(XI, 29)

However, Shakespeare got it wrong. The mysterious music, according to
Plutarch, was the god *Dionysus* deserting Antony. It fits better: when he
returned for Trapnel in the Hero of Acre, 'the fountains ran with wine,
more precisely with bitter and scotch' (XI, 32; Plut. *Ant.* 75).

What is important in all this is precisely its casualness. It is not a display
of learning, however effortless. Rather it is the unaffected working of a
historically conscious mind, one that knows and loves the tradition of
Western culture and sees it as a whole, in a continuous perspective right
through from antiquity to contemporary life.

Where the effortless erudition *does* come in, to beautiful effect, is with
a character not yet mentioned who appears in the last two volumes of
the work. Dr (later Dame) Emily Brightman is formidably well-read,
authoritative at a moment's notice on American literature, Florentine
tapestries, Casanova's *Memoirs*, Dostoevsky, or the personal habits of
Alexander the Great and Julius Caesar. Jenkins treats her with an only
slightly ironical respect—'you outrun my literary bounds' he tells her at
one point (XI, 48)—and evidently regards her intellect as of a different
order from his own. Certainly her conversational style is not his:

'Personally I am devoted to the Parthenopaean shore, although once victim of a most unseemly episode at Pompeii when younger. It was outside the lupanar, from which in those days ladies were excluded. I should have been affronted far less within that haunt of archaic vice, where I later found little to shock the most demure, except the spartan hardness of the double-decker marble bunks. I chased the fellow away with my parasol, an action no doubt deplored in these more enlightened days, as risking irreparable damage to the responses of one of those all too frequent cases of organ inferiority.' (XI 18–19)

Naturally the classical world falls within the range of her expertise. When the Quiggin twins disrupt the Magnus Donners Prize dinner with a stink bomb, Dame Emily fans herself with a menu and observes: 'This compares with the Mutilation of the Hermae' (XII, 113).

Her powers as a polymath are fully displayed in expounding the 'Bragadin Tiepolo'. From the painter's technique and the Venetian politics of his patron, through the variants of the Gyges and Candaules story and its analogies in Thomas Vaughan and the Book of Esther, she proceeds triumphantly to Gautier and Gide and their respective interpretations of *le roi Candaule*. She is brilliant on the Lydian background, anticipating by eight years the discovery by Professor Hanfmann's team of a sub-Mycenaean horse burial near Sardis,[8] but there is something wrong with her discovery of Gautier's sources for the name of Candaules' queen (XII, 57f.). Ptolemy Chennus, yes—he gives 'Nysia' along with three other possible names. But 'Niklaus of Damascus in his *Preparatory Exercises*'? Nicolaus of Damascus told the story of Gyges in book 6 of his *Universal History*, where the king is Sadyattes, not Candaules, and his consort, whom Gyges inherits, a Mysian princess called Tudo. It was another Nicolaus, professor of rhetoric at Constantinople five centuries later, whose *Progymnasmata* included an exercise to show the implausibility of the Candaules story as told by

---

8. Explaining Plato's story of Gyges and the bronze horse (*Rep.* 2.359D): 'The historical Gyges may well have excavated the remains of some Bronze Age chieftain, buried within a horse's skin or effigy. Think of the capture of Troy. I don't doubt they will find horses ritually buried around Sardis one of these days . . .' (XI, 87, dramatic date 1958). See *AJA* 71 (1967) 171 on the discovery of 'the skeleton of an equid' in the 1966 season of excavations.

Herodotus; he does not name the queen at all.[9] Still—it was very late at night when Dame Emily was looking up the references in her college library. And she was drinking gin and tonic at the time.

Faces in their time

Identify the following:

—— was more like a caryatid . . . though for that reason no less superb.

. . . his dark, shiny hair . . . rolling away from his forehead like the stone locks of a sculpted head of Caracalla.

She was like a strapping statue of Venus conceived at a period when more than a touch of vulgarity had found its way into classical sculpture.

. . . an appearance at once solid and forcible, a bust of the better type of Roman senator.

——'s air had something faintly classical about it . . . a touch of the figures in the train of Bacchus or Silenus.

The young Byzantine emperor had become an old one; Herod the Tetrarch was perhaps nearer the mark.

Answers, respectively Bijou Ardglass (II, 126), Ted Jeavons (IV, 22), Mona Templer (IV, 105), Buster Foxe (VII, 162), Colonel Van der Voort (IX, 89), and Louis Glober (XI, 79; cf. 66). They represent the antique end of Jenkins' interest in art as physiognomy.

---

9. Ptolemy Hephaestion *al.* Chennus; summarised in Photius *Bibl.* 190 (Budé ed., III, 63). Nicolaus of Damascus (fl. 20–5 BC): *Fragmente der griechischen Historiker* 90F47, 6–13 (ed. Jacoby, IIA, 350f.). Nicolaus of Myra (fl. AD 470–490, according to the Suda): *Progymnasmata* 5.3, in *Rhetores Graeci* (ed. Walz, 1832) I, 287f. Gautier could have got his 'Nyssia'—with two s's—from Cramer's *Anecdota Graeca* III (1836) 351: a scholiast on Tzetzes *Chil.* 1.144 quoting Ptolemy Helphaestion.

In fact, Van der Voort's Bacchic features are not wholly antique, but 'naturally conceived in Dutch or Flemish terms'; they are part of Jenkins' musing on Belgian and Dutch physical types, most of which remind him of the Middle Ages or the Renaissance:

> . . . emaciated, Memling-like men-at-arms on their way to supervise the Crucifixion or some lesser martyrdom, while beside them tramped the clowns of Teniers or Brouwer, round rubicund countenances, hauled away from carousing to be mustered in the ranks. (IX, 88)

The medieval world had earlier been evoked during Jenkins' regimental duties, not only by the men on parade at Castlemallock, 'cohorts of gargoyles' who could hardly be inspected without hysterical laughter (VII, 172), but also by that military romantic, Captain Gwatkin:

> He had draped a rubber groundsheet round him like a cloak, which, with his flattish-brimmed steel helmet, transformed him into a figure from the later Middle Ages, a captain-of-arms of the Hundred Years War, or the guerrilla campaigning of Owen Glendower. . . . Rain had wetted his moustache, causing it to droop over the corners of the mouth, like those belonging to effigies on tombs or church brasses. Persons at odds with their surroundings not infrequently suggest an earlier historical epoch. (VII, 76)

We are edging here away from art towards history proper, and history—or the no man's land of history and legend—is what the physical features of the men of the Welch Regiment insistently conjure up in Jenkins' mind throughout *The Valley of Bones*.

Sergeant Pendry is tall, blue-eyed, fair-haired—a 'Brythonic type', Nick supposes—while CSM Cadwallader has a stern nobility of feature 'suggesting a warrior from an heroic epoch, returned with dragon banners to sustain an army in time of war' (VII, 8, 6). Both descriptions refer back to the splendid long passage at the beginning of the book—the introduction, in a sense, to the second 'sextet' of the whole work—in which 2nd Lieut. Jenkins ponders his family history.

The subject interested Nick even as a boy. 'Well, our ancestor, Hannibal Jenkins, of Cwm Shenkin, paid the Hearth Tax in 1674—' (I, 24). Uncle Giles shows some irritation at that, as does Russell Gwinnett much later when Jenkins asks about someone's background (XI, 73). It matters to him: he is fascinated by ancestry, whether individual (is Theoderic descended from Queen Victoria? is Dicky Umfraville Pamela Widmerpool's father?) or ethnic, as when he looks for Welsh characteristics among the Free French officers from Brittany (IX, 139). Gwatkin mentions the possibility of his being related to Lord Aberavon, but is wholly indifferent to Nick's suggestion, based on Aberavon's obituary ('the details had appealed to me': VII, 187), that he might therefore be descended from the sinister Vortigern: 'thought of Lord Aberavon's business acumen kindled him more than any steep ascent in the genealogies of ancient Celtic Britain' (VII, 188).

How different from the modest pride of Nick Jenkins himself, wondering about his own ancestors in the opening scene of *The Valley of Bones*:

> In medieval times they had been of more account in war; once, a long way back—in the disconcerting, free-for-all-manner of Celtic lineage—even reigning, improbable as that might now appear, in this southern kingdom of a much disputed land. One wondered what on earth such predecessors had been like personally; certainly not above blinding and castrating when in the mood. A pale, mysterious sun glittered on the circlet of gold round their helmets, as armed men, ever fainter in outline and less substantial, receded into the vaporous, shining mists towards intermediate, timeless beings, at once measurably historical, yet at the same time mythically heroic: Llywarch the Old, a discontented guest at the Arthurian Table; Cunedda—though only in the female line—whose horsemen had mounted guard on the Wall. For some reason the Brython, Cunedda, imposed himself on the imagination. Had his expulsion of the Goidels with great slaughter been at the express order of Stilicho, that Vandal captain who all but won the Empire for himself? I reviewed the possibility as we ascended, without breaking step, a short, very steep, very slippery incline of pavement. . . . A gale began to blow noisily up the street. Muffled yet disturbing, the war horns of Cunedda moaned in the frozen wind, as far away he rode upon the cloud. (VII, 2–3)

A steep, slippery ascent it certainly is, in genealogical terms, to trace your lineage to the fifth century, especially without breaking step. Here is another continuity, more startling than that of the cultural tradition—a succession of generations connecting Nick Jenkins directly with the last defenders of the ancient world.

A European royal house might plausibly claim an ancestry reaching back to the final years of Rome—the names of Prince Theoderic and his

Proustian forebear Odoacer certainly suggest such a thing (IX, 120)—but in Britain only a Welshman could hope to do it. Celtic genealogy brings us back to Dr Emily Brightman, who corresponds about Gallo–Roman personal names (with special reference to Brittany, XI, 47), and neatly elucidates the provenance of Button Gwinnett, signer of the American Declaration of Independence: '"Gwinnett", of course, "Gwynedd", meaning North Wales—the Buttons, a South Wales family, probably *advenae*' (XI, 49). Her main work is on the 'Triads of Britain', that compilation by Iolo Morganwg of traditional Welsh lore purporting to record the main events and personalities of the chronicles of Britain from the Celtic settlement of the islands to the coming of the Saxons.[10] Vortigern, Cunedda, and Llywarch the Old all appear in the Triads, along with much else of legend and tenuous history—'intermediate beings', their war horns blowing like the conches of tritons.

Jenkins, as ever, doesn't give much away about his feelings. But he goes to some lengths to contact his old regiment on the advance into Germany, and pays an unobtrusive but not insignificant farewell tribute to the antiquity of the Celts:

> Perhaps as a result of Kedward's exhortations, the fatigue party began to sing ['Guide me, O thou great Jehovah', of course]. The L. of C. captain and I walked up the road in the direction of the cars, leaving them to move eastward towards the urnfields of their Bronze Age home. (IX, 177)

Anthony Powell is often described as an essentially *English* author. In a sense that is true, and obvious; but to leave out of account the European and Celtic aspects—respectively in art and literature and in consciousness of ancestry—is to ignore a vital part of his resources as a writer.

---

10. See Rachel Bromwich, *Trioedd Ynys Prydein: The Welsh Triads* (Cardiff: University of Wales Press 1961). In *John Aubrey and his Friends* (above, n. 5, p. 20), Anthony Powell records the families of Bromwich, Button, and Powell among those of Welsh or Cambro–Norman descent who migrated from the Welsh Marches to Wiltshire; for the history of the Powells, see the first chapter of his *Infants of the Spring* (above, n. 1), especially p. 3 on Llywarch the Old and Coel Hên Gautepec, 'possibly last *Dux Britanniarum*, whose government extended to—perhaps went beyond—Hadrian's Wall.'

In the same way, although he received at Eton a traditional public-school classical education, his use of antiquity is far from merely conventional: 'Good idea to get away from all that—what is it, *Eheu fugaces*, something of that sort, never any good at Latin. All that sentimental stuff, I mean' (X, 64). Thus Alfred Tolland on school reunions; and throughout the work, those who used tired classical tags are treated with some irony (Mr Deacon, II, 118; General Conyers, VI, 54; Sir Gavin Walpole-Wilson, X, 109). 'The classics' proper are conspicuous by their absence. Jenkins/Powell at school must have read plenty of Demosthenes and Cicero, Pindar and Horace, but they have not contributed in any detectable way to his imagination. It is true that there is Latin in his style; but what matters in his work is not the classic authors but the ancient world itself, mysterious, a bit sinister, but visible and real.

As a last example of the subtlety of its influence, let us look at the description of Pamela Widmerpool, at the height of her powers, under the Tiepolo in the Bragadin Palace:

> She stood, legs thrust apart, staring upward. White trousers, thin as gauze, stretched skin tight across elegantly compact small haunches, challengingly exhibited, yet neatly formed: hard, pointed breasts, no less contentious and smally compassed, under a shirt patterned in crimson and peacock blue, stuck out like delicately shaped bosses of a shield. (XI, 82)

'Contentious', an inconspicuous Latinism, expresses a sexual com-bativeness indicated equally by the concluding simile. Already in the previous volume, Pamela's sex life had been described as 'gladiatorial' (X, 62); now we see the gladiator's arms displayed. The image extends to Gwinnett and Glober, two very different competitors for the privilege of taking her on; 'one thought of the gladiator with the sword and shield; the one with the net and trident' (XI, 99). There is no striving for effect here, just the selection of the precise illustration from a mind well stocked from childhood.

In *At Lady Molly's*, Jenkins finds himself in a bar 'designed by someone who had also [like Mr Deacon] brooded long and fruitlessly on classical themes' (IV, 169). Precisely the contrary can be said of his creator. Mr Powell has no need to brood on what seems to come so naturally, and the result is just the opposite of fruitless. Of all the many characters in *A Dance to the Music of Time*, none is more aptly named than Miss Orchard.

6

A ROMAN VILLA

Horti Lolliani

There are two city walls of ancient Rome. The first circuit was built about 380 BC, of stone from the quarries of newly-conquered Veii. At its highest and most vulnerable point, behind the promontories of the Quirinal, Viminal and Esquiline hills, it incorporated an earth rampart and ditch which the Romans, probably rightly, attributed to king Servius Tullius in the sixth century BC.

This wall was built after the archaic city had been sacked by a Celtic war-band. It was defended against Hannibal in 211, and again during the civil wars of 89, 87 and 82 BC, but by the time of Augustus it was obsolete, in some places not even traceable among the buildings that had grown up around it.[1] For three hundred years Rome needed no walls; during the *pax Romana*, her defences were at the imperial frontiers.

So it was an ominous sign when Aurelian in AD 271, six and a half centuries after his republican predecessors, built the great wall that bears his name.[2] It has defended the city ever since, not always successfully. The walls could not keep out the Visigoths under Alaric in 410, the Vandals under Genseric in 455, the Ostrogoths under Totila in 546, the Normans under Robert Guiscard in 1084, or the imperial mercenaries under Charles Duke of Bourbon in 1527. Nor, finally, could they defend papal Rome against the Italians; on 20 September 1870, Aurelian's wall was breached at the Porta Pia, and the crumbling, backward, picturesque

---

1. Dionysius of Halicarnassus IV 13.5; G. Säflund, *Le mura di Roma repubblicana* (Rome 1932).
2. Ian A. Richmond, *The City Wall of Imperial Rome* (Oxford 1930).

71

Rome of Pius IX was dragged into the modern world as the capital of the Kingdom of Italy.

In medieval Rome, less than a third of the area within the imperial walls was occupied.[3] Essentially, that was still the situation in 1870. But the next thirty years saw a huge expansion of population, and a corresponding building boom as new quarters to house the citizens of *Roma capitale* were hurriedly constructed. One such area was between S. Maria Maggiore and the Baths of Diocletian, on what had been the gardens of the Villa Montalto-Negroni-Massimo.

The usual rectangular grid of streets was laid out. Behind the *palazzo* of the Villa (now demolished), at the intersection of what would be the Via Principe Umberto and the Via del Viminale, workmen digging foundations for the new block in 1883 came upon two Roman boundary stones.[4] One inscription read simply 'PR'—that is, presumably, *pr[ivatum]*. The other named the owner of this private estate:

TI. CLA.
CAISARIS
AVG. GER.
AREA HORT.
LOLL.

Tiberius Claudius Caesar Augustus Germanicus was the emperor Claudius (AD 41–54), and this imperial property was called *hort[i] Loll[iani]*, Lollius' gardens.

'Gardens' is really a misnomer. What *horti* meant, in the Rome of the late Republic and early Principate, was a luxury villa on the edge of the city.[5] The prime sites were as attractive to wealthy Romans as they were later to cardinals and princes. Two of the most sumptuous late-republican *horti* were those of Lucullus and of Sallust, which became,

---

3. Richard Krautheimer, *Rome: Profile of a City, 312–1308* (Princeton 1980), map at p. 245.

4. *Corpus Inscriptionum Latinarum* VI 31284–5.

5. Nicholas Purcell, *The Gardens of Rome* (forthcoming), and in E. MacDougall (ed.), *Ancient Roman Villa Gardens* (Dumbarton Oaks 1987) 187–203. For the *Horti Maecenatis* and *Lamiani*, see the splendid monograph-length article by Ruth Christine Häuber in *Kölner Jahrbuch für Vor- und Fruhgeschichte* 23 (1990) 11–107.

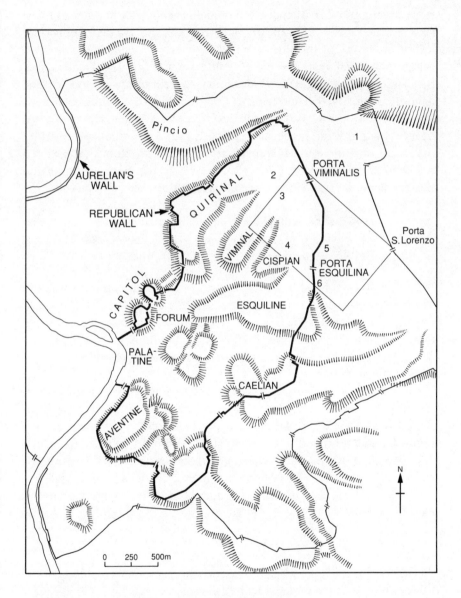

Figure 3

The site of ancient Rome and its walls. The rectangle indicates the area mapped in figs 4, 5, 8 and 9. 1: Barracks of the Praetorian Guard. 2: Baths of Diocletian. 3: Find-spot of *horti Lolliani* inscription. 4: Basilica of S. Maria Maggiore. 5: Find-spot of *horti Tauriani* inscription. 6: Approximate position of the *horti* of Maecenas.

respectively, the Villa Medici on the Pincio (1540) and the Villa Ludovisi (1621) which was sold in the 1880s to become the Via Veneto quarter.

The discovery of the Horti Lolliani boundary stones, along with two others found ten years earlier,[6] revealed a whole string of luxury villas that were created in the late first century BC both inside and outside the now obsolete city wall and rampart. The building of the Julian aqueduct by Agrippa in 33 BC had greatly improved the water supply to this healthy high ground, much of which had previously been occupied by the ancient cemetery of archaic and republican Rome. Substantial redevelopment followed: Propertius refers to 'the New Fields' of the 'watery Esquiline', and Horace celebrates the fact that

> Nowadays it's healthy to live on the Esquiline,
> and on the rampart you can walk in the sun, where once
> there was only a gloomy view of a field of white bones.[7]

Horace no doubt had in mind the *horti* of his patron Maecenas; to the north, also just outside the rampart, were the *horti* of Taurus; and beyond them, within the old wall, were the *horti* of Lollius. All three men, like Agrippa, were close friends of the young Augustus;[8] naturally, the most prominent supporters of the new regime were best placed to exploit the situation.

Marcus Lollius organised Augustus' huge new province of Galatia (central Turkey) in the late twenties BC; he was then moved to Macedonia, from where he brought the Bessi of Thrace under Roman control, and after that to Gaul. In 16 BC he suffered a defeat at the hands of marauding Germans, but recovered his position sufficiently for Horace a few years later to celebrate him as a victor in arms as well as a wise counsellor and an incorruptible magistrate.[9] In 1 BC he went to the East as advisor to C. Caesar, Augustus' adopted son and heir, in his

---

6. *CIL* VI 29771: 'cippi hi finiunt hortos Calyclan. et Taurianos.' Found in 1874–5 when the garden wall of S. Eusebio was demolished (at the other end of the Via Principe Umberto development).

7. Propertius IV 8.1–2, Horace *Satires* I 8.7–16.

8. T. Statilius Taurus (consul in 37, triumphed in 34, consul again with Augustus in 26) 'stood second only to Agrippa as a soldier and an administrator': Ronald Syme, *The Roman Revolution* (Oxford 1939) 325.

9. Eutropius VII 10.2, Dio Cassius LIV 20.3–6, Horace *Odes* IV 9.30–44.

negotiations with the king of Parthia. Denounced by the king for plotting and accepting bribes, Lollius took his own life, and earned a posthumous name for rapacity and dissimulation.[10]

Ill-gotten or not, Lollius' wealth descended to his heirs. Nothing is known of his son, but his grand-daughters were Lollia Paullina and Lollia Saturnina, two society beauties of the time of Gaius 'Caligula'. They were both married to prominent senators who would one day, though in very different circumstances, be named as potential emperors themselves.[11] Saturnina's husband was Valerius Asiaticus, who owned the luxurious *horti* of Lucullus. No doubt it was Paullina who occupied those of their grandfather Lollius, since her husband Memmius Regulus was not wealthy on Asiaticus' scale.

Both women attracted Caligula's attention. Asiaticus had to endure the mortification at an imperial banquet of hearing the emperor loudly complaining about Saturnina's sexual performance. As for Paullina, she at least briefly became an empress. Gaius summoned her from the province her husband was governing, and married her with Regulus himself giving the bride away. He soon divorced her, but forbade her to have intercourse with anyone else.[12]

A few months later Gaius was assassinated, much to the satisfaction of Valerius Asiaticus ('I wish *I* had done it!'), but we are not told whether Lollia Paullina continued to obey the imperial interdict. All we know of her social life is the frank enjoyment with which she flaunted her wealth. At one private party, for a betrothal, a young equestrian officer was among her fellow guests. His moral outrage was still burning thirty years later, when he included in his encyclopaedia a passage on luxury and empire which needs a pen from the Puritan age to do it justice in English:[13]

---

10. Velleius Paterculus II 97.1, 102.1. Tiberius detested him: Suetonius *Tib.* 12–13, Tactius *Annals* III 48.2
11. Tacitus *Annals* XI 1–3 (Messallina on D. Valerius Asiaticus), XIV 47 (Nero on P. Memmius Regulus). See Ronald Syme, *The Augustan Aristocracy* (Oxford 1986) 176–8 and Stemma XI.
12. Seneca *de constantia* 18.2; Dio Cassius LIX 12.1, Suetonius *Gaius* 25.2.
13. Pliny *Nat. Hist.* IX 117–8, trans. Philemon Holland (London 1635) 1.256–7. As a concession to modern weakness, I have divided his first paragraph into two.

I my selfe haue seen *Lollia Paulina* (late wife, and after widdow,[14] to *Caius Caligula* the emperor) when she was dressed and set out, not in stately wise, nor of purpose for some great solemnity, but only when she was to go to a wedding supper, or rather vnto a feast when the assurance was made, & great persons they were not that made the said feast: I haue seen her, I say, so beset and bedeckt all ouer with hemeraulds and pearles, disposed in rewes, ranks, and courses one by another; round about the attire of her head, her cawle, her borders, her peruk of hair, her bondgrace and chaplet; at her ears pendant, about her neck in a carcanet, vpon her wrest in bracelets, & on her fingers in rings; that she glittered and shon again like the sun as she went. The value of the ornaments, she esteemed and rated at 400 hundred thousand Sestertij: and offered openly to proue it out of hand by her bookes of accounts and reckonings.

Yet were not these jewels the gifts and presents of the prodigall prince her husband, but the goods and ornaments from her owne house, fallen to her by way of inheritance from her grand father, which he had gotten together euen by the robbing and spoiling of whole prouinces. See what the issue and end was of those extortions and outrageous exactions of his: this was it, That *M. Lollius* slandered and defamed for receiving bribes & presents of the kings in the East; and being out of fauor with *C. Caesar*, sonne of *Augustus*, and hauing lost his amitie, dranke a cup of poison, and preuented his iudiciall triall: that forsooth his neece *Lollia*, all to be hanged with jewels of 400 hundred thousand Sestertij, should be seene glittering, and looked at of euery man by candle-light all a supper time.

If a man would now of the one side reckon what great treasure either *Curius* or *Fabricius*[15] carried in the pompe of their triumphs; let him cast a proffer and imagine what their shews were, what their seruice at table was: and on the other side, make an estimate of *Lollia*, one only woman, the dowager of an Emperor, in what glory she sitteth at the bourd; would not he wish rather, that they had been pulled out of their chariots, and neuer triumphed, than that by their victories the state of Rome should haue grown to this wastfull excesse & intollerable pride?

But luxury villas were not easy for a private citizen, however wealthy, to hold on to. The *horti* of Maecenas had passed to Augustus in 8 BC, and those of Sallust to Tiberius in AD 20, both by bequest. That was too slow

---

14. Not in fact his widow: Pliny just says 'Gai principis matrona'.
15. Proverbially frugal heroes of the old Republic (third century BC).

a method for Claudius and his avaricious wives. In 47 Messallina got Valerius Asiaticus arrested on a trumped-up charge, and took possession, after his enforced suicide, of the *horti* of Lucullus. (The following year she met her own death there.) In 53 her successor Agrippina did the same to Statilius Taurus, the grandson of Augustus' friend, and the Horti Tauriani became imperial property too.[16]

Lollia Paullina had been one of the other candidates for the position of empress after Messallina's execution. Agrippina was jealous of a potential rival. The charge was astrology and magic; Claudius reported to the Senate that Lollia was banished, and her property forfeit; an officer of the Praetorian Guard was despatched to make sure she killed herself.[17] 'Private property of Claudius Caesar.' The boundary stones found in 1883 marked the end of a story of greed and tyranny.

Villa Montalto, Villa Negroni

This latest imperial acquisition was situated at the head of a steep little valley between the *mons Cispius* and the *collis Viminalis*, with a south-west aspect and a view straight down to the temples and basilicas of the Roman Forum. Through it or past it (no doubt discreetly walled off) ran the Vicus Patricius, the route up the valley from the city to the Viminal Gate in the old wall and rampart. Beyond the gate were the barracks of the Praetorian Guard.

Except for a rebuilding in the second century (attested by a brickstamp of AD 134),[18] we know nothing of the history of the Horti Lolliani as an imperial property. From the early fourth century, the old villa was overshadowed by the great Baths of Diocletian to the north, and in the fifth there rose to the south an even more significant neighbour, the basilica of Santa Maria Maggiore. No doubt the villa had been long in ruins when Vitigis' Goths in AD 537 cut the aqueducts that had made the *horti* possible in the first place. There would be no fountains playing on the 'watery Esquiline' for another thousand years.[19]

---

16. Tacitus *Annals* XI 1, 37, XII 59.
17. Ibid. XII 1–2, 22.
18. *CIL* XV 515.a.3.
19. Procopius *Bellum Gothicum* I 9.13 and 18; Rossella Motta, in *Il trionfo dell'acqua: acque e acquedotti a Roma* (Rome 1986) 203–5.

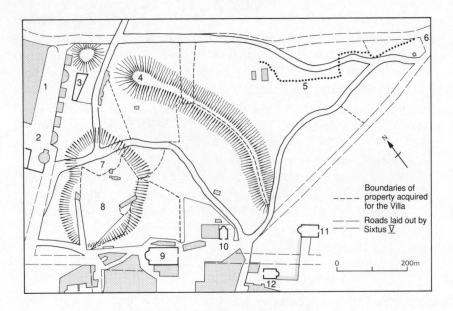

Figure 4

The area of the Villa Montalto in 1576 (from the map in V. Massimo, *Notizie istoriche della Villa Massimo*, 1836). 1: Baths of Diocletian. 2: Piazza di Termini. 3: Roman reservoir. 4: Mound of the 'Servian Wall': site of later Monte della Giustizia. 5: Line of Roman aqueduct. 6: Porta S. Lorenzo. 7: Cappelletti vineyard, site of the Roman 'underground house'. 8: Site of Sixtus V's *casino*. 9: S. maria Maggiore. 10: S. Antonio Abbate. 11: S. Eusebio (wrongly oriented on Massimo's plan). 12: S. Vito.

It was the popes of the counter-reformation, restoring their faith and their city after the horror of 1527, who brought back the running water. Pius V in 1570 restored the Acqua Vergine (debouching at the Trevi fountain), which watered the lower parts of the city. His successor Gregory XIII aimed higher, and planned an aqueduct which would bring water to the Piazza di Termini, by the ruins of the Baths of Diocletian.[20] In anticipation, he began a new papal palace on the Quirinal. The high ground was going to be made habitable again, as it had been in the ancient city.

In the summer of 1576, also in anticipation, Cardinal Felice Peretti bought, through an intermediary, some vineyards just north of S. Maria

---

20. Maria Grazia Tolomeo and Rossella Motta, *Il trionfo dell'acqua* 205–8, 220–5.

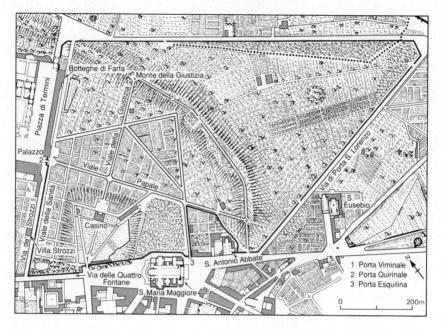

Figure 5
The Villa Montalto in 1748 (from the plan of Rome by G. B. Nolli).

Maggiore, at the top of the steep valley between the Viminal and the Cispian. Here he commissioned Domenico Fontana to build him a villa and surround it with formal gardens.[21] Though he didn't know it, this prince of the church was doing exactly what Augustus' friend Marcus Lollius had done in the same place.

In 1585 Peretti became Pope Sixtus V. Among the many projects of urban development that filled the five years of his pontificate was the completion of the new aqueduct, named Acqua Felice. It ended at the 'Moses fountain' at the Quirinal end of the Piazza di Termini, but before

---

21. The standard works on the Villa Montalto are: Vittorio Massimo, *Notizie istoriche della Villa Massimo alle Terme Diocleziane* (Rome 1836), and Maria Giulia Barberini, *Guide rionali di Roma: Rione XVIII Castro Pretorio*, part 1 (Rome 1987).

it got that far it had been tapped by the papal architect for the gardens of the new estate, which would feature 'copia grandissima di fontane'.[22]

The elegant villa which had been suitable for Peretti the cardinal did not satisfy Sixtus the Pope. He now bought up more land, and in 1588 got Fontana to build him a *palazzo* above and behind the earlier villa (which was henceforward called the *casino*). The new building faced the Piazza di Termini, on the line of the outer circuit of the Baths themselves. Indeed, much of the Roman masonry was incorporated into the building, which featured a long row of workshop premises known as the *botteghe di Farfa*; Sixtus had transferred the annual fair at the abbey of Farfa to the Piazza di Termini, which he intended to develop as a commercial centre.[23]

The grounds of the villa now extended far beyond the gardens of the original *casino*, even beyond the rampart of the republican wall, which still survived as a long grassy mound and was now, as in Horace's time, a place to stroll and enjoy the view. The height of the mound varied according to the height of the ruined wall within it, and at its most elevated point—which was also the highest point in the whole of Rome—Sixtus placed a seated statue of the goddess Roma which had been found in the Baths of Constantine on the Quirinal a few years before. She was identified as the goddess of Justice (fig. 6), and her high seat, with its cypresses and umbrella pines, became the Monte della Giustizia.

Looking south-east from that point of vantage, the visitor could see the arches carrying the Acqua Felice from the Porta S. Lorenzo, half a mile away at the far end of the villa grounds. To the west, a broad flight of steps led down to the Viale della Giustizia, one of the two main axes of the gardens. The original villa, now the *casino*, was on the line of this avenue, which continued beyond it down to what had been the main entrance, the 'Porta Viminale', in the valley below the apse of S. Maria Maggiore (Plate IIIb).

Since 1588, however, the main entrance was the 'Porta Quirinale', next to the new *palazzo* on the Piazza di Termini. That led straight into

---

22. Domenico Fontana, *Della transportazione dell'obelisco vaticano et delle fabriche di nostro Signore Papa Sisto V* (Rome 1590) 37.
23. Barberini, op. cit. (n. 21) 12–14, 28–30, 50–55. He even planned to build a canal from the Anio.

Figure 6
'Giustizia'.

the Viale Papale, the other axis of Fontana's layout, which intersected the
Viale della Giustizia about 100 m behind the *casino* and continued out
beyond the formal gardens to a *belvedere* at the southernmost point of
the rampart mound. There, a left turn took you on the high path back to
the Monte della Giustizia; a right turn brought you down to a gate by the
church and monastery of S. Antonio Abbate. Beyond S. Antonio, looking
out on the facade of S. Maria Maggiore, was the third principal gate of the
villa, the 'Porta Esquilina'.

The whole property was defined by roads which Sixtus himself had
laid out, straightening the old winding lanes. The southern boundary, the
Via di Porta S. Lorenzo, was one of the new roads radiating from S. Maria
Maggiore which were such a feature of his urban planning. Another of
them, the Via delle Quattro Fontane, defined the north-western corner of
the villa, which towered above it on a large retaining wall. A door at
street level gave access to a two-storey belvedere (later known as the
Caffehaus) which at its upper level formed the terminus of the third main
avenue in the gardens, the Viale della Sanità. This ran along the northern
wall above the Via de' Strozzi, past the 'Porta Quirinale' and behind the
palazzo and the *botteghe di Farfa*—a south-facing suntrap 700 metres
long. (See fig. 5, p. 79.)

Fontana's creation was known as the Villa Montalto, after Sixtus'
nephew Cardinal Montalto, who inherited it in 1590. Its impact may be
judged by a description of 'la délicieuse *Villa Montalta*' (*sic*) offered by
a French observer a century later:

> Le jardin contient plusieurs parterres pleins de fleurs; des allées à perte
> de vue, ornées de Statues, entr'autres une de *Neptune* du Cav. *Bernini*;
> des Bois, Orangers, et autres agrumes plantés et dans les vases; un Parc
> pour les bêtes fauves, et grand nombre de Fontaines, Jets d'eau,
> Cascades, et Bassins, dont plusieurs sont remplis de poisson.

But already by then it was in decline. In 1696, the last of Sixtus' family
to own the villa lost his fortune and sold the contents of the *palazzo*,
including the library and art collection.[24] Not only that, Deseine goes

---

24. Francois Deseine, *Rome moderne, première ville de l'Europe, avec toutes ses
     Magnificences et ses Délices* (Leiden 1713) 3.655. For the date, see Barberini,
     op. cit. 30.

on, but

> [il] a vendu aussi la vigne à M^r le Cardinal *Negroni*, qui en a ôté les
> canaux de plomb qui faisoient jouer mille jets d'eau, et a fait planter des
> choux, de l'ail, et des oignons dans les plus beaux Jardins et parterres.
> On n'a jamais vû une pareille désolation; et ce n'est pas sans raison qu'il
> n'y laisse entrer personne.

The Romantic Age preferred it as a desolation. 'The negligence of the
present owners through many years,' commented a visitor in 1787, 'has
again established nature to its former rights; it now gives us true
pleasure.'[25] And William Beckford of Fonthill found there 'what his soul
desired',[26]

> thickets of jasmine, and wild spots overgrown with bay; long alleys of
> cypress totally neglected, and almost impassable through the luxur-
> iance of the vegetation; on every side, antique fragments, vases,
> sarcophagi, and altars sacred to the Manes, in deep, shady recesses,
> which I am sure the Manes must love. The air was filled with the
> murmurs of water, trickling down basins of porphyry, and losing itself
> amongst overgrown weeds and grasses.

Despite all Sixtus' ambitious plans, the economic centre of Rome had
not moved up to the Piazza di Termini. There were now villas and
gardens on the high ground, as well as churches and ruins, but that was
all. In May 1783, pursuing his beloved Countess of Albany (wife of the
Young Pretender), the poet Vittorio Alfieri moved into the Villa Strozzi,
just opposite what was now the Villa Negroni. It was, he tells us,[27]

> a delightful retreat. The whole long mornings I passed in study, never
> moving from the house, except for an hour or two spent in riding over
> those immense solitudes of the uninhabited neighbourhood of
> Rome . . . An existence more gay, more free, more rural in the confines
> of the great city one could never find, nor one more agreeable to my
> nature, character and occupations.

25. Quoted in Chr. Elling, *Rome: the Biography of its Architecture from Bernini to Thorwaldsen* (Tübingen 1975) 460.
26. Guy Chapman (ed.), *The Travel-Diaries of William Beckford of Fonthill* (Cambridge 1928) 1.273, from a letter of 30 June 1782.
27. *Vita di Vittorio Alfieri* 4.10; trans. Cecil Roberts, *And so to Rome* (London 1950) 189.

Figure 7
The *palazzo* of the Villa Montalto-Negroni, from the Piazza di Termini; at the right, the
'porta Quirinale'. (Giuseppe Vasi, *Magnificenze di Roma*, 1753.)

As it had been since the Middle Ages, the high ground above the Quirinal
and Esquiline was the *disabitato*, merging into the deserted Campagna
beyond the walls.

The main industry of eighteenth-century Rome was selling antiquities
and works of art to the wealthy English. The statuary Beckford saw was
all sold four years later to Thomas Jenkins, the principle agent in this
trade. That is why Bernini's *Neptune and Triton*, commissioned by
Cardinal Montalto in 1620 to adorn the great oval fishpond at the end of
the Viale della Sanità, is now in the Victoria and Albert Museum.[28]

Some of the sculpture was ancient, discovered only a few years before
the sale. It had come to light during a spectacular excavation, which the
painter Thomas Jones, of Pencerrig in Radnorshire, recorded in his
journal for 5 July 1777:

---

28. R. Wittkower, *Burlington Magazine* 94 (1952) 68–76. For Jenkins, see
Brinsley Ford, *Apollo* 99 (1974) 416–25.

Went with *Tresham* to see the Antique Rooms just discovered, by digging for antient bricks, in the Villa Negroni—The painted Ornaments much in the Chinese taste—figures of Cupids bathing &c and painted in *fresco* on the Stucco of the Walls—The Reds, purples, Blues & Yellows very bright—but had a dark & heavy effect—NB Tresham made a purchase of these paintings for 50 Crowns, to be taken off the walls at his Own Expence—

Jones evidently made a sketch of the scene which he later turned into a finished oil painting, now in the Tate Gallery (Plate IIIa). It shows the excavation of a substantial house of at least two storeys, but is topographically very unhelpful. The site of the excavation was probably the 'underground house' in what two centuries earlier had been the Cappelletti vineyard; that is, between the *casino* and the *palazzo*.[29]

Jones' companion Henry Tresham sold the detached wall-paintings to the eccentric Bishop of Derry (soon to be fourth Earl of Bristol), but they never reached either England or Ireland. Presumably they were part of the Earl-Bishop's collection of antiquities that was captured and plundered by the French in the invasion of 1798. Mercifully, they had been copied, and the published engravings (fig. 8) caused quite a sensation. But the house itself was destroyed; once the paintings had gone, the brickwork could be dismantled and reused. A schematic plan (fig. 9) is all that survives of what must have been the second-century rebuilding of the *horti Lolliani*.[30]

It seems an oddly small house to be so sumptuously decorated. But this is a plan only of the lowest level, where the painted plaster was best preserved. It is significant that the entrance did not lead straight through on a central axis, as is usual, but turned left to the stairs. Only subsidiary routes gave access to the rooms on this level; the main business of the house was evidently on the upper floor, and the upper floor, to judge by Jones' painting, may well have been more extensive. Since the only

29. Barberini, op. cit. (n. 21) 78–80. Memoirs of Thomas Jones: *Walpole Society* 32 (1951) 62. Francis W. Hawcroft, *Travels in Italy 1776–1783* (Manchester 1988) 46f., 57; see pp. 230f. below.
30. Details and discussion in the excellent article of Hetty Joyce, *Art Bulletin* 65 (1983) 423–40. For the Earl-Bishop, see Brinsley Ford, loc. cit. (n. 28) 426–34.

Figure 8

A wall-painting from the Roman house. Ariadne and Dionysus: one of three Bacchic scenes
in the dining-room (fig. 9, room D).

outside windows were at the front,[31] it is a reasonable surmise that this
part of the house was a semi-basement, built into the slope of the hill.
Room D, which had the most elaborate paintings (all of Bacchic scenes),
was evidently a northeast-facing summer dining room, cool and shady,
illuminated only through the two-storey light-well of the peristyle.

The plan makes most sense if we think of it as the lowest floor of a
house built at the head of a V-shaped valley; and that fits exactly with the
suggested site. The continuity is perfect: since 1600 years' accumulation
of debris and washed-down topsoil had moved the edge of the valley
perceptibly westwards, Cardinal Peretti's *casino* was the exact equivalent of Marcus Lollius' *horti*.

Villa Negroni, Villa Massimo

The *marchese* Francesco Massimo acquired the property in 1789, but the
name 'Villa Negroni' persisted, particularly among the English and

---

31. Above the front door, and high up in the front wall of room B (Joyce, op. cit.
    424f.).

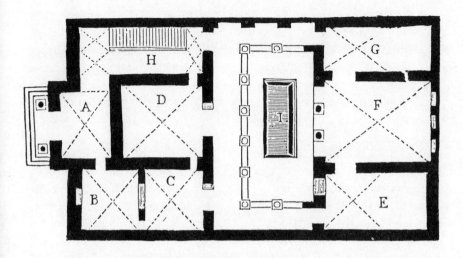

Figure 9
Plan of the Roman house excavated in 1777 (after Massimo 1836). D: dining room.
I: peristyle. E, G: Bedrooms. No scale, but overall dimensions are given as 125 × 70 *palmi*;
a Roman *palmo* was about 25 cm.

Americans who were its principal visitors once the Napoleonic occupation was over. Pope Pius VII was restored from exile in January 1814; the next fifty-six years, briefly interrupted by Mazzini's Republic of 1848–9, saw the long evening of papal Rome, impoverished and picturesque, condemned as a medieval anachronism and treasured as the one place safe from the modern world. In the crumbling city of Pio Nono, Ferdinand Gregorovius found the 'spell-bound silence', Henry James the 'golden air', which they knew was both doomed and irreplaceable. Unified Italy would destroy it all. As Gregorovius wrote in his journal,[32] 'Rome will lose everything—her republican atmosphere, her cosmopolitan breadth, her tragic repose.'

Some of those in thrall to this enchanted place were escaping from puritanical New England—artists especially, the originals of James'

32. *The Roman Journals of Ferdinand Gregorovius 1852–1874* (Eng. trans., London 1907) 132, 4 April 1861.

Roderick Hudson and of Kenyon in *The Marble Faun*.[33] Among them
were the painter Luther Terry, who landed from Connecticut in 1833,
and Thomas Crawford of New York, who came to study sculpture under
Thorwaldsen in 1835; they were to be close friends, and successive
husbands of the same woman, Louisa Ward of Rhode Island.[33] Terry
made a decent unspectacular career, but Crawford was a shooting star
from the moment his *Orpheus* was accepted by the Boston Athenaeum in
1840.

Louisa Ward came to Rome in 1843 to join her sisters Annie and Julia
and Julia's husband Samuel Gridley Howe. It was, in fact, the Howes'
honeymoon, and they stayed in the city until their first child (Julia
Romana) was born in March 1844. By then Louisa was engaged to
Thomas Crawford, who used all his charm and energy to break down her
family's opposition to the match. They were married in New York City
in September 1844, and returned to Rome a year later. Their first child,
Annie, was born in January 1846, their second, Jennie, in November
1847. In January 1848, Louisa wrote to her uncle John Ward, who
controlled her allowance, with the news that they were going to rent 'a
very lovely place' for six years, at $250 per annum:

> We could not take it for less time, without paying a higher rent, and
> then it is a divine place and quite like living in the country it will be,
> with its immense extent of garden behind it.

Prince Massimo had let them the Villa Negroni *palazzo*, keeping only the
ground floor rooms for his own use; Crawford could use the *botteghe di
Farfa* as his studios.[35]

Early in March 1849, the Crawfords entertained the sculptor W.W.
Story and his wife, and Margaret Fuller, author of *Woman in the Nineteenth Century*, who was correspondent for the New York *Tribune* and a
close friend of Giuseppe Mazzini. The Pope was in exile in Gaeta; Crawford had joined the newly-recruited Civil Guard; a French army was

---

33. For the background, see William L. Vance's superb book, *America's Rome*
    (Yale 1989).
34. See pp. 232f. below for genealogy and bibliography.
35. R.L. Gale, *Thomas Crawford* (Pittsburgh 1964) 64–6; studios illustrated in
    his Plate VIII.

on its way to put down the Roman Republic; and in little more than a year, Miss Fuller, Count Ossoli and their child would be drowned in a shipwreck off Long Island. But Henry James, coaxing out the memories fifty years later, was oblivious to such drama. This is his version of the scene:[36]

> Our friends breakfast immediately with the Crawfords at Villa Negroni,
> where the irrepressible Margaret again joins them. What has become of
> Villa Negroni, dim, denied, engulfed, more or less, to a certainty now,
> but where three small inhabitants, dedicated each, by the admirable
> scene itself, as we make out, to distinction, grew up, or at least began
> to, and laid up memories? Nothing will induce me, however, to insist
> on an answer to my question; one must never, in Rome at this hour, for
> penalties and pangs, insist on such answers. There were two little girls
> of the villa, and there was one [Edith Story] brought to play, and *she*
> remembers well how they picked up bitter oranges in the alleys to pelt
> each other with. Thirty years ago, and later, in any case, the place was
> there still, but with that indescribable golden air about it (according to
> my faded impression) of a paradise closed and idle, where the petals of
> the Roman roses in the spring, all ungathered, might be thick on the
> Roman walks, where happiness unmistakably *had* been.

James was there in 1869; the happiness he remembered sensing was the life of the Crawford children between October 1850 and April 1856.

Crawford had taken his family to the United States in the spring of 1849, shortly before the French assault. When they returned, the revolution was over and the Pope was back in the Quirinal. They brought with them Louisa's sister Julia Ward Howe, who caught the magic of the place in the style of the time:[37]

> Then the enchantment of an orange grove
> First overcame me, entering thy lone walks
> Cloistered in twilight, Villa Massimo!
> Where the stern cypresses stand up to guard
> A thousand memories of blessedness.

---

36. *William Wetmore Story and his Friends* (Boston 1903) 1.122f.; for the
background, see the romantic narrative (not always accurate) of Joseph Jay
Deiss, *The Roman Years of Margaret Fuller* (New York 1969).
37. Anon.[Julia Ward Howe], *Passion Flowers* (Boston 1854) 13f., from 'Rome'
(pp. 8–25).

There seemed a worship in the concentrate
Deep-breathing sweetness of those virgin flowers,
Fervid as worship is in passionate souls
That have not found their vent in earthly life,
And soar too wild untaught, and sink unaided.
They filled the air with incense gathered up
For the pale vesper of the evening star.
Nor failed the rite of meet antiphony—
I felt the silence holy, till a note
Fell, as a sound of ravishment from heaven—
Fell, as a star falls, trailing sound for light;
And, ere its thread of melody was broken,
From the serene sprang other sounds, its fellows,
That fluttered back celestial welcoming.
Astonished, penetrate, too past myself
To know I sinned in speaking, where a breath
Less exquisite was sacrilege, my lips
Gave passage to one cry: God! What is that?
(Oh! not to know what has no peer on earth!)
And one, not distant, stooped to me and said:
'If ever thou recall thy friend afar,
Let him but be commemorate with this hour,
The first in which thou heard'st our Nightingale.'

(Mrs Howe was a small woman; Thomas Crawford was tall.)

Crawford had won the commission for the Washington Equestrian Monument at Richmond, Virginia, and soon added to that the pediment sculpture and bronze doors for the Senate and the House of Representatives, and the 'Armed Liberty' statue for the top of the Capitol dome. The studios at the Villa Negroni, which he shared with Story, were full of activity. The third daughter, Mary, was born in April 1851, and the longed-for son, Francis Marion, in August 1854. In the spring of 1856, Louisa Crawford took the four children again to the United States; her husband followed in July. But he never returned to the Villa Negroni. He died in London in 1857 of a tumour on the eye.

William Story remembered his friend in *Roba di Roma*, that wonderful kaleidoscope of life in papal Rome which also provides the last contemporary description of the villa still intact.[38] Its southern

---

38. W.W. Story, *Roba di Roma* (London 1863) 1.141, 2.119.

boundary, Sixtus V's Via di Porta S. Lorenzo, was the way to the cemetery: 'you pass from the city through a long avenue of acacias and elms, between villa walls, to the curious old gate . . .' Its northern boundary was a good place to play bowls:

> In the Piazza di Termini numerous parties may be seen every bright day in summer or spring playing this game under the locust-trees, surrounded by idlers, who stand by to approve or condemn, and to give their advice. The French soldiers, free from drill or guard, or from practising trumpet-calls on the old Agger of Servius Tullius near by, are sure to be rolling balls in this fascinating game. Having heated their blood sufficiently at it, they adjourn to a little *osteria* in the Piazza to refresh themselves with a glass of *asciutto* wine, after which they sit on a bench outside the door, or stretch themselves under the trees, and take a *siesta*, with their handkerchiefs over their eyes, while other parties take their turn at the *bocce*. Meanwhile, from the Agger beyond are heard the distressing trumpets struggling with false notes and wheezing and shrieking in ludicrous discord, while now and then the solemn bell of Santa Maria Maggiore tolls from the neighbouring hill.

Another continuity: the French forces that garrisoned Rome between 1849 and 1866, to protect the Pope, were quartered on the site of the barracks of the Praetorian Guard.[39] Why not? Its defences were still there, incorporated into Aurelian's wall.

As for the Villa itself, it comes to Story's mind when he writes of cabbages ('O mighty Cavolo!—how have I dared omit thy august name?'):[40]

> Saunter out at any of the city-gates, or lean over the wall at San Giovanni (and where will you find a more charming spot?), or look down from the windows of the Villa Negroni, and your eye will surely fall on one of the Roman kitchen-gardens, patterned out in even rows and squares of green . . .
>
> As one looks from the Villa Negroni windows, he cannot fail to be impressed by the strange changes through which this wonderful city has passed. The very spot on which Nero, the insane emperor-artist,

---

39. Gregorovius (n. 32 above, 202) reports a great concert there in March 1864 by Liszt and the papal choir, 'for Peter's Pence'.
40. *Roba di Roma* 1.154f., 155f.

fiddled while Rome was burning has now become a vast kitchen-garden, belonging to Prince Massimo (himself a descendant, as he claims, of Fabius Cunctator), where men no longer, but only lettuces, asparagus, and artichokes, are ruthlessly cut down. The inundations are not for mock sea-fights among slaves, but for the peaceful purposes of irrigation. And though the fiddle of Nero is only traditional, the trumpets of the French, murdering many an unhappy strain near by, are a most melancholy fact. In the bottom of the valley, a noble old villa [the *casino*], covered with frescoes, has been turned into a manufactory of bricks, and the very Villa Negroni itself [the *palazzo*] is now doomed to be the site of a railway station. Yet here the princely family of Negroni lived, and the very lady at whose house Lucrezia Borgia took her famous revenge may once have sauntered under the walls, which still glow with ripening oranges, to feed the gold-fish in the fountain,—or walked with stately friends through the long alleys of clipped cypresses, and pic-nicked *alla Giorgione* on lawns which are now but kitchen-gardens, dedicated to San Cavolo. It pleases me, also, descending in memories to a later time, to look up at the summer-house built above the gateway, and recall the days when Shelley and Keats came there to visit their friend Severn, the artist (for that was his studio), and look over the same alleys and gardens, and speak words one would have been so glad to hear,—and, coming still later down, to recall the hearty words and brave heart of one of America's best sculptors and my dear friend, Thomas Crawford.

That was written in 1858. At the end of 1862 Gregorovius wrote in his diary:[41] 'The railway to Naples was opened on December 1; the Central Station has been removed to the Baths of Diocletian. A great event in the annals of the city!'

The *palazzo* had gone, and about one-third of the villa grounds. The Monte della Giustizia survived, but the goddess was cut off from her Sixtine avenue by tracks and wagons and steam engines (Plate IVa). The rest of the grounds were still accessible, 'possessing a delightful terrace, fringed with orange-trees [the Viale della Sanità]—which is a most agreeable sunny walk in winter—and many pleasant shady nooks and corners for summer.'[42] But the age of innocence was over.

---

41. Op. cit. (n. 32) 173.
42. Augustus Hare, *Walks in Rome* (London 1871) 29. Hare was born in 1833 at the Villa Strozzi, just opposite the Viale: *The Story of My Life* (London 1896) 1.42.

No more the *vetturino*'s cry of 'Ecco Roma', as the carriage breasted the rise on the road from Civitavecchia from where St Peter's dome could be seen across the desolate Campagna. Now the visitor arrived by rail, 'at a very prosaic and commonplace station', as Julia Ward Howe found it when she visited her sister in 1868.[43] Soon, that station itself would be the object of fond nastalgia, 'the little old Termine of our Roman days—the funny little station so far away, with few porters or cabs, and comparatively few voyageurs.'[44] After 1870, the Roman days were a thing of the past.

The capital of united Italy required a large modern station, and a large modern city. Naturally, the area around the station itself was among the first to be developed. Massimo was one of the 'black' aristocracy, faithful to the Pope—no problem about expropriating *his* land. Gregorovius' journal, 12 January 1873:[45]

> Building is proceeding at a furious pace; the Monti quarter is turned entirely upside down. Yesterday saw the fall of the lofty walls of the Villa Negroni; streets are being laid out even there; a new quarter of the city is already rising on the Praetorian Camp, another on the slopes of the Coelian beside the Quattro Coronati. Building is also going on beside S. Lorenzo in Paneperna. Almost every hour witnesses the fall of some portion of ancient Rome. New Rome belongs to the new generation, while I belong to the ancient city, in whose spell-bound silence my history arose.

According to Augustus Hare, 'it was in vain that the aged Prince Massimo . . . prayed for redress; and when the cruel seizure was complete, and the magnificent old cypress and orange trees of the villa fell under the axe of the spoiler, he died of a broken heart.'[46]

Gregorovius' 'new generation' included the son of Thomas Crawford, now a best-selling novelist. In *Don Orsino* he addressed the modernisation issue, and Del Ferice, his spokesman for the developers, is portrayed with understanding and not just hostility:[47]

43. Julia Ward Howe, *From the Oak to the Olive* (Boston 1868) 48.
44. M.K. Waddington, *Italian Letters of a Diplomat's Wife* (London 1905) 42, from a letter written in 1880.
45. Op. cit. (n. 32) 437.
46. *Walks in Rome* (12th ed., London 1887) 2.34 n. 3.
47. F. Marion Crawford, *Don Orsino* (London 1892) 111. For Crawford's Roman novels, see Vance, op. cit. (n. 33) 2.228–54.

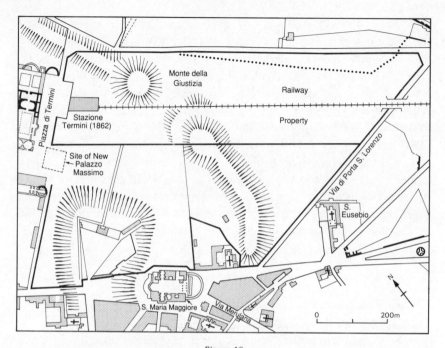

Figure 10
The Villa Negroni-Massimo in 1869 (from Murray's *Handbook of Rome and its Environs*, ninth edition). The new Palazzo Massimo was not constructed until 1886.

'Oh, I am not going to defend all we have done! I only defend what we mean to do. Change of any sort is execrable to the man of taste, unless it is bought about by time—and that is a beautifier which we have not at our disposal. We are half Vandals and half Americans, and we are in a terrible hurry.'

Crawford's description of the effect of it is eloquent enough:[48]

The cab entered a sort of broad lane, the sketch of a future street, rough with the unrolled metalling of broken stones, the space set apart for the pavement being an uneven path of trodden brown earth. Here and there tall detached houses rose out of the wilderness, mostly covered by scaffoldings and swarming with workmen, but hideous where so far finished as to be visible in all the isolation of their six-storied nakedness. A strong smell of lime, wet earth and damp masonry was blown into Orsino's nostrils by the scirocco wind.

---

48. Ibid. 185f., *Ave Roma Immortalis* (London 1899) 1.153f. = (1903) 141.

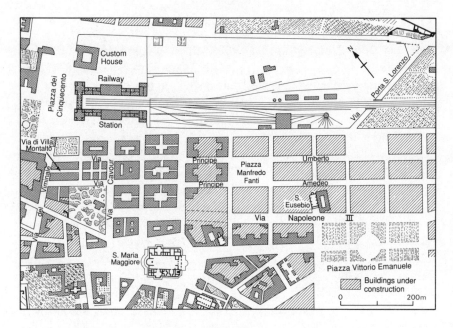

Figure 11

The area of the Villa Negroni-Massimo in 1882 (from S. Russel Forbes, *Rambles in Rome*).
At this early stage the *casino* still survived, but not for long. The new railway station was
completed in 1874.

In Roman times, and again (or still) in the *disabitato* of the papal city, the high ground had been full of humps and hollows, slopes and sunken lanes (Plate IVb).[49] No more; the new city must be built for traffic. 'The villas have disappeared,' wrote Rodolfo Lanciani:[50]

> their magnificent ilexes have been burnt into charcoal, their great pines used for timber, their hills and dales cut away or filled up to a dead level, and their deliciously shady avenues destroyed to make room for broad, straight, sun-beaten thoroughfares.

Quite literally, the Villa Negroni had been flattened.

---

49. Livy XXVI 10.6: 'inter convalles tectaque hortorum et sepulcra et cavas undique vias'.
50. R. Lanciani, *The Ruins and Excavations of Ancient Rome* (London 1897) 418; cf. his *Notes from Rome* (ed. A.L. Cubberley, London 1988) 411 and 427 on 'the modern craze for levelling heights and filling in valleys'.

Mimoli

The left-hand bronze door of the Senate wing of the Capitol in
Washington shows scenes from the immediate aftermath of the
Revolutionary War. At the top, the laying of the cornerstone of the
United States Capitol; below it, the inauguration of George Washington
as first President; below that, an ovation for Washington at Trenton, New
Jersey; and finally, at the bottom, an allegorical scene of 'Peace and
Agriculture with Infancy, Maternity, Childhood, Youth and Manhood
grouped around a plow' (Plate V).[51] It was this bottom panel that caught
the eye of Mrs Howe at some Capitol function: 'Why, this is my family!'
she exclaimed. 'That is Louisa with Frank, Annie and Mimoli.'[52]

Thomas Crawford was working on the design of the Capitol doors
between October 1854 and May 1855.[53] His daughter Annie had her
ninth birthday during that time, and Jennie her seventh. It is possible that
Mrs Howe thought the boy on the right was based on Annie, but he
seems too old, and too modest.[54] About the baby and the little girl,
however, there can be no mistake. Mary, known to all as Mimoli, was
four that April, and little Frank (born the previous August) was a babe in
arms.

Mimoli had her fifth birthday in Paris, en route to the United States.
The Atlantic crossing terrified her, amid fog and icebergs, and the
reunion with her adored father at her aunt's house in Newport was a brief
one; he went back, and six months later her mother went back after him,
leaving the children at the other sister's house in Bordentown, Mass.,
where the little girl suffered from night terrors. A few months later came
the news of her father's death. She was six and a half.

Louisa Crawford and her children were away from Rome for nearly
three years. It was not all unhappiness for Mimoli (she took little Frank in
hand, and taught him to read), but the return to Villa Negroni must have
been a joy to her. That was in the winter of 1858-9, and the family was

51. J.M. Goode, *The Outdoor Sculpture of Washington D.C.* (Washington D.C.
    1974) 62.
52. Elliott, *Three Generations* 72. For abbreviated titles in this section, see
    p. 233 below; unless otherwise stated, biographical details are from Mrs
    Fraser's memoirs.
53. Gale, *Thomas Crawford* 133-9.
54. See Fraser, *A Diplomatist's Wife*, opp. p. 2.393 for a portrait of the arrogant
    and tempestuous Annie.

still there in March 1860.[55] But the demolition men would soon be in, and decisions had to be made.

Mrs Crawford married Luther Terry the painter in September 1861, and the family moved to a house near the Pincio; Margaret Terry, known as Daisy, was born in August 1862, and a month later Mimoli (11) and Jennie (nearly 15) were taken by their stepfather to school in England. After three years at Miss Sewell's on the Isle of Wight, the girls returned to an enlarged family (Arthur Terry was six months old) which was now established in some luxury in the Palazzo Odescalchi.

The American civil war was over, and the Ward finances had survived it intact. Louisa's sister Julia Ward Howe was now famous as the author of *The Battle Hymn of the Republic*, and her adventurous brother Sam was beginning his Washington career as 'King of the Lobby'.[56] For the next ten years the Terrys maintained at the Odescalchi a style as *signorile* as that of the Storys at the Palazzo Barberini. It was to this household that Mrs Howe came through the prosaic little station in 1868—and when she arrived, she reflected that the whole of her modest house in Boston would fit into the largest of those lofty rooms.[57]

Gentle Jennie died of typhoid in 1866. That left Mimoli six years junior to the headstrong Annie, three years older than brother Frank (on whom they all doted), and eleven years older than Daisy, the observant half-sister. 'The Crawfords were different from us,' wrote Margaret Terry many years later; 'all three were handsome, proud, and brilliant.' With Annie, the pride was pathological ('I hate equality; I want inferiors'); hard as flint, Henry James thought her. Frank was superbly handsome, but vain and self-indulgent until he found his *métier*. Mimoli was the best of them—'pleasanter to live with, easier to love. She had grace and charm, she had a delicately outlined face with very blue eyes; she was kind and gay and generous . . .' (Plate VI).[58]

Unlike her sister, who was twenty-seven before she found someone willing to take her on (a Prussian *Junker*, Erich von Rabe), Mimoli was married soon after her twenty-third birthday. Her bridegroom was Hugh

55. Dates: Pilkington, *Francis Marion Crawford* 19; Elliott, *Uncle Sam Ward* 460.

56. See Tharp, *Three Saints and a Sinner*.

57. Op. cit. (n. 43) 49f. Cf. Henry James, *Letters* (ed. L. Edel, Harvard 1974) 1.346 on 'the rival houses of Story and Terry' (1873).

58. Chanler, *Roman Spring* 26f.; Henry James, *Letters* 1.347; Annie's revealing comment quoted in Elliott, *My Cousin* 29.

Fraser, aged thirty-eight, son of Sir John Fraser K.C.M.G. He was a career diplomat who had already served in various embassies and missions from Guatemala to Peking.[59] They had met at Bagni di Lucca, while Fraser was on long leave before going back to Peking as Secretary of Legation. The newly-weds sailed from Venice in August 1874, and for most of the next four years Mimoli was in China.

In later life, Mrs Fraser's comments on her husband were just slightly double-edged:[60] 'affectionate but awe-inspiring . . . nerves always overstrung . . . rather a queer person in some ways.' And most revealingly:

> I always leave my real self in storage when I go to England, and my dear Hugh had very little use at any time for the Mediterranean-born side of my personality.

He had a temper, he could be moody, and he probably didn't much care for her glamorous brother Frank. But at least there is no sign of any friction between them when her family suffered a financial disaster in the first year of their marriage. Charles Ward, Louisa Terry's cousin and trustee, gambled with her money and lost it. 'The poor Terrys of former fame,' reported Henry James, 'are down in the world, having lost two thirds of their property.' (Annie and the von Rabes behaved abominably about it.)[61]

Mimoli came home to the Odescalchi in May 1878, with her two little boys. Her husband joined her a year later, and took her to England to await his next posting. After a two-year stint at the embassy in Vienna, in the spring of 1882 Hugh Fraser was transferred, at his own request, to Rome.

Mimoli wanted to be near 'her own dear people' (now living more economically at the Palazzo Altemps). But it was not a success:[62]

59. For his career, see *The Times* 5 June 1894 p. 5.
60. *Further Reminiscences* 19, 13, 309.
61. Henry James, *Letters* (n. 57) 2.142, November 1877; Chanler, *Roman Spring* 51–5.
62. *Further Reminiscences* 106. The Terrys were at Palazzo Altemps from 1879 to 1887, and then moved back to the Odescalchi (but to a less grand apartment than before).

In order to be in the same quarter as the embassy, we had taken an apartment on the Esquiline, looking into the Piazza of Santa Maria Maggiore. It went against me like a sacrilege, for the raw, showy, newly-built house stood exactly over the spot where, in my childhood, the side-gate of Villa Negroni, my birth-place, shut our fairyland off from the world outside.

When the maid they had brought from Vienna died of typhoid, Mrs Fraser was convinced that the developers had opened up unhealthy ground on the site of ancient cemeteries, 'and the miserably bad drainage arrangements did the rest.' Anxiety for her children affected her own health; she began to be haunted by ugly apparitions, from which she could not free herself for many years.

1882 was a bad time, with 'endless trouble and continuous illness in the family.' Erich von Rabe died, leaving Annie in Prussia with two young children; Frank Crawford was in Boston trying to find an occupation, and succeeding only in attracting gossip about his relationship with a married woman;[63] 'Uncle Sam' Ward had to leave secretly for England in November to avoid his creditors; Daisy Terry and Mimoli herself were both about to join their brother Frank in the Roman Catholic church, against fierce opposition from their mother, Luther Terry and Hugh Fraser.

One anxiety was resolved in 1883, when Frank the wastrel suddenly blossomed into F. Marion Crawford the successful novelist; and another when the Frasers moved house, closer to the embassy at Porta Pia (but there was trouble with the drains there too). With her husband kept in Rome to deputise for the ambassador, Mimoli had a wonderful family summer at Sorrento. But her elder boy was seriously ill, and the religious crisis still unresolved. In her brother's judgement, Mimoli's troubles were very great.[64]

Mrs Fraser was thirty-three when her husband's Rome posting came to an end in 1884. For the next ten years she was away from her native city and the demanding intensities of her family. The two boys were at school in England, and she was fulfilling her role as the wife of Her Britannic Majesty's Minister Resident and Consul General at Santiago (1885–7) and

63. Louise Hall Tharp, *Mrs Jack* (Boston 1965) 78–81.
64. Elliott, *Uncle Sam Ward* 674, 679 (drains at 35 Via Palestro); *My Cousin* 180 for Crawford's comment (April 1884).

Envoy Extraordinary and Minister Plenipotentiary at Tokyo (1888–94). She was now a Roman Catholic, and to judge by her letters from Japan,[65] her new faith may have helped her peace of mind. But in June 1894, in Tokyo, Hugh Fraser died.

'I think we are well rid of him,' wrote F. Marion Crawford to his wife:[66]

> I hope you have managed to write a letter of condolence to Mimoli. I have not! I really do not know what to say, under the circumstances, but I must write something. The question seems to be whether it was better that Fraser should make a hell for Mimoli on earth, or a hell for himself on the other side. It seem to me that he has chosen the better part. The only trouble is about Mimoli's supporting herself.

Instead of the ambassadress she might have become, at forty-three Mimoli was a widow. She returned to Italy, not to Rome but to Sorrento, where her brother and his family were now living in magnificent style.[67] He cheered her up with sumptuous amateur dramatics (Henry James among the appreciative audience), and encouraged her to write. It was the second time he had given that advice to a widowed sister. Annie had managed two pseudonymous novellas and then sunk into depression and despair. (Only the previous year Crawford had installed her in a sanatorium near Vienna, under the care of Dr Krafft-Ebing.)[68] Mimoli had more stamina than that.

She began with children's stories, then moved on to romantic tales not unlike her brother's, often set in Japan or Italy. Much of her writing was done at his Sorrento villa, but she was sometimes in Florence, sometimes

----

65. *A Diplomatist's Wife in Japan* (London 1899).
66. 26 and 28 June 1894 (Crawford expected Mimoli to marry again). The letters are in the possession of Professor Robert L. Gale of the University of Pittsburgh; transcripts kindly made available by Gordon Poole on behalf of the F. Marion Crawford Memorial Society.
67. See Pilkington, *Francis Marion Crawford* 87–90 on the Villa Crawford, and the novelist as 'Prince of Sorrento'.
68. Annie's vampire story *A Mystery of the Campagna* (1887) was republished in 1982, with a valuable biographical introduction by John C. Moran (New York: Adams Press, for the Count Dracula Club). The sanatorium is mentioned in two letters from Crawford to his wife (see n. 66) dated 8 and 9 May 1893.

in Rome. Mrs Terry was still holding her Wednesday receptions at Palazzo Odescalchi until her death in 1897, and Luther Terry lived on there until 1900. Not long before he died, Mimoli was dining with her cousin Maud Howe (Mrs Elliott) at Palazzo Rusticucci. It was the time of the 'Boxer rebellion', and she had known several of the people butchered at the embassy in Pekin. 'She is very fascinating', wrote Maud.[69] Mimoli could tell a good story, and her life had been an eventful one.

Her English sons were now grown up. Despite her antipathy to England, she must sometimes have stayed with them; in December 1898 she dated the preface to her published letters from Japan at 'The Warren, Torrington'. Hugh Fraser the younger served throughout the South African war (he was wounded three times), and then emigrated to the new state of Washington on the American Pacific coast. There he was joined by his brother John, and in 1906 by Mrs Fraser herself, en route from New York to Japan. She was ill with some sort of mental disorder— what she calls 'the misery known to brain-workers as "broken-head"'. The Methow Valley cured her, and among the books she wrote in the seven years she stayed there were three volumes of memoirs.[70]

In 1914 she was back in Rome, still writing hard. This time it was stories from Italian history, but still with a dash of personal reminiscence.[71] Her sons too had left America, and both of them collaborated in her literary industry. But their country was at war. Hugh Fraser was killed in 1918.[72] His elder brother, who had been so ill in Rome as a little boy, survived again. In 1922 John Fraser was living at Woodchester Park, a country house in the Cotswolds, with his mother at the nearby Park Farm. And that is where Mimoli died, on 7 June 1922, of a heart attack. She was seventy-one.

---

69. Elliott, *Three Generations* 257f. (Mrs Terry), 302 ('Mimo'). Augustus Hare was a regular visitor at Palazzo Odescalchi: *The Story of My Life* (n. 42 above) 3.375f. for the first mention (June 1870), 6.415 for the last (April 1896).
70. Mrs Hugh Fraser, *Seven Years on the Pacific Slope* (New York 1914) 9–12; see p. 233 below.
71. *Italian Yesterdays* (London 1914), *More Italian Yesterdays* (London 1915), *Storied Italy* (New York 1915). Also *The Patrizi Memoirs: A Roman Family under Napoleon* (London 1915); Mrs Fraser spent Christmas 1914 at the Palazzo Patrizi (*Storied Italy* 75f., 94f.).
72. Elliott, *Three Generations* 297.

A child's eye view

The life of Mary Crawford Fraser is important for our purpose because it
is only through her that we can still *sense* the Villa Montalto-Negroni-
Massimo. And to understand her testimony we need to see why it
mattered so much to her. Our witness is not just the little girl in the
paradise garden; she is also the desperate young mother in the house
poisoned by its destroyers, and the widow of fifty-five summoning her
memories to heal her mind in the clean air of the Washington mountains.

In 1900, Mrs Fraser published a novel called *The Splendid Porsenna*.
(It is not about the legendary king of Clusium; her Porsenna are plural, an
imaginary Roman aristocratic family like the Saracinesca in her brother's
trilogy.) The first four pages are pure childhood memory. For 'Honora',
read Mimoli; for 'Peppino', read Pietruccio, the Villa Negroni gardener;
for 'Lady Eva Dering', read Louisa Crawford.

> The blazing Roman noon was at its full, and there was no street or
> piazza where the tide of sunshine did not sweep all before it in one
> breathless vibrating wave of heat. But in the garden of a palace on the
> high outskirts of the town[73] there were nests of shade, and deep
> bowers where the warm air was sweetened with countless roses and
> violets, and where the high glare of midday entered not. There were
> paths flecked with mimic branches of green and brown that waved in
> the shadows under your feet, but did not trip you up, because they
> were reflections of the dance that the real branches were dancing
> overhead. There the smell of the earth was cool and strong, and
> vivified with mats of cypress needles and tiny cones shaken down at
> the roots of some black-green spire, soaring solemnly above the lower
> billows of orange-trees and oleander boughs. But mostly the orange-
> trees had been taught their places by the wise gardener who planted
> them some three hundred years ago, and stood only in long lines in
> their own *viale*; for who does not know that orange-trees love the
> damp black earth and are not good neighbours for either flowers or
> human beings? It is true that the violets and the blue Roman hyacinths
> ran all along their roots at one side of the way; but every gossiping bee
> and poppy in the garden knew that it was not for the sake of the
> orange-trees, but because a sweet runnel of fresh water trickled in a
> stone trough down that side of the walk; and who would not plant

---

73. She calls it Palazzo Peretti (p. 6), which is hardly a disguise at all.

himself near running water if he could? Of course the orange-trees did not understand that, and in bloom time were always raining down scented white petals to greet their little friends below.

The avenue was a quarter of a mile long, and Honora had learnt to walk there, running after enormous golden balls which the beneficent giant in charge of her used to pull off the trees somewhere near the sky (sky or tree-top, it is all one when you are two years old), and sent rolling away over large boulders in the gravel for Honora to chase.

And Honora would start off in good faith, keeping her eyes too steadily on the orange to look at her feet, and generally got some dreadful tumbles over the boulders before she reached the golden ball; and perhaps one little blue shoe would get wrecked on the way. But she always scrambled to the goal somehow, and pounced on the orange with a triumphant lurch that nearly sent her over again, and then hugged it to her little heart in an ecstasy of triumph; giving it up very reluctantly to the dear giant father who would send it spinning away once more into the distance so that Honora might run after it again and grow strong and firm on her feet.[74]

When she was big enough not to tumble at every third step, there came another joy into her life, and that the orange-trees taught her. They had a way of dropping their leaves—the greenest and most shining ones—into the runnel at their feet, and the leaves sometimes went spinning down the length of the *viale* till they came at last to the iron grating that led into the bowels of the earth. So Honora would climb up and pick the leaves, one, two, three, of the strong young ones, and pin them up at either end with a tiny twig from the spiraea bush, and then follow their course anxiously till ruin took them at the iron grating, where the bubbles went through with an angry swirl, and where there was always a little tangle of garden wreckage waiting for Peppino and his rake.

But Peppino had tertian fever most of the year, so that the garden had rather an independent time of it on the whole. It was Honora's joy in the hot summer days to slip away from the sun-steeped garden into the vast vaulted space on the ground floor of the palace, where Peppino stored his pots, and flowers, and garden culch, on shelves round three sides of the damp peeling walls. On the fourth side was a kind of scaffolding like a stage cottage—having a door for the hero to

---

74. The same scene in *A Diplomatist's Wife* 1.30f., with an additional detail: 'behind us usually stalked "Moro", a black cat of enormous size and corresponding dignity.'

disappear through when he had scaled the crazy steps, and a window for the heroine to shriek from after she is sure that he has really got in.

Peppino slept at the top of the stairs, and used his bed chiefly as a place under which to hide his own small ventures in cuttings or bouquets from Honora's sharp young eyes; but sometimes he would lie there shivering or burning for several days, and Honora's mother would send him down bowls of soup from the mediaeval kitchen in the attic of the palace, and by-and-by Peppino would come out, looking deathly yellow and incredibly thin, and would totter off to his work again. Once, when a very little child, Honora had scrambled up to Peppino's nest and seen him lying, grey-faced and hollow-eyed, in his dark corner; and the next moment she had flown up the frescoed stone stair-case to where Lady Eva Dering sat, a fair woman in a flood of sunshine, by a great window, whence she could gaze her fill on the classic stretch of the Campagna, and make out the gleaming villages on its boundary hills.

The gardener's private enterprise is mentioned in *Storied Italy*:[75]

The breeze that came up from the south sang among the cypresses very gently, just swaying their delicate crowning spires, but without disturbing the massed foliage below or shifting a single grain of the fragrant dust that its falling had piled for centuries around their roots. These had struck so deep that it seemed as if earth could hold no more, and they had risen and spread above it in upstanding buttresses velveted with moss, between whose deep arms a child could creep in and lie for hours on the sifted gold-brown mould, watching the play of branches in the sun against the blue, a thousand miles overhead; dreaming of the great past that made itself felt all around, even to untutored senses; and of an enchanting future limited to the blooming of *the* moss rose-tree, whose whereabouts just then was the most wonderful secret in the world—one's own alone; or else of how many bunches of big dark purple violets could be smuggled upstairs in one's pinafore before the old gardener woke from his nap and came hobbling after one to snatch them away. For the gardener had illicit dealings with flower-sellers, through the scrolled iron-work of the gate that looked to St. Mary Major; and one of the chief joys of life was to outwit him, and pick armfuls of violets and hyacinths while he was asleep.

---

75. Pp. 50f., in a chapter on S. Susanna.

That was the 'Porta Esquilina', which must be the gate Story referred to as Joseph Severn's studio:[76]

> Just here the orange 'viale' used to end in a beautiful deep-arched gateway two stories high, containing a studio and dwelling-rooms, and frescoed within and without in fine Renaissance style. Through its iron *cancello* Marion and I used to watch the doings of the outer world and listen to the bells of Santa Maria Maggiore, our own special church. A friendly French artist had rented the studio from my father, and we had an intimate friend in a hoary cheerful old beggar who sat all day on the stone seat outside and into whose battered peaked hat we dropped many a *baiocco* on festa days. To him I proudly presented my first piece of knitting, I remember—a woollen scarf of all the colours of the rainbow, of which I was enormously proud.
>
> In May there was another great attraction just outside that gate, a wonderful little altar, all smothered in roses and pansies, in the midst of which stood a picture of Our Lady, flanked—when the altar tenders had had good luck—with lighted candles. This was the poor children's way of celebrating the Month of Mary. Before almost every doorway in the humbler quarters of the town stood a little table, sometimes only a straw-bottomed chair, on which, during the whole month, the 'Madonna' of the family was displayed, surrounded with flowers, and passers-by were solicited to drop a copper into the cup on the *altarino* to buy more candles with.

Across the piazza from the 'Porta Esquilina' was the road that ran to S. Giovanni in Laterano, the Via Merulana:[77]

> I have the most delightful recollections of the walk from Santa Maria Maggiore, our own church, to the great free spaces round the Lateran. The last part of the way led through the Via San Giovanni, on the right side of which were scarcely any buildings at all, but only a long wall overhung in the late spring with masses of yellow Banksia roses, their trailing wreaths hanging so near our heads that we had but to spring and snatch to carry away big handfuls of the flowers. And what flowers! Yard-long arcs of ruffled honey tossed up against that Roman blue, every petal of the million a wing of translucent gold in sun and breeze; no stem, no foliage visible through the crowded blooms,

---

76. *Further Reminiscences* 104f., cf. p. 92 above.
77. *Italian Yesterdays* 134–6.

except where the trailers tapered to the last tiny cluster of unopened buds, set like yellow pearls in the green calix—tapered to a point so delicate that the faintest breath would set them waving and quivering as if mad to burst their bonds and flutter in the sunshine like the rest. And their perfume, that perfume of warm wax, the purest and sweetest in this world, filled the whole street—not altogether honestly perhaps, for, by a rare harmony of the eternal fitness of things, the long wall on which they grew sheltered, in the middle of a beautiful garden, a wax factory where church candles of every size were made, from the four-foot pillar, painted like a missal, that serves for the Paschal candle in church, to the slim taper that the poorest could buy to light before the picture of their patron Saint.

It was worth while to be young, with every sense unspoiled, and to go dancing along that road on a summer afternoon; to stop where a low gateway led into the hidden garden and buy from the gardener's wife some of her fat bunches of red carnations and lavender—for the sake of the Blessed St John, whose especial flowers they are—also, the cones of lavender made by tying a bundle just below the flowers, then turning the stalks back over these and tying them again to form an egg-shaped casket from which nothing could escape, and within which the flowers themselves could crumble to fragrant dust that would keep your linen sweet for at least ten years from the day they were gathered.

At the other end of the villa, the *palazzo* itself looked out on the Piazza di Termini. Mrs Fraser remembers the 'Porta Quirinale':[78]

The most beautiful gate of all was the one to the right of the house—an immense decorated archway leading into the *piazzale* of the Villa, a vast round, ringed with cypresses, and delimited by stone pillars which stood in a semi-circle, with huge iron chains swinging low between. This was planned as a waiting-place for the coaches and sedan chairs after they had put down their freight at the foot of the state staircase, under the *porte-cochère*.

When Mimoli was about nine years old, she and little Frank were blessed by Pius IX, whom they had met on the Pincio. Mrs Fraser saw that as a deeply significant moment,[79] and the recollection of it leads

---

78. *Storied Italy* 51f.
79. For her reactionary Catholicism, see Vance, op. cit. (n. 33) 2.215–23.

directly into her most detailed, and explicitly nostalgic, account of the Villa Negroni:[80]

For days afterwards we could think and speak of nothing else. When I was allowed to go and sit alone in our old drawing-room, from whose open windows I could look over the whole Campagna—windows through which the sun poured on vast stretches of crimson carpet, giving me a heavenly sense of magnificence and solitude—I used to dream that the Holy Father would open the door and come and sit in the big gilt chair and tell me all I wanted to know about himself.

Our villa had been the home of another Pope, Sixtus V, whose arms were painted all over the stairways and ceilings, and I felt it would be quite a proper place to receive his successor in . . .

Far on the upper outskirts of the city this stood, a great pile, golden grey with age, its enormous windows set foursquare to the world, its topmost terrace open to the winds, and commanding a view of the entire city below. Soracte and the 'dark Ciminian hills' lay to the north; the Sabines, jewelled with villages, to the east; the exquisite lines of the Alban hills to the south; and towards the fairy west the wide stretches of the Campagna rolled softly to the sea, their gold and purple emptiness touched here and there with the shaft of a ruined watch-tower, where shy, dark-eyed shepherds herded their flocks at night. The Campagna was so near, the villa so vast, that the gardens stretched away and lost themselves in it long before their boundary was reached.

In all the years that we played there my brother and I never got outside the grounds on the southern side, though we walked our little feet tired in trying to find out where they ended. But long before our time the outlying spaces had ceased to be gardens, and had been turned to agricultural uses. They were dotted with the stone huts of the peasants, who patiently planted cabbages and lettuce, fennel and Indian corn round broken fountains and tumbled pedestals;[81] who used the Temple of Minerva Medica and a beautiful but deserted Renaissance palace on the outskirts as storehouses for grain, and who sometimes crept into the gardens proper on dark nights, to steal the fruit on the old orange trees in the 'Viale', which ran the whole length

---

80. *A Diplomatist's Wife* 56–9. For her brother's recollection of the villa, see F. Marion Crawford, *Ave Roma Immortalis* (London 1899) 1.147f. = (1903) 136.

81. See G.M. De Rossi, *La riscoperta di Roma antica* (Rome 1983) 197: vegetable gardens at 'Minerva Medica'.

of the distance from the Piazza di Termini (now Delle Terme) to the Piazza of Santa Maria Maggiore, now called the Esquiline. At right angles to this Viale, a quadruple avenue of enormous cypresses slowly rose to terminate, far away south, in a steep artificial hill crowned with the 'Belvedere', the pavilion commanding the widest possible view, without which no pleasance would have been complete for the beauty-loving magnates of the later Renaissance.[82]

The cypresses were everywhere in that old garden; for century after century they had shed their needles on the ground, till the soil round their huge, upstanding roots was as velvety and fragrant as powdered sandalwood; but their newest topmost plumes waved in feathery freshness at the level of our upper windows—delicate dark lace against the matchless Roman sky.

The house itself was built of materials filched from the Baths of Diocletian, whose huge sulky-looking arches covered several acres of ground near us. There is no destroying that titanic masonry; and though many a palace had been built with the stone and marble that could be removed, even the Vandals who have ruled Rome since 1870 have had to utilize and build round the masses of bricks and concrete, which nothing short of dynamite would dislodge.

My dear father, who loved old grandeur and needed much space, fell in love with the Villa Negroni, and took it on a life-long lease from the owner, Prince Massimo, who reserved for himself a vast warren of rooms on the first floor,[83] and gave up all the rest to us. He only brought his family there in the spring and autumn for a short time; the winter saw him housed in the forbidding Palazzo Massimo, down in the oldest part of the city, and the summer months were spent at Arsoli, his feudal castle in the Sabines. He gave my father permission to erect a series of studios on the eastern side of the house, over the ancient reservoir of the Baths of Diocletian; and in these studios I often took refuge from nursery tyranny, and sat for whole days among the shining white statues, perfectly happy with a ball of clay and a modelling stick, listening to the delicate ring of chisel on marble, still to me the sweetest music in the world.

My father joyfully abetted me in these escapades, and I remember that when people came to look for me, he used to lift me up and hide me away, far above their heads, in the body of the charger which had been cast in sections for the Richmond monument.

---

82. The Viale della Sanità and the Viale Papale? Or the Viale Papale and the Viale della Giustizia (in which case 'south' must be an error)?
83. I.e. presumably the ground floor.

From the studios, I could slip out through a dark ilex grove always full of singing birds, and climb a little hill on which sat a colossal statue of Roma Imperatrix, looking down with stony eyes on her vassal city, while above her head waved the spires of some giant cypresses planted by Michelangelo, who used to walk in these gardens with his friend the great Pope Paul III. Up in the crimson drawing-room I wanted to see Pio Nono, but here, under his own trees, I wished Michelangelo would come and talk to me, and tell me why I loved his statues and was so horribly afraid of his paintings.

It is all gone now. The railway runs where the ilex grove broke in gold and green rustlings over my head; the railway station stands on the site of our studios; gone are the orange walk and the cypress avenue, and the lovely fountain court guarded by stone lions and encircled by cypresses wreathed to their crests with climbing roses. The fountain had been playing for three hundred years; and the palace was so quiet and remote that, when we children looked down from our nursery windows on moonlit nights, we used to see a ring of little Campagna foxes drinking silently out of the low marble basin.

Epilogue

The modern railway station, the third in succession, is set further back than its two predecessors. Instead of coming out on to the Piazza di Termini, the arriving traveller is now faced with the vast expanse of the Piazza dei Cinquecento. This desert of tarmac is not wholly featureless, however: to the right, as you emerge from the concourse, is a splendid stretch of the republican city wall. That is what was inside the long tree-lined mound that ran through the villa grounds. The trees, the mound and what was left of the ancient rampart, were removed in the 1870s and the full height of the wall revealed.[84]

The highest place, the Monte della Giustizia with its goddess enthroned, was at the point closest to the modern building, next to the station cafeteria. You must imagine the clipped cypresses of the Viale della Giustizia sloping down from there, below the taxi rank (or the queue where the taxis should be), and out of your sight in the direction of the Via Cavour. The other end of it, Fontana's 'Porta Viminale', was, I suppose, somewhere in the underground car park at the top of the Via Urbana.

---

84. De Rossi, op. cit. (n. 81) 206–215.

Another part of the wall survives in the Piazza Manfredo Fanti, in what was meant to be a park (now locked and overgrown) in front of a pretentious Pantheon-like building (now in disrepair). It looks like a theatre or an opera-house; but no, the inscription above the entrance— below Venus with tritons in a sea-shell on the roof—reads 'ACQVARIO ROMANO construito MDCCCLXXXV'. The same date, with a proud 'SPQR', appears above a boarded-up door in the Via Turatti to the south-east. Here, where once the road to Porta S. Lorenzo, with its elms and acacias, bounded the villa to the south, are the HQ and depot of the Sixth *Compagnia di Sossistenza* of the national Military Commissariat; some of it looks abandoned, and the rest has the scruffy, run-down air characteristic of army property.

Not all the *ottocento* dates are so depressing. In the Via del Viminale, once the Via de' Strozzi, just a few metres down from the site of Fontana's 'Porta Quirinale', is a tiny establishment which boasts 'dal 1890 Porchetta Romana. Bibite. Vino dei Castelli'. Just about here the boundary-stones of the Horti Lolliani were found in 1883. And between the wine-shop and its neighbour is an arch that leads to an alley called Via di Villa Montalto. This humble reminder of a glorious past serves the back entrances of hotels and other premises in the Via Principe Amedeo and the Via Giovanni Amendola. Most of the doors are anonymous, but one has a name. Perhaps its associations are not wholly inappropriate for the pleasure gardens of Lollia Paullina. It reads: 'American Workout Studio, Beverly Hills California'.

7

WITH BONI IN THE FORUM

The transformation of Rome after 1870, from the old papal town to the capital of united Italy, was reflected not only in the building boom but also in the new government's attitude to the ruins of the ancient city. In particular, the excavation of the Roman Forum was systematically taken in hand. In 1882–3 Rodolfo Lanciani extended the excavated area right up to the Arch of Titus, and in 1898–1902 Giocomo Boni achieved spectacular results with deep explorations down to the level of the archaic city.[1]

In Eva Tea's biography of Boni, much of the narrative of the crucial 1899 season of excavations is taken from the archaeologist's letters to an English friend, St Clair Baddeley.[2] Baddeley is now a forgotten figure. But he was much involved with Boni's epoch-making discoveries, and wrote about them in various English newspapers and magazines. Moreover, in the County Library at Gloucester a substantial collection of his papers survives, including notebooks and diaries of the times he spent in Rome. The story of his involvement with Roman archaeology is well worth digging out.[3]

Abbreviations:

NFR: R. Lanciani, *Notes from Rome*, ed. A.L. Cubberley (London 1988).
RDF: St Clair Baddeley, *Recent Discoveries in the Forum 1898–1904, by an Eyewitness* (London 1904).

1. See G.M. De Rossi, *La riscoperta di Roma antica* (Rome 1983) 26–36, for a well illustrated synthesis.
2. E. Tea, *Giacomo Boni nella vita del suo tempo* (Milan 1932) 2.26–33: 'lettere che formano tutt'insieme un vero giornale di scavo' (p. 27).
3. Full documentation in *Rivista dell'Instituto Nazionale d'Archeologia e Storia dell'Arte* series 3, 8–9 (1985–6, publ. 1987) 119–49.

1856–1895

Welbore St Clair Baddeley was born at St Leonards on 30 September 1856, the third and youngest son of Major (later Lt.-Col.) John Fraser Lodington Baddeley, Royal Artillery, and Emma Welbore Ellis. His father had served in the Crimea and been severely wounded at Inkerman in 1854; he does not appear in the *Army List* after 1862. Baddeley was educated at Wellington College from 1868 to 1872, but did not go to university; instead, he 'chose the education of world travel',[4] visiting Brazil and Argentina at the age of 18–19.

In April 1879 he was introduced to Edmund Christy, twenty-nine years his senior, and began a long and devoted friendship in which Christy took the place of the father Baddeley had lost: 'I was in fact a son to him, and he was my dearest foster-father for twenty-three years.' In September of that year, the day before his twenty-third birthday, he and Christy left together for Italy. The tours they made that winter and the next remained vividly in Baddeley's memory:[5]

> In 1879 the writer was taken to visit an ancient Venetian lady who had never left the city, and boasted that she had never seen a cow . . .

> I can recollect in the winter of 1881 seeing the Arno at Florence being skated upon, and icicles like a prodigious portcullis hanging from the Ponte Vecchio . . .

Rome, however, he found 'sultry and depressing'.

1883 found Baddeley in Calabria with Christy in March, and in Moscow with his brother John in the summer, visiting 'Count Paul Schouvaloff, brother to his and our family friend Count Peter.' The same pattern was followed in 1884 (July and August in Finland and Russia), and this time the winter in the south was spent in Rome, where Rodolfo Lanciani was now in charge of the Forum excavations. In 1882 Lanciani had opened up the whole area from the Arch of Titus to the Campidoglio by demolishing the surviving baulk between S. Maria Liberatrice and S. Lorenzo in Miranda; now he was excavating the House of the Vestals, and Baddeley (at twenty-seven, ten years younger than Lanciani himself) was one of the interested observers.

---

4. *St Andrews Citizen* 1 July 1933: 'Laureation address' for Baddeley's honorary degree.
5. *Notes and Queries* 11.1 (1910) 384, 9.2 (1898) 104.

What looms larger in his diary, however, is the social life of the Anglo-American 'colony' in Rome. He meets F. Marion Crawford (newly famous as a novelist) at the Palazzo Altemps one day in January 1884, and in the evening attends a reception by W.W. Story at the Palazzo Barberini. These talented Americans were much more fun than the English set, 'exclusive, dull, pretentious, keeping much aloof',[6] and Baddeley had a certain claim on their attention as a budding 'man of letters'. For he already had five books of verse to his credit—historical romances and 'lyrical dramas', eked out with sonnets and other short occasional poems, of a literary quality best illustrated by the fact that when the present writer looked at them in the Cambridge University Library in 1984, their pages were still uncut after more than a century. The day after his return from Italy, he met Browning while out walking in London; he was already an acquaintance of Sir Richard Burton; and he was careful to record in his diary the day he was introduced to Tennyson and invited to a country walk with him. But the romances of Marion Crawford and Ouida better reflect his own literary level.

In 1885 Baddeley's travels took him to France, Switzerland and Austria; but in March of the following year he and Christy settled into a room 'under the thick ilex on the terrace in front of the Medici Villa and Trinità dei Monti', with a view across to St Peter's—'the dear old view, so often contemplated before.' That note of nostalgic affection (Baddeley was only twenty-nine!) coincides with a new interest in Rome and its history. 'Much progress has been made in excavating the Vestals since we were here two years ago,' he notes; and his diaries now contain extended passages of description—on the Ghetto, the Forum, etc.—which look like draft material for a book of travel essays. (Baddeley published two such books in the next three years, but as it happens none of the essays they contain was on Rome.)[7]

In one such passage, he takes a consciously 'progressive' view of the post-1870 modernisation of the city:[8]

> Rome from the foreigner's point of view is a sacred deposit of past History, an eternal Museum, a palace of aesthetic antiquarian pleasure and delectation which ought to be secured and guaranteed against the

6. Frances Elliott, *Roman Gossip* (London 1896) 297–9.
7. *Tchay and Chianti, or Wanderings in Russia and Italy* (London 1887); *Travel-Tide* (London 1889).
8. Gloucester MSS, notebook 2 (17 March 1886); cf. *Tchay and Chianti* ix–xii.

invasion of the Spirit of the Age, or any other financial revolution. The gardens of the villas must be insured against their owners, the ancient picturesque streets where man and beast are herded together in one crowd must never be made wider or more practical, for that would spoil the pleasure of the eye and memory of a hundred thousand English and American frequenters of Rome. There must be no interference with the ruins in order to benefit national wants. Rome was made for the sentimentality of the amateur and the dilettante, not for the heart and centre of a regenerate people, the core of her new industrial life. Yet the palaces so universally admired and lauded were built by the popes and their minions out of the Coliseum and the temples of the Roman deities of old.

But forsooth, the English in their conceit, being a fly on the chariot wheel, imagine they control the wheel's motion. They will see that to be impossible, and that the hard-won cause must express itself as it does because the spirit of industry is the spirit of the age: and the spirit of the people takes hold of the actual present, and not of the ideal past which is the joy and pensive pleasant melancholy of the indulged traveller.

The popes should be taken to Madame Tussauds, and the Englishmen too, and pickled . . .

Self-irony was not one of Baddeley's characteristics (he took himself too seriously for that); but 'the sentimentality of the amateur and the dilettante' and the 'pensive pleasant melancholy of the indulged traveller' are in fact a good description of his own attitude, as revealed all too clearly in his poems.

His next book of verse was a sumptuous quarto volume entitled *Lotus Leaves*, published in 1887 after Baddeley's return from an extensive tour through Greece, Turkey and the Balkans. He had stopped at Venice on the way back, and 'At Venice' was one of the poems in the new collection:

> The waterways are silent now,
>   And eventide is sweet and clear.
> A full moon cloven by the prow
>   Gleams faintly on our gondolier.
> Velvet as night we glide between
>   Cool oozy beds of trembling green,—
>   Save the low whispering of the stream
>   That makes the twilight round us seem
>   As life's own dream.

I quote these lines both as an example (mercifully brief) of Baddeley's poetic style, and because it was during that stay in Venice, as a result of just such an evening cruise, that Baddeley first met Giacomo Boni. The gondola had passed the Doge's Palace, where there was scaffolding up. Baddeley's companion explained that there had been some subsidence, and introduced him to the man in charge. Boni was twenty-eight, Baddeley thirty-one. 'E furono amici per sempre', says Eva Tea.[9]

More travels: North Africa in 1888, France in 1888 and 1890, Canada in 1891. In the meantime, Baddeley had met his future wife. On 1 February 1890 he was introduced to Helen Georgiana, second daughter of O.E. Grant Esq., Clerk of the Table at the House of Lords, and sister of the Katherine Grant whose portrait by Herkomer (as 'The Lady in White') had been the sensation of the Royal Academy exhibition five years before.[10] His next book of verse, which appeared in 1891, was entitled *Love's Vintage*.

However, Baddeley was preparing to widen his literary horizons beyond verse and travel essays to the more scholarly genre of history. In 1889 he began to contribute to *Notes and Queries*, and his next trip to Italy, in 1892, was evidently undertaken with a specific project in mind, a biographical account of Queen Joanna I of Naples. The book was published in 1893, and immediately damned by the serious reviewers. The *English Historical Review* had this to say:[11]

> Mr Baddeley's sumptuously got-up book on Joanna of Naples consists of a series of diffuse sketches and essays on various historical points, which are not always very closely related to the life of his heroine, and which convey a minimum of historical information with a maximum of cheap eloquence. The book has no substance at all about it. The style is singularly bad . . .

The author, meanwhile, was back in Italy collecting material for a sequel, *Charles III of Naples and Urban VI*, which he published in November.

In the spring of 1894, *Notes and Queries* printed a very hostile attack on *Queen Joanna of Naples* by 'L.L.K.'; Baddeley made a good, dignified reply, which scored a few points off his critic but could not answer the

9. Baddeley, *Lotus Leaves* (London 1887) 101; Tea, op. cit. (n. 2 above) 1.190.
10. J. Saxon Mills, *Life and Letters of Sir Hubert Herkomer* (London 1923) 149–55.
11. *EHR* 8 (1893) 398.

main charge ('that my account cannot be described by myself, nor by others, as an absolute history, or even as purposed fiction, maybe brands it as an undesirable literary hybrid'); and the controversy continued throughout the year.[12] In May, Baddeley was in Italy again, and he was able to take credit for further research when the *Charles III* book was published; by the end of June his opponent had read it, and 'was pleased to notice various signs of progress in the transformation process from historical romance to serious history.'[13]

Fortified, perhaps, by this evidence that he might one day be taken seriously as an historian, and with the satisfaction of three books published in eighteen months,[14] Baddeley married the beautiful Helen on 4 September 1894. After a honeymoon at Dunster on the Somerset coast, he took his bride to Italy; with the inseparable Christy, the Baddeleys spent the winter at Rome and Salerno, returning to England at the end of April. Their son was born on 10 June 1895, and named after his godfather, Edmund Christy.

Baddeley was thirty-nine. It was about this time that he bought the old Cotswold manor house—Castle Hale, Painswick, near Stroud—which was to be home for him and Helen for nearly fifty years.

1895–1898

As a family man with a settled abode, Baddeley redirected the focus of his activity from travel to scholarship. He had left Wellington at fifteen, and had no formal academic training; but wide reading, much experience of the world, a capaciously retentive memory and a gift for languages more than compensated for the lack. The pages of *Notes and Queries*—to which he was a particularly avid contributor during the five years after his marriage—testify to the variety of his interests and the breadth of his knowledge.

---

12. *NQ* 8.5 (1894) 261–4, 301–3; 369–72 (quotation from p. 369), 429–31; 509–11; 8.6 (1894) 29–31; 169–71, 229–31; 369–72, 429–31; 8.7 (1895) 49–52.
13. Baddeley, *Charles III of Naples and Urban VIII* . . . (London 1894); L.L.K., *NQ* 8.5 (1894) 511.
14. I.e. the two historical works, and *Tennyson's Grave* (London 1893), a poem of eighteen stanzas published as a separate volume, in which Baddeley made the most of his brief acquaintance with the great Laureate.

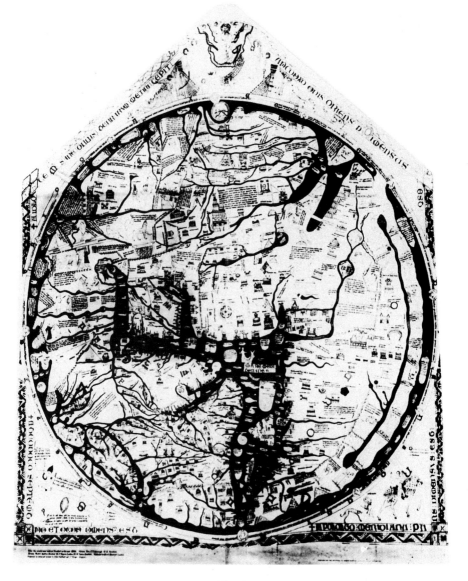

Plate I
The Hereford *mappa mundi*. The inscription recording Julius Caesar's world survey runs
round the edge, starting at the top left-hand corner.

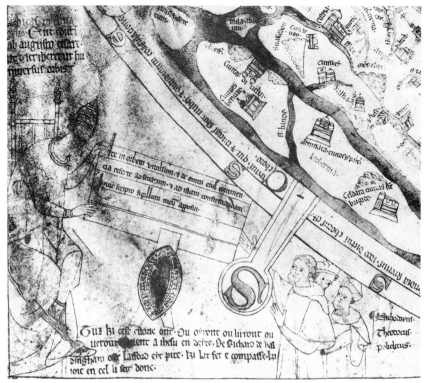

(a)

(b)

Plate II
(a) Detail from the *mappa mundi*: Augustus and the three surveyors.
(b) Augustus with a 'T-O' map, from Lambert's *Liber Floridus*.

(a)

(b)

Plate III
(a) Excavation of a Roman house in the Villa Negroni, 1777 (painting by Thomas Jones).
The church in the background is probably imaginary: that is where the *palazzo* should be.

(b) S. Maria Maggiore (Parker no. 2124). On the left, part of the Villa Negroni-Massimo; the
'porta Viminale' is behind the building at the bottom left. The pine-trees in the distance
mark the *belvedere*, behind the church and monastery of S. Antonio Abbate.

(a)

(b)

Plate IV
(a) The papal Stazione di Termine, from Monte della Giustizia (Parker no. 1741). In the left background, the Baths of Diocletian.

(b) Preparing the ground for development: the Villa Negroni-Massimo in 1874 (Parker no. 3185). Note the remains of Roman buildings being dismantled; no other record of them survives.

Plate V
Detail of the bronze doors of the Senate wing of the Capitol, Washington D.C. Thomas
Crawford's allegorical group includes portraits of his wife (with their baby son) and their
four-year-old daughter 'Mimoli'.

(a)

(b)   (c)

Plate VI
Mary Crawford, Mrs Hugh Fraser: a detail from the Washington group (Plate V), and
frontispiece portraits from two of her volumes of memoirs.

(a)

(b)

(c)

Plate VII
(a) Group at the *lapis niger*, 12 January 1899 (detail from a photograph by Thomas Ashby).
Left to right: *custode*, A. Bartoli, Wickham Steed (?), Giacomo Boni, St Clair Baddeley (?).

(b) W. St Clair Baddeley, *c.* 1930.

(c) G. McN. Rushforth F.S.A., 1937.

Plate VIII
W.F. Jackson Knight, 1895–1964. 'J.K. at Caroline House 1953', by Jean Creedy (Jean
Howard, U.C.S.W. 1937–1939); Queen's Building, University of Exeter. A colleague
commented: 'That's right for J.K.; he always was at a slight angle to the universe.'

Two particular projects now occupied his time in the study at Castle Hale: a new book on Angevin Naples, to show the critics of his earlier work that he could satisfy their scholarly standards, and the local history of Painswick, his new home, beginning with its church. For the latter, he had to go no further afield than Gloucester, Oxford and London; the former, however, needed research in Naples itself and in the Vatican Library, so the Baddeleys spent the winter of 1895–6 in Rome. The result was gratifying. When *Robert the Wise and his Heirs, 1278–1352* was published in 1897 (dedicated 'To My Wife'), it included a 54-page appendix of hitherto unexploited documents from the Vatican archives, and the reviewers were duly impressed.[15]

No diary survives for 1897, so we cannot tell what turned Baddeley's enquiring mind from Naples to the Roman Campagna. But it is an obvious guess that Lanciani had something to do with it. We have seen Baddeley taking an interest in the Atrium Vestae excavations in 1884 and 1886; and he met Lanciani himself in 1893. The publication of *Ancient Rome in the Light of Recent Discoveries* (1888), *Pagan and Christian Rome* (1893) and *The Ruins and Excavations of Ancient Rome* (1897) had by now made Lanciani's name synonymous with Roman archaeology in the minds of English-speaking readers (he also had a 'Notes from Rome' column appearing regularly in the London journal *Athenaeum*);[16] so we can be sure that Baddeley made a point of renewing his acquaintance while he was staying in Rome.

At this time the Forum excavations were in abeyance, and Lanciani was concentrating on exploring the Campagna. As Thomas Ashby was to put it many years later:[17]

> He thoroughly explored the Campagna, in every direction, particularly in the company of his English friends—the late Contessa Gautier, Miss D.E. Bulwer (a skilled photographer), my late father and myself . . . At least once or twice a week there were excursions, by train or carriage.

---

15. E.g. B. Croce, *Arch. stor. prov. nap.* 23 (1898) 425–30. For a balanced but favourable assessment, see E.-G. Léonard, *Histoire de Jeanne Ire* (Monaco and Paris 1932) I xiv–xv.

16. Now published in book form by the British School at Rome (*NFR*).

17. T. Ashby, *Arch. R. Soc. romana di storia patria* 51 (1928) 126: my translation.

Miss Bulwer's photographs vividly illustrate these expeditions into the countryside; the company varies, but two figures are always present—an elegant middle-aged lady in black (Mme Gautier?), and Lanciani, usually in a bowler hat, staring confidently at the camera.

Ashby himself was twenty-three years old at the time, just down from Oxford with a first-class degree in Literae Humaniores. The survival of his diary for 1897–8 shows how Lanciani's outings captured his imagination.[18] It begins with daily trivia; from late December 1897 it concentrates on outings only, with detailed notes of finds; from April 1898 alternative pages are left blank for additional notes; finally the diary format is abandoned, inessentials (such as names of companions) are omitted, and we have simply the dated annotations of a serious scholar.

Baddeley was nearly twenty years older than young Ashby; but it seems that on him too, at just this time, the effect of Lanciani's guidance was much the same. His diaries recommence at the beginning of 1898, with the Baddeleys in Rome, evidently staying at the Hotel Eden in the new Via Ludovisi. On 3 January they went to tea with Mme Lanciani at 2 via Goito. On 7 and 10 January Baddeley examined the nymphaeum of Sallust's gardens, just round the corner from the hotel, in the new Piazza Sallustio. He was accompanied by a lady called Daisy Hilton-Green, with whom he went to hear Lanciani lecturing at the Baths of Caracalla on 11 January. Lanciani invited Baddeley to come out with him to Frascati the following week, 'excavating a villa and mapping out'.

> Tuesday 18 January 1898.
> To Marino with Lanciani. Albano. Find villa remains. Stamped tiles.
> Descend by vineyards to Squarciella and Frascati 4 miles further.
> Lunched in cavern. Happy day.

That was the first of many expeditions with Lanciani in the next three months, mainly to the Albano-Frascati area, during which Baddeley became, if not an archaeologist, then at least an ardent seeker after brickstamps and inscriptions.

Young Ashby too was regularly accompanying Lanciani, sometimes on the same trips as Baddeley, sometimes with his father or other English friends like Dr Charles and his wife, more often on his own. (He and Baddeley walked out to Porta Furba on the Via Tuscolana one afternoon

---

18. British School Archive, Rome.

in February, and found some brickstamps and a fragmentary inscription.) What strikes one most is Lanciani's energy—he was regularly lecturing and giving guided tours throughout this period—and the generosity with which he spent his time on these English amateurs. With Ashby at least, his efforts were well rewarded.

Baddeley's more dilettante attitude appears in his diary entry for 1 March:

> To Albano with Lanciani and the Ashbys. 9.15. Glorious sun. We are to visit the rock-cut sepulchres of the Parthian legion of Severus which had its barracks out by the Cappuccini above Albano—that is their Cemetery. We spend an hour turning over a stone. Huge centipedes. Orange-coloured. The Professor Lanciani photographs me in the act of digging on hands and knees. We are not lucky, however! Later, we come upon one of those hobby-horse-shaped Parthian tombstones and can make out 'qui vixit annis XXVIII' and a few other letters. Enormous toads in pairs. Smaller always uppermost. We traverse the old Monte Cavo road from Ariccia, which the generals used for their triumphs on M. Alba.

Three days earlier, Baddeley had been present when the excavations below SS. Giovanni e Paolo were shown to the public; he wrote a paragraph on it for *Notes and Queries*, recording how, 'while wandering by taper-light', they heard 'the deep monotonous chanting of the Passionist monks in the medieval basilica above.'[19] The emphasis on atmosphere rather than historical detail is very characteristic.

By now Baddeley considered himself an authority on Rome and Roman history. On 31 March he took a guided tour round the site of the old Ghetto; the following day, lunching at the Ashbys', he was discussing Roman Gloucester with F.J. Haverfield, Senior Student of Christ Church, Oxford. Haverfield had been young Ashby's tutor until the previous year. Now he was in Rome with his elder colleague H.F. Pelham, the Camden Professor of Ancient History, during the University's Easter vacation.[20] On 4 April Lanciani took Pelham, Haverfield, Baddeley and the two Ashbys to Tivoli; three days later, however, when the Oxford

---

19. *NQ* 9.1 (1898) 225f.
20. For this visit, see T.P. Wiseman, *A Short History of the British School at Rome* (London 1990) 3.

visitors went with Lanciani and the Ashbys to Nettuno, Baddeley was not with them. He was giving a lecture at the Lateran.

The following week, there were trips to Ostia and Palestrina, with Helen Baddeley now joining the party; the week after that, on Friday 21 April—the anniversary of the foundation of Rome—Baddeley lectured in the Forum itself to an audience of 25, including several members of the Anglo-American community whose names he thought worth recording in his diary.[21] The following Sunday the Baddeleys left Rome for a leisurely return to England.

Among his contributions that summer to *Notes and Queries* Baddeley published an article on Alba Longa, contesting Gell's identification of the site as Palazzolo:[22]

> I was fortunate enough to discover an inscribed marble block, showing the surrounding remains to have belonged to a doubtless sumptuous villa pertaining to the Galba family. I am driven, therefore, to infer, with Prof. Lanciani, after six days entirely devoted to careful research on the ground, that the remains seen by Sir William Gell belong to a period centuries later than the destruction of Alba Longa.

Baddeley lends the weight of his authority to Lanciani's identification of Castel Gandolfo as the true site.

The article was evidently important to him (he recorded its appearance in his diary), and it is interesting that he referred in it to young Ashby's identification of Lake Regillus in the *Rendiconti dei Lincei*.[23] He clearly felt that these publications conferred enhanced status on their authors as experts in Roman archaeology. At any rate, when he and his family returned to Rome in December, Baddeley went straight to the Ashbys' on arrival; two days later he was out with them up the Via Nomentana. It was the first of a series of expeditions (more than twenty in the next four months), often with the Ashbys, sometimes with Lanciani, occasionally

21. Gloucester MSS, notebook 18: 'Lecture in Forum at 10.30–1. 25 people. Capt. & Mrs Mahan among them; Mrs J. Ward Howe and Mrs Elliott. Mr & Mrs Terry. Will. and Leon. Darwin and Mrs Darwin. The 3 Whitiers.'
22. *NQ* 9.2 (1898) 201–2.
23. T. Ashby, *Rend. Linc.* 7.2 (1898) 103, presented by Lanciani; cf. *Classical Review* 12 (1898) 470–2.

with other English friends. But what his diary records is picturesque scenery and 'marble hunts'.[24]

Meanwhile Guido Baccelli (Minister of Public Instruction) had appointed Boni to resume the Forum excavations, which had lapsed since Lanciani's campaign of 1882–3. On 9 December Baddeley notes:

> Lanciani, Bacelli [*sic*] and G. Boni are to meet at the Forum this afternoon to confer. It is important.

This seems to be the first time Boni's name appears in the diaries (the story of their meeting in Venice was told by Baddeley to Eva Tea much later); but it may be significant that a statement by Boni of his proposals for excavating the Forum, dated apparently the previous day, survives among Boni's letters to Baddeley.[25] Perhaps Boni had sent it to his old acquaintance in the hope of engaging his interest and support. The document is scathing about earlier work (evidently alluding to Lanciani, though not by name), and Boni may have felt he needed allies.

It was Lanciani, however, who took Baddeley and his wife round the first of Boni's excavations (the *cella* of the Vesta temple) on 12 December; and Baddeley did not interrupt his trips into the Campagna to keep up to date with the new work. It is not until 29 December that we find him talking to Boni in the Forum, by which time excavation was proceeding in the 'Temple of Romulus', by the Rostra, at the Arch of Septimius Severus and along the Sacra Via.

1899, Winter and Spring

In the new year, under Lanciani's guidance, Baddeley concentrated his attention on Tivoli, and in particular on the villa complex at S. Stefano, just south-east of Hadrian's Villa:

> Tuesday 10 January 1899.
> To Tivoli with Ashbys and Miss Bulwer. Work away at Monte
> S. Stephano [*sic*] behind Hadrian's villa. Find a good inscription.

---

24. Cf. Matilda Lucas, *Two Englishwomen in Rome* (London 1938) 3, on J.H. Parker's advice to English visitors: 'Ladies, steal what bits of marble you can find.'

25. Boni papers, Instituto Lombardo, Milan.

Saturday 14 January.
To Tivoli walking with Lanciani and Ashby. Last Tuesday L. couldn't accompany us: so we went alone with Miss Bulwer . . .

Friday 20 January.
To Bagni with Robertson. Lovely spring day . . . Thence up to S. Stefano past Villa Bulgarini. Found a fresh piece of the inscription: delighted beyond measure. We luncheon there. Old woman boils eggs for us. Carry off our prize to Tivoli . . . 4.10 train to Rome. Smoke. Glorious afternoon. Olives glitter and gleam. Emerald wheat in plain below grey rock above. Rocca Giovane in shadow, lonely and lofty Lunghezza: tell Lucretia's story. Leave the prize at Lanciani's: 2 via Goito.

And again with the Ashbys on 29 January, with the Ashbys and Lanciani on 4 February, 17 and 18 March.[26] (The diary entries may give an unfair impression of dilettantism: Baddeley was also making detailed notes and drawings in his pocketbook.) The inscription, of which further fragments turned up in March and July that year, turned out to refer to C. Iulius Plancius Varus Cornutus, Pliny's colleague in the consulship of AD 100. Lanciani first published the fragments and paid due credit to their discoverer, 'sig. Welbore St Clair Baddeley, l'illustre storico della Regina Giovanna e di Robert il saggio ecc.' Baddeley had already told *The Times* Rome correspondent about the find; it was duly reported on 24 February.[27]

Meanwhile, however, matters of greater moment were taking place in the field of Roman archaeology, as the readers of *The Times* were already aware. On 9 January, Prof. Richard Norton of the American School of Archaeology in Rome had contributed a lengthy letter on the new Forum excavations, praising Boni and condemning the incompetence of his predecessors.[28] As it happens, it was late in the evening of that very day that the workmen uncovered the *lapis niger*—the black paving-stones of

---

26. See *Thomas Ashby: un archeologo fotografa la campagna romana tra '800 e '900* (Rome 1986) 53–6, nos 32–3: Ashby's photographs taken on 4 February.
27. Lanciani, *Bull. Com.* (1899) 33–4; *Times* 24 Feb. 1899 p. 13, 4 March 1899 p. 15.
28. *Times* 9 Jan. 1899 p. 14 = *NFR* 241–7.

the Comitium. Boni was not able to verify it till the following morning, so 10 January is the canonical date for the discovery.[29]

No wonder Lanciani coudn't come to S. Stefano that day! Baddeley found his inscription, but missed the great discovery. He later alleged that he had been with Boni at the site the day before, and later still contrived to give the impression that he had been present at the discovery itself.[30] In fact, his diaries at first betray little interest in Boni's activities, though he was certainly aware of them. Now, however, he started taking them seriously. Baddeley may well be the figure on the right in Ashby's photograph of the *lapis niger* site on 12 January (Plate VIIa). Certainly he took the trouble to inform himself about it. Wickham Steed's report for *The Times*, sent on 16 January, was based on notes supplied by 'the well-known English historian and archaeologist Mr St Clair Baddeley'; the previous day Baddeley himself had written to *The Athenaeum* 'to acquaint your readers with the interesting discovery made last Wednesday . . .' Both pieces refer also to the supposed column base in the niche at the front of the Divus Iulius temple, at the excavation of which Baddeley had been present.[31]

But he was not spending all his time in the Forum. On 19 January he was at Sette Bassi; on 22 January he took Helen to Naples for a few days, thus missing the opportunity to hear from either Boni or Lanciani about the Lincei session on the 'black stone' and its significance. On 31 January he lectured to the British and American Archaeological Society on 'The Sacred Trees of Rome'; the elder Ashby was in the chair, and Baddeley noted with satisfaction that the audience numbered about 100. The following morning he lectured at the Lateran:

2 hrs. 15 people. Lady Brabourne, Lady Susan Byng. 2 Princesses Calitzino, Miss Ozanne, Mrs Ransom Hill, Mrs Trotter, Major Urmston,

29. See Boni's letter to Ruskin on 11 January, printed in *Rivista politica e letteraria* 6.2 (Feb. 1899) 135–7, Tea (op. cit. n. 2 above) 2.15–17, and *Studi romani* 7 (1959) 269.
30. Baddeley, *Archaeologia* 57 (1900) 175f.; *RDF* 15.
31. *Times* 20 Jan. 1899 p. 7; *Athenaeum* 3717 (21 Jan. 1899) 90. Cf. Ashby's notes on these excavations: *Archaeologia a Roma nelle fotografie di Thomas Ashby 1891–1930* (Rome 1989) 159–64 (*lapis niger*), 117f. (Divus Iulius).

> Mrs Taylor, Mrs Dixon. Afternoon went to look at 'scavi' in Forum.
> Nothing new.

That entry shows where his main interests lay.[32]

Baddeley's lectures and guided tours were clearly a great social success with the Anglo-American community. The Lateran lecture (subject not recorded) was repeated by request of Baddeley's friends at the Hotel Eden on 11 February. One of those present was Richard Norton of the American School, whose letter to *The Times* had urged the destruction of the modern street above the so-called Basilica Aemilia (really the Basilica Paulli). Another was Douglas Murray, a friend of the British Ambassador, Lord Currie; the following day Baddeley was showing both Murray and the Ambassador round the Forum, and dining at the Embassy. On 17 February Lord Currie was in Baddeley's audience at a lecture in the Forum. A plan was formed, to find the funds needed to expropriate the houses and enable the Basilica to be excavated.

Murray and the Ambassador introduced Baddeley to Mr Lionel Phillips, a wealthy Englishman recently arrived from Pretoria, and Baddeley invited Phillips to his next lecture. On 3 March at the Colosseum, on the subject of Aemilius Paullus' triumph, Baddeley dwelt on the glories of the 'Basilica Aemilia' and the lamentable shortage of finance which stood in the way of its exploration. Phillips was inspired to make an offer.

Eva Tea gives a romanticised version of the story, but the realities appear more clearly from two memoranda composed by Baddeley soon afterwards.[33] The first runs as follows:

> In Feb. G. Boni informed me that the Government estimate of House-buying-up, necessary for excavating the 'Forum' Aemilia [*sic*], amounted to 64,000 lire. Friday 4th [i.e. 3rd] I gave a lecture about the grandiose triumph of Aemilius (Lucius Paullus, BC 179) over Perseus, after battle of Pydna. Douglas Murray, Mr Lionel Phillips, Miss Allen, and others; Earl Spencer, Ld. Tweedmouth. Afterwards Mr Lionel Phillips made the request to offer £500 (sterling) towards this excavation. I accepted; and wrote to On. Baccelli (Minister of Public Instruction), telling him of this v. generous offer and asking if it was

---

32. The 'sacred trees' lecture was printed in the *Journal of the BAASR* 3.1 (1898–9) 7–20.
33. Gloucester MSS, notebook 20; cf. Tea, op. cit. (n. 2 above) 2.22.

acceptable. He has not yet thought fit to reply: although ten days have now passed since I wrote. My letter was personally delivered to his Engineer, Sig. G. Boni, an old acquaintance of mine, and one of John Ruskin's special friends. He directs the 'scavi' now going on at the Forum in various sites.

On Tuesday [i.e. 7 March?], Signor Boni called on me, and told me my letter had caused surprise and then pleasure; and had been shown to Deputies, and finally to the King. But no word at all, even of acknowledgement (of my letter and the offer), had been vouchsafed me.

I felt hurt: and anxious (for the Donor has now left for Paris). I wrote to the Phillips's at Florence and wired them that a reply would, no doubt, soon come![34]

On Friday, however, I called, and left a fresh letter written before breakfast at (3 Piazza Campitelli) On. Baccelli. No response! Next day [i.e. 11 March?] I told Mr Steed about it and he resolved to awaken the official energies so markedly dormant. He wired to SS. Canevaro and Fortis, and then had favourable hints from these and might go and see them later.

Canevaro sent a written card of admiring thanks on Saturday morning to Steed which the latter presently brought to me. After 2 p.m. (12.3.'99) [i.e. 11 March?] Signor Bernabei brought personally a letter from Baccelli acknowledging the noble gift and expressing a desire that an appointment to meet shall be made between myself and him on Monday next [20 March]. He also [illegible] . . .

Also, that the Government should 'not be placed in too delicate a position?' This puts a fresh complexion upon the matter—chilling delay.

Only part of the second memorandum survives. Where the text begins, it seems that Baddeley is being briefed by the Ambassador, Lord Currie, before his interview with Baccelli:

. . . i.e. as if I was myself a Government official, and to let him know that the money will be handed over to Ld. Currie by the 'Donatore' at any moment for the said purpose. *We should like to be kept acquainted with whatever steps the Minister will take towards carrying out the*

---

34. Added later: 'Heard augmentation of gift at night L 64,000' (£2400 according to Steed, *Times* 22 Jan. 1901 p. 12).

proposals. 'Reasonable speed is too vague' (Ld. C.). He regards it as an act of friendship to Italy, and will not otherwise regard it.

Consequently, I interviewed Baccelli at 2 Piazza Campitelli for over half an hour. Professor Bernabei was, perforce, present. But twice I noticed that they spoke with their eyes.

The *Messagero* had an incorrect account of the Donation the very morning. I inserted a correction; which duly appeared 2 days later, to the effect of the Donor's exclusive aim and purpose. Evidently their corrupt press is under official thumbs; and we have to count on that for certain.

Boni's work had made the Forum interesting to the general public, and Baddeley's facility as a lecturer meant that he was in demand to explain it. On two successive days in the middle of the 'Baccelli affair' he was in action again—on 14 March sharing a lecture tour of the Forum with Lanciani (who took over at the Comitium), on 15 March showing Lord Currie and Miss Sullivan over the Palatine 'in order to complete their inspection'. The diaries show that his interest in the Campagna was still strong—the excursions with Lanciani and/or the Ashbys continued throughout February and March—and his work in Rome itself was not confined to the Forum.[35] But the new excavations were where public attention was concentrated, and Baddeley could never resist public attention.

Soon the 'Basilica Aemilia' would be revealed, and the 'mountains of exquisitely carved marbles' that Lanciani was confident it still contained.[36] Meanwhile, Boni was already excavating below the *lapis niger* pavement. On 28 March he found the bronze statuette of an augur with a *lituus*, on 31 March part of the archaic altar, identified as the pedestal for one of the stone lions at the supposed tomb of Romulus. Baddeley immediately communicated these events to a London newspaper, the first of a regular series of reports in *The Globe* during the next twelve months. He and Helen and young Edmund were to leave Rome three days later, but he evidently arranged with Boni to keep him immediately informed of any new developments; Baddeley would then report them as if from Rome. So from 8 April to 9 June the Rome

---

35. He claimed to have recognised a fragment of the Ara Pacis in the Gesù (*RDF* 105); according to Lanciani (*NFR* 386) it was 'discovered by accident'.
36. *NFR* 262.

correspondent of *The Globe* was operating from Painswick,
Gloucestershire.[37]

Lanciani reported the 'lion pedestal' find in his *Athenaeum* column,
with generous praise of Boni:

> The work of exploration has been carried out with great care and skill
> by Cavaliere Boni, and it has already led to important results, showing
> how wrong we all have been in disbelieving every particular of Roman
> traditional history (if I can use such an expression) previous to the
> Punic wars.

Lanciani and Baddeley himself were on excellent terms. We have seen
Baddeley working at S. Stefano under Lanciani's guidance, and the
esteem in which he held him was expressed in public at the Comitium on
14 March:

> S[ignor] L[anciani] has been gifted with the happy power among his
> many talents of, I may say, holding the mirror up to the monuments of
> Roman History, and making his listeners aware of their very form and
> presence. The monuments, the very wrecks of monuments, under the
> spell he commands, seem to resume their functional beauty and
> practically live for us: and I feel that the vote of thanks, which it
> becomes my agreeable duty to propose to him today, will be most
> cordially received.

In the light of what happened later, it is good to have that on record.[38]

1899, Summer

Boni's first letters, in April and May, are addressed formally to 'Dear
Mr Baddeley'—though with *saluti alla signora* and *un bel bacione* to
little Edmund which show that he was on good terms with the family—

---

37. *Globe* 24 April 1899 p. 6 ('Rome, April 22'), based on Boni letter received on
    19 April; 8 May p. 4 ('Rome, May 5'), written at Painswick on 6 May; 6 June
    p. 4 ('Rome, June 2'), based on two Boni letters, the second dated 21 May:
    Boni papers, Instituto Lombardo, Milan.
38. *NFR* 257; Gloucester MSS, notebook 20 ('Points for the other or *Upper
    Forum Lecture* Tues. 10.30, 14.3.99').

'and contain purely factual details of his most recent finds. But then comes a very sudden change, both in style and content:[39]

> My dear Baddeley,
> They even denied that the *niger lapis* was marble, they called my belief 'an entirely untenable opinion'—like a sick hallucination, they mocked me as the archaeological 'medium' of the Roman Forum (as if intuition were not the sum of positive data which escape the eye of the masses); they have tried to remove me from the monuments that I love more than myself. But as long as I live I shall remember that while the academies were academizing, while the scholarly mob was making mischief, Minister Baccelli used to grasp my hand and say: Courage!!

What had happened to produce this sudden outpouring?

On 28 May the Reale Accademia dei Lincei had met to discuss the new finds—including the most recent, a well which Boni believed to be the Puteal Libonis, full of material which Boni believed to be votive offerings. The academics deplored such confident identifications: as Lanciani observed, 'the black stones are likewise transformed into the grave of Romulus'.[40] On 31 May Boni was under the black stones, dosed with quinine against a high fever, and made the sensational discovery of a stele with an archaic inscription. Hence his cry of triumph and defiance:[41]

> To reach the 'Tomb of Romulus', I seem to have been navigating for five months on the high seas with no compass but that of faith.

From now on, Boni's defence of his faith becomes a crusade; and the chief of the infidels is identified as Lanciani.

In a postscript to the same letter, Boni tells Baddeley that he has started to uncover the ancient paving of the Sacra Via near the Basilica of Maxentius: 'sta a due metri di profondità da quello del tardo medioevo'. What Boni calls the late-medieval paving is what Lanciani had laid bare in 1882, and described in his most recent book as 'the queen of streets'.[42]

---

39. Boni papers, 'Roma, Giugno 1899' (my translation). Baddeley left Painswick for Rome on 9 June, and was 'with Boni Forum' on 12 June.
40. *NFR* 264. Cf. 260f. for the well.
41. N. 39 above.
42. Lanciani, *Ruins and Excavations of Ancient Rome* (London 1897) 190, 208f.; cf. *NFR* 253f. for his defence against implied criticism of his own excavations.

Baddeley was about to return to Rome for a month's visit; if he was to be involved in these dramatic events, as he clearly intended, then he would have to make up his mind whose side he was on.

As soon as he got to Rome, Baddeley lost no time in inspecting the new finds and showing them to his friends. Day by day the diaries reveal him with Boni in the Forum, picking up all the information he could for his now regular column in *The Globe*. On 15 June, for instance:[43]

> Afternoon. Sultry. Went to Forum at 5. Met Lanciani with Boni and Peroni coming back from the scavo by Basilica of Constantine. We all went together to the Tholus of the Regia. Boni has got out of it today 26 styli of bone and a fragment of travertine margo with early bold mouldings. Curious indeed, if not amazing, it is inscribed on the lip or ledge REGIA. This is a poser for us all . . .

That last phrase is revealing. It suggests, not only that Baddeley now thought of himself as an archaeologist on equal terms with Boni and Lanciani, but also that he was still unaware of the rancour between them. His innocence did not last much longer.

The following day he wrote a piece for *The Globe* which contained a minor disagreement with Lanciani; but most of it was a harmless description of the convolvulus growing up through the *lapis niger* pavement. Two days later, however, he was inspecting the Sacra Via pavement, and on that subject Boni must have had plenty to say. At this point Baddeley's diary contains the draft of a *Globe* article on the irritation felt by those whom Boni's discoveries had refuted; but he mentions no names, and gives the impression that it was Huelsen in particular he had in mind.

By 21 June, however, Baddeley had taken sides:

> 5.15 p.m. To Forum with Boni . . . Lanciani appeared on the scene, silk-hatted, and trying seriously to pick Boni's brains, as usual. But B. was too alert for him and it was amusing to watch. The fact is that Lanciani is furious at having to go away to Britain, as he says, 'to these

---

43. Gloucester MSS, notebook 20. *Globe* 19 June 1899 p. 4; 26 June p. 4; 28 June p. 3; 30 June p. 4; 3 July p. 5; 4 July p. 3; 10 July p. 4; cf. *RDF* 9f. (giving the false impression that he had been present at the discovery of the archaic inscription), 32f. on the Regia *tholos*.

dull Scotchmen, who have induced me to lecture to them'! I fancy he
will find them the reverse of 'dull', though I can penetrate his causes of
irritation.

(Lanciani had been invited to give the Gifford Lectures at St Andrews,
later published as *New Tales of Old Rome*.) That evening Baddeley
completely re-wrote his piece for *The Globe*, with Lanciani now cast in
the role of jealous detractor:[44]

> Certain archaeologists, even eminent ones here, are now suffering from
> an acute dejection; and this is not due to this capricious and somewhat
> unseasonable June. It is due, rather, to the fact that there has arisen, and
> is still arising, from below familiar levels, a Forum which they do not
> know, and full of problems which they cannot solve. 'Hinc illae
> lachrymae!' Some of them have written popular volumes already
> crammed full of errors; others, in good, though too dogmatical, faith,
> have hitherto believed the Comitium to have been situated much
> further North than it is now proved to have been. Signor Boni, who is
> the most trustworthy, industrious, and patient of workers, is roundly
> abused by some for not leaving things as they were. They suffer a
> certain shock every time a fresh monument or inscription comes to
> light. It is only justice to him to say that he pursues an even course,
> unmindful of their folly, forming his own generally sound opinions and
> knowing full well that of bookmaking there is no end, and that even
> the latest works will perforce have to be rewritten, even from Jordan's
> invaluable 'Topography of Rome' down to that last vermilion volume
> of 'Excavations' in which, owing to characteristic negligence, its author
> has, of all desperate things, omitted the 'Circus Maximus'—a sort of
> 'Hamlet', with the King's part left out. Such, indeed, are the natural
> conditions of archaeological literature—somewhat resembling
> quicksands which are safe for only short periods of time.

It is very unlikely that Lanciani ever read *The Globe*, and the article was
in any case anonymous ('from a Correspondent'); but Baddeley followed
it up a few days later with a signed piece in *The Athenaeum* criticising
various points in Lanciani's recent 'Notes from Rome' column in that

---

44. *Globe* 26 June 1899 p. 4, dated 'June 21'. The earlier draft (Gloucester MSS,
    notebook 20) is undated, but between 18 and 21 June.

journal, and including an attack on the account of the Sacra Via in his latest book (the 'vermilion volume').[45]

The ostensible purpose of both these articles was to report progress on the 'Basilica Aemilia' excavation. The houses were being steadily demolished, and bits of cornice and columns were being dug out underneath them. Boni was digging on other sites as well, and Baddeley made the most of having witnessed the excavation of the 'Volcanal' on 27 June, in 'a veritable blaze of perfect sunshine'; 'on the Palatine the poppies blazed, while the nightingales gave a chorus'.[46] But it was the Basilica, not surprisingly, that he cared most about, and Boni took care to keep him well informed about the magnificent inscription to L. Caesar that was discovered just after Baddeley had gone back to England in July.

As before, Baddeley's absence from the city did not inhibit the Rome correspondent of *The Globe* from sending his reports.[47] In fact, Baddeley was now busy excavating Hailes Abbey for the Bristol and Gloucestershire Archaeological Society; but Boni's letters were very detailed, and there is no sign of any slackening-off in his interest in the Roman scene. He was in any case at work translating Boni's account of the Comitium excavation for *Archaeologia*.[48]

Besides the news of the 'Basilica Aemilia', Baddeley passed on to the readers of *The Globe* Boni's discovery of the 'sacred seismograph' of the Regia, the *sacrarium Martis* where the *hastae Martiae* were hung, emphasising, as Boni had done, the coincidence of an earthquake that very day. 'Three days ago, during the earthquake, I conceived the idea . . .', just as the idea of the *cella* of Vesta had come to him the year before at the first light of dawn. ('Where do your ideas come from?' asked Benedetto Croce; Boni spread his arms, raised his eyes to heaven, and said solemnly, 'They come.')[49] In a letter to Baddeley on 8 August, expanding what he had told Ruskin in January, Boni gave a list of the occasions when he had known beforehand what was going to happen. After finding the black pavement, for instance, he had told his friend

45. *Athenaeum* 3741 (8 July 1899) 72 = *NFR* 262f.

46. *RDF* 24, 27.

47. *Globe* 19 July 1899 p. 4; 24 July p. 6; 26 July p. 4; 28 Sept. p. 5.

48. Baddeley, *A Cotteswold Shrine* (Gloucester and London 1908) vii, 36, 53; G. Boni, *Archaeologia* 57 (1900) 175–84.

49. B. Croce, *Scritti di storia letteraria e politica* vol. 33 (Bari 1940) 208f.

Marchese de la Penne what he would find beneath it; urged to excavate immediately, he had waited for three months, 'lasciando altri malignare accademizzare'.

The next sentence is very revealing:[50]

> It grieves me that you, my best friend, cultured spirit and noble and beautiful soul, were described to me last winter as the pupil and 'follower' of that false man who in reality was exploiting your penetrating intelligence!

Here I think we are close to understanding the motives for Baddeley's *volte-face*. The context of the letter, on Boni's intuition and the jealousy of the academics, reminds us that neither Boni nor Baddeley had any scholarly qualifications in history or anthropology. Boni was trained as an architect; Baddeley was a poet and essayist who had made himself a scholar, and he knew from experience how scornful the academic establishment could be towards amateur historians. I think Boni's flattery undid the bracing effect the reviews of *Queen Joanna* had had on Baddeley, and made him value the superficial mode of thought that came more naturally to him as if it were a superior sensibility. Hence the emphasis on the earthquake for the *sacrarium Martis*, and the favour of the divinities of light and fire as the 'Volcanal' was revealed. Boni found in Baddeley a kindred spirit, even to some extent a fellow mystic so far as trees and flowers were concerned, and he was able to communicate to him his detestation of the *uomo falso*, Lanciani.[51] What Baddeley owed to Lanciani in archaeological guidance was now forgotten.

The enemy had to be attacked on his own ground, and shown to be lacking not in sensibility but in scholarly standards. Some comment of Lanciani in the summer of 1899 caused Baddeley to draft the following paragraph, perhaps a rejected version of the piece in *The Globe* quoted above:[52]

---

50. Boni papers, Instituto Lombardo, Milan: letter dated 8 August (my translation).
51. Volcanal: *RDF* 27. Trees and flowers: Baddeley, *Nineteenth Century* 54 (1903) 629–41, and 58 (1905) 100–115; Boni planted laurels round the Regia, and named one of them after Helen Baddeley (*Times* 1 March 1945 p. 8).
52. Gloucester MSS, notebook 149: undated, but 'Rome 1899 Summer' on the previous page.

I confess I am one of many who have long ceased to regard Prof. Lanciani anything like as seriously as he would have us regard him. To him Rome is a market for the Bookmaker, and for him apparently the more volumes he can turn out, the better: but if he would consider his public a little better, he would not foist upon them a work like the last volume on Rome, with the Circus Maximus quietly left out of all consideration. Certainly some people become inaccurate, some have inaccuracy thrust upon them, by printers, but there are some who seem to have been born inaccurate: and to this last category Prof. Lanciani sometimes appears to belong.

The attack would concentrate on the two main achievements of Lanciani's Forum campaign of 1882–3, the Sacra Via and the Atrium Vestae.

By late August, Lanciani had left for St Andrews—to convert the Scots, said Boni, who enjoyed mocking Lanciani's devout Catholicism. In his lectures—partly cannibalised from his articles in *The Athenaeum*—he took the opportunity to dismiss Boni's exploration of the Atrium Vestae, and counter-attacked strongly on the question of the Sacra Via. (He also belittled the 'Basilica Aemilia' excavations, reversing his earlier opinion—still strongly held by Boni and Baddeley—that there had been no plundering of the building during the Renaissance.)[53]

Boni meanwhile was conducting his own propaganda on the site. 'Now come and look at the true Via Sacra; you see it lies several feet below the road we used to call the Sacred Way. Do you observe how much finer this earlier pavement is than the later paving?'[54] On 22 July he gave his friend clear instructions:

When you find stupid people, stone headed ones or sentimental lovers of modern cobble stones (simply because they believed for seventeen years that they had walked over the promenade of Horace) tell them, please, that the arguments I had at disposal, when I dared to move the selci, were three: the quality of the *silex* (lava basaltina), the workmanship of each stone, and the way in which they were laid . . .

---

53. Lanciani, *New Tales of Old Rome* (London 1901) 58, 86f., 134f. (cf. *NFR* 262).
54. Maud Howe, *Roma Beata: Letters from the Eternal City* (Boston 1904) 253–61, quotation from p. 258.

> The sentimental selci were joined together by the inhabitants of Campo
> Vaccino, while the ancient ones were themselves worthy companions
> of other manifestations of the greatness of the builders of the
> TEMPLUM SACRAE URBIS and of the BASILICA MAXENTII.

Baddeley did his best: 'I have the satisfaction to inform your readers', he
told *The Athenaeum* in September, 'that eighty metres of the real Sacra
Via have now been laid bare . . .'[55]

Meanwhile, Boni was bombarding the Minister with telegrams to get
permission to remove the electric tramway in front of S. Adriano, and
thus enable the Curia and the rest of the Comitium to be excavated.
Success came in early October: now the programme that Baddeley's
eloquence and Phillips' generosity had made possible could be carried to
its logical conclusion. Substantial new funds had been made available for
an extended programme of excavation; no doubt the sensational
discovery of the Comitium inscription had helped, but it was Phillips'
donation above all that had enabled Baccelli to get the supplementary
grants.[56] Boni might well feel grateful. Now he was counting the days to
Baddeley's return, 'desioso di mostrarle quel poco che ho fatto'.

1899–1902

Baddeley had just passed his forty-third birthday. His young friend
Ashby, now twenty-five, had spent the summer excavating the Roman
town of Caerwent (*Venta Silurum*) in South Wales. Baddeley visited the
site in October, and gave Ashby some admiring publicity in *The Globe*.[57]
A few weeks later Ashby was dining with the Baddeleys in Rome. One
would very much like to know what Ashby thought about Baddeley's
new attitude to his friend and mentor Lanciani.

On his way to Rome on 25 October, Baddeley had been present at a
meeting in London to discuss the possibility of setting up a British School
of Archaeology in Rome. It was a small but distinguished committee
(chaired by Pelham), and the fact that Baddeley was invited is a measure

---

55. Boni papers, Instituto Lombardo, Milan (original English); Baddeley,
    Athenaeum 3751 (16 Sept. 1899) 394, based on Boni's letter of 26 August.
56. R. Norton, *Times* 13 Feb. 1900 p. 15 = *NFR* 299.
57. *Globe* 16 Oct. 1899 p. 5: 'one of the most experienced and painstaking of the
    younger Roman archaeologists.'

of the reputation he now enjoyed.[58] Another indication that he was taken seriously is the fact that his name appears as an authority in the notes Ashby took in the Forum from November onwards (no doubt catching up with all that had happened since he left in May.)[59] Baddeley joined Ashby for two Campagna expeditions in November, but his main interest was now in Rome itself: in contrast with the previous year, the diaries mention only six trips in the country all that winter.

The next big story broke on 17 November. As Baddeley told it later,[60]

> I was up in the Forum office with Commendatore Boni, when the Foreman of the works came in, dripping and breathless, to say that gold had been found. We went down together. Only that very morning we had remarked upon the unusual scarcity of coins hitherto found during the excavations. Upon reaching the spot the man beside the drain was throwing out spadefuls of mud, and the fast-falling rain here and there was revealing the coins lying in it.

It was, in fact, a fifth-century hoard of 397 gold coins in mint condition. Baddeley dashed off a piece for *The Globe* that evening, not missing the opportunity for polemic:

> The merits of these discoveries in the Vestal Convent are entirely due to Signor Boni's complete disregard for Professor Lanciani's statements to the effect that everything had been discovered that was to be discovered in this locality. But Professor Lanciani, like many of those he has so freely condemned as bad excavators, never went deep enough, nor took really correct measurements. But perhaps this need be no matter for regret.

After a tutorial session with Boni on 7 December, he also sent a report to *Notes and Queries* on the quality and weight of the coins.[61]

---

58. See p. 150 below; and Wiseman, op. cit. (n. 20 above) 3f.
59. *Archeologia a Roma* (n. 31 above) 159f.—including three exclamation marks for an egregious misdating by Baddeley.
60. *RDF* 39.
61. *Globe* 20 Nov. 1899 p. 2; *NQ* 9.4 (1899) 513f.

On Tuesday, 16 January 1900, the British and American Archaeological
Society of Rome held its first meeting of the new session. The American
Ambassador presided, the British Ambassador and Lady Currie were also
present. The lecture 'was delivered before a large and distinguished
audience, by Mr W. St Clair Baddeley, on the subject of the recent
excavations in the Basilica Aemilia.' The hoped-for haul of statuary had
not materialised, but the architectural remains were interesting enough,
and allowed for a little sniping (both on this occasion and in *The Globe*)
at those authorities—studiously unnamed—whose theories were now
exploded.[62] Later in January—too late for the lecture, alas—more
dramatic finds were made: part of the architrave inscription, PAVL[. . .]
REST[. . .], and a large collection of fourth-century bronze coins, badly
oxidised but offering vivid evidence of the heat of the fire that destroyed
the building.[63]

The houses bought with the Phillips donation had been demolished
the previous summer, but a bank of earth had had to be left in order to
support the houses behind, so only about 40 per cent of the area of the
Basilica could be excavated. (Another £2500 was needed to buy up the
other houses.) However, the consequent obsolescence of the road, and
its short-lived tramway, meant that the rest of the Comitium could now
be excavated.

What lay under the road was the medieval cemetery of S. Adriano:
already by November, 55 skeletons had been disinterred. Now, on
1 February, the workmen made an aperture into the front of the church
itself, fifteen feet below its floor level. Inside was the marble floor of
Diocletian's Senate-house. Boni and Baddeley climbed in, to the
gesticulating protests of the Spanish monks, leaning out of the windows
above.[64] The monks complained to the Spanish ambassador; the

---

62. *Journal of the BAASR* 3.2 (1899–1900) 55, 61, 66.
63. *Globe* 23 Jan. 1900 p. 4; 1 Feb. p. 4; 22 Feb. p. 6; cf. *NFR* 296f. On the
    inscription, discovered after Baddeley had left Rome, see *RDF* 60 n. 1: 'it
    would be difficult to convey the feelings experienced when on washing the
    fragments we saw those significant letters.'
64. St Clair Baddeley and Lina Duff Gordon, *Rome and its Story* (London 1904)
    41, 43. Cf. Lanciani, *Wanderings in Ancient Roman Churches* (Boston 1924)
    28f. on the Curia marble: 'I have seen a small section of this fine work
    creeping by stealth through a hole burrowed by Commissioner Boni under
    the threshold of the front gate.'

aperture was closed, and exploration of the Senate-house suspended for several years. One of the monks told Baddeley that he had heard his original lecture on the Basilica Aemilia the year before,[65]

> and he knew not only that he was an out-and-out Pagan, but that he made others so, and 'spread the poison everywhere by means of a vain enthusiasm'. 'You'll want S. Lorenzo in Miranda next, or S. Maria Liberatrice!'

That story had been improved by Baddeley when he told it in 1904; for S. Maria Liberatrice had already been expropriated (for 375,000 lire compensation) and was even then being demolished. 'The orange-trees, which the nuns cultivated behind S. Maria, will be removed to the Palatine and elsewhere.'[66] The site revealed the so-called Augusteum, with a ramp to the Palatine, and the eighth-century frescoes of S. Maria Antiqua. (The following year, S. Maria Antiqua was to be the subject of the first of the *Papers* of the British School at Rome, by the first Director of the School, G. McN. Rushforth.)

Meanwhile, the argument about the Sacra Via had reached the pages of *The Times*. Richard Norton, now Director of the American School and a loyal Boni supporter, wrote a long 'follow-up' to his letter of January 1899, summarising what had been done in the intervening year. His remarks on 'the complete incompetence of earlier excavators', for not going deep enough, and 'the careless, or rather stupid character of the earlier excavations' at the Atrium Vestae, were clearly aimed at Lanciani but did not name him. As for 'the real Sacra Via', Boni had found it 'several feet below the late road that Lanciani had mistaken for the Sacred Way.' Lanciani replied ten days later, firmly repeating his identification of the street he had uncovered in 1882, which Boni had now removed, as the Maxentian Sacra Via, part of the rebuilding programme after the great fire of 283. He said the same, and in much the same words, in his *Athenaeum* article on 3 March. Norton came back with a list of reasons for supposing the road medieval, very reminiscent of Boni's letter to Baddeley the previous July. It is clear that Boni briefed his Anglo-

---

65. R.H. Edlestone, *Letters from Rome in 1903* (Darlington and London 1904) 50; *RDF* 20f.
66. *RDF* 78; *Globe* 5 Jan. 1900 p. 4 (compensation), 22 Feb. p. 6 (demolition).

American supporters very carefully.[67] Naturally, Baddeley did not
remain silent, and his attack in *The Globe* gave the impression that he and
Boni had done the excavation together:

> . . . beneath the former 'medieval' road we found remains of a ninth
> century church, and two medieval walls covered entirely over, full of
> medieval fragmentary pottery and relics of destroyed pagan buildings.
> Signor Boni was for some time inclined to put its construction only as
> late as the twelfth century, when suddenly underneath the same noble
> avenue [Lanciani's phrase] we found coins of Sixtus IV (1484)! The
> basalt blocks, however, told a practised eye their story quite plainly:
> for they were clumsily rounded with hammers, and not carefully
> dressed with chisels after the ancient manner . . .

The reader is clearly meant to infer that the 'practised eye' was
Baddeley's own.[68]

It is easy to mock: Baddeley had had little more than two years'
experience of Roman archaeology. But they had been very intensive
years, with the best instructors, and his powers of rapid assimilation were
considerable. What he knew may not have been very firmly rooted, but
it was enough to make him look like an authority. He was, of course,
much in demand for lectures and guided tours, and now he was even
going to lecture in the United States. Perhaps it was thanks to his ally
Richard Norton, or to the American Ambassador, who had chaired the
meeting on 16 January; at any rate, Baddeley was invited to Massa-
chusetts, to lecture at Harvard and at the Lowell Institute.[69]

We do not know when the Baddeleys left Rome (probably in May), nor
how long Baddeley stopped in England before crossing the Atlantic.[70]
The next piece of evidence is a letter from Boni in August, thanking him
for his telegram of sympathy (King Umberto had been assassinated on
29 July), bringing him up to date on recent work, and adding a
characteristic postscript on the jasmines and roses he had planted in the
Atrium Vestae.

---

67. *Times* 13 Feb. 1900, p. 15, 23 Feb. p. 15, 16 March p. 15 = *NFR* 298–303.
68. *Globe* 13 March 1900 p. 7; cf. 17 April p. 4.
69. Tea, op. cit. (n. 2 above) 2.45.
70. On his return, Baddeley brought with him the bell of S. Giovanni Calabita on
    the Tiber island, which he had rescued from the breakers: *NQ* 9.9 (1902)
    406.

The Baddeleys spent Christmas in Venice, and then came straight to Rome; no doubt their luggage contained copies of his new book of poems, *Autographs of Cloud and Sunbeam in England and Italy*, which included one on the *lapis niger*, dedicated to Boni.

The 'Basilica Aemilia' project was hanging fire: it could not continue until S. Adriano and S. Lorenzo in Miranda had been expropriated, and the monks were holding out for a very high figure in compensation. What attracted attention now was S. Maria Antiqua. When the Director of the newly-founded British School at Rome wrote to *The Times* in January 1901, talking over from Norton the task of bringing English readers up to date with the new excavations, nearly half of his long letter was devoted to this 'Sistine Chapel of the Eighth Century'.[71] Baddeley inspected the site, and lectured on it to the Archaeological Society on 5 February. By the beginning of May the Baddeleys had left Rome; Boni wrote to report on a visit by Phillips, who was very satisfied with the result of his benefaction, and hoped the excavation could be completed.

This impression of a flying visit may be misleading, the result of poor documentation. The following winter (1901–2) the Baddeleys again arrived late in December and left in April, but his surviving pocket-books show that he was taking almost daily notes on Boni's excavations in the Atrium Vestae and elsewhere. He was present at the excavation of one of the wells beside the Clivus Sacrae Viae, and wrote a poem about a flute found in the debris it contained.[72] He went on Campagna expeditions with Ashby—even with Lanciani in the party. He gave lectures and guided tours for the Archaeological Society, to which he and Boni were now elected as honorary members.

Yet the impression remains that Baddeley was now less deeply engaged. The intense excitement of 1899 could not be kept up; and it may be that his position as 'the well-known lecturer and archaeologist'[73] was less easy to sustain now that a British School of Archaeology had been established in Rome. He got on well with Rushforth, and Ashby was an old friend, but he must have known that he could never approach the scholarly standard of Rushforth's account of S. Maria Antiqua or Ashby's

71. G. McN. Rushforth, *Times* 9 Jan. 1901 p. 13 (cf. leader comment at p. 7).
72. Gloucester MSS, notebooks 26 and 28; Baddeley, *From Cotteswold and Beyond* (Painswick 1920) 39.
73. The phrase used of him by the British and American Archaeological Society of Rome: see its *Journal* 3.4 (1901–2) 135, 3.5 (1902–3) 195.

'Classical Topography of the Roman Campagna', both now published in the first volume of the *Papers*. Besides, he was increasingly committed to the local history of his own county. His book on Painswick Church appeared in 1902, and he was already busy going through the documents in preparation for a sequel, on the town itself.[74]

It is not surprising, therefore, that his correspondence with Boni in 1902 is mainly about subscriptions for rebuilding the S. Marco campanile in Venice. And the death of Edmund Christy in December that year removed one with whom Baddeley's earliest memories of Italy and Rome were always associated.

1903–1907

The family did not winter in Rome in 1902–3; little Edmund was now seven, and presumably at school. In March 1903, Baddeley left his beloved Castle Hale for a five-week visit on his own, carefully setting out his reasons:[75]

> My main object, in going off to Rome, now, is threefold.
> 1. To revise the works of A. Hare.
> 2. To lecture and help Boni.
> 3. Attend Congress of Historic Studies.

Augustus Hare had died on 22 January. Baddeley went to the funeral, where he discussed copyright with the executors. The first 'Baddeley edition' of *Walks in Rome* appeared in 1903, of *Venice* and *Florence* in 1904, of *Sicily* in 1905, of *Days near Rome* in 1906, and of *Cities of Southern Italy* in 1911. Even for the minimal revision Baddeley provided, that must have taken his attention away from the Forum excavations during the next few years.

As for lecturing and helping Boni, on 8 April Baddeley repeated his exploit of four years earlier: at an 'open-air demonstration' in the Forum, Baddeley described the 'Basilica Aemilia' excavations, and explained that the remaining houses prevented completion of the project. The

---

74. Baddeley, *A History of the Church of St Mary at Painswick* (Exeter and London 1902); *A Cotteswold Manor, being the History of Painswick* (Gloucester and London 1907).

75. Gloucester MSS, notebook 31 (11 March 1903).

government estimate for expropriation was 4000 *lire*. 'Mr Lionel Phillips therefore offered to place this further sum at Mr Baddeley's disposal for the completion of the work, and the Italian Government, we understand, has consented to avail itself of this offer.'[76]

At the International Congress of Historical Sciences, which was held in Rome early in April, Baddeley represented the British and American Archaeological Society of Rome. All we know of it from his diary is that he was only 25 feet from the King at the opening session on the Campidoglio. 'The Queen is plain, but tall and striking . . .' It is surprising that he did not stay for King Edward's state visit at the end of April—the first by an English sovereign to Rome since the days of Canute. (Did he want to avoid seeing Lanciani in a place of honour at the Quirinal?)[77]

Baddeley had a closer encounter with Victor Emmanuel III the following year. Below the so-called Equus Domitiani, Boni had discovered a group of five perfectly preserved archaic vases, the largest containing a piece of quartz with pure gold in it. That was on 11 March. Boni waited nine days before removing them.

> At half-past eight on the morning of March 20 (1904), the sun filled the Forum with light, while the wrens, smallest of birds, filled the place of the Emperors with song. At nine o'clock Comm. Boni, having arranged to lift the votive vases from the dedicatory pit and examine their contents, Professor Huelsen, the correspondent of the *Times*, and another, were invited to take part. We did not know that King Victor Emmanuel was to be present . . .

No, of course not! The biggest vase came up wrapped in Baddeley's handkerchief, and was taken to the temporary museum, 'the King looking on highly interested'.[78]

How long Baddeley was in Rome this time is not clear. He gave his now annual lecture to the Archaeological Society (on 'Dante's Emperor in Rome') in February or early March, and may have been present at the

76. *Athenaeum* 3938 (18 April 1903) 505, unsigned.
77. Edleston, op. cit. (n. 65 above) 9–20, esp. 16 (27 April) for Lanciani.
78. *RDF* 48–51; for the site, see now F. Coarelli, *Il foro romano: periodo arcaico* (Rome 1983) 282–98.

discovery of the Lacus Curtius on 19 April. He probably spent most of his time writing. His 'handbook for travellers', *Recent Discoveries in the Forum 1898–1904, by an Eye-witness*, and the sumptuous volume *Rome and its Story*, of which he contributed the first part, both appeared later that year; the former contained the episode of the King's visit, which was evidently written in Rome immediately after the event.

The handbook shows signs of haste, no doubt because of the rival volume by E. Burton-Brown, which had already gone to the press. Mrs Burton-Brown was evidently a professional guide ('A Weekly Course of Two Lectures is given in the Forum throughout the Winter season by the Author'), and the disobliging account of the book's origin in Tea's biography of Boni no doubt reflects Baddeley's irritation at being pushed into second place by a mere *cicerone*. In fact, the Burton-Brown book is a much better piece of work, less anecdotal and far more useful to the visitor, as Ashby observed in his notice of the two books.[79] But Baddeley was an eye-witness, as his title page proclaimed; his map was 'made for this work by order of the Director of the Excavations'; he had lived in the Forum 'both beneath it and above, as few can have done, for considerable portions of the last six years'; he acknowledged the help of 'my personal friend Comm. Giacomo Boni'; the illustrations were mainly his own photographs, including the Frontispiece, which showed the demolition of 'the houses purchased by Mr L. Phillips'—to whom the work was dedicated, 'in memory of days in the Forum'.

Not surprisingly, the old quarrels were not forgotten. Boni's programme was begun 'in the teeth of spiteful opposition and envious depreciations'; spiteful, too, was the opposition to Boni's exposure of the Clivus Sacrae Viae on the part of 'certain archaeologists' who believed the existing pavement to be Maxentian.[80] Baddeley quotes Lanciani's letter to *The Times*, as follows:

> '*This most beautiful specimen of the architectural and engineering skill of the third century is no more* . . . it has been obliterated to lay bare the Sacred Way and its surroundings of a later (*sic*) date.'

---

79. E. Burton-Brown, *Recent Excavations in the Roman Forum 1898–1904: a Handbook* (London 1904); Tea, op. cit. (n. 2 above) 2.168; Ashby, *Classical Review* 19 (1905) 78.
80. *RDF* 7, 34, 64f.

The italics were Baddeley's, not Lanciani's. More important, what Lanciani had written was '. . . surroundings of an earlier date'![81] The misquotation is emphasised, as if Lanciani had been foolish enough to think that lower strata could be later. Was Baddeley just careless, or deliberately malicious? He certainly enjoyed hearing gossip to Lanciani's discredit, and even in later life, it seems, he went out of his way to ridicule him.[82] The spite and envy were not all on one side. Baddeley's attitude is in strong contrast with that of Ashby, who remained a loyal friend and admirer of Lanciani all his life; but Ashby was not committed to the Boni camp.

Meanwhile, Baddeley had become a collector. In 1904–5 he acquired two important items—P.S. Bartoli's *Libro delle pitture antiche* (a collection of drawings of ancient paintings done for Cardinal Camillo Massimi), and a sixteenth-century panorama of Rome by Anton von den Wyngaerde—which were both subsequently published by Ashby.[83] (Ashby was now Assistant Director of the British School, and became its Director in 1906.) A third acquisition, for which Baddeley aspired to be his own interpreter, was made in March 1905 at S. Stefano near Hadrian's Villa, where Lanciani had first directed him six years before.

Baddeley had arrived in Rome on 20 February, and immediately got to work on the introduction to Hare's *Sicily*. Ashby was urging him to contribute to the British School's series of open meetings, held in the Library of the School's apartments in Palazzo Odescalchi and 'attended by English residents and visitors and by representatives of the other foreign schools and of the principal learned bodies in Rome.'[84] Baddeley was in fact committed to the Archaeological Society, to talk about the

---

81. *RDF* 64; Lanciani, *Times* 23 Feb. 1900 p. 15; *NFR* 301f., cf. 296 ('of the time of Domitian'), *New Tales of Old Rome* (n. 53 above) 87 ('of the time of Commodus or Domitian').

82. A photograph of a Campagna excursion (with Pelham, Haverfield and the Ashbys), inserted in Gloucester MSS notebook 81, was later annotated by Baddeley: '. . . myself "the Guide", Lanciani the chief "Talker"—tho' constantly in needless terror of the invisible sheepdogs!'

83. T. Ashby, *Papers of the British School at Rome* 6 (1913) 489–91, 8 (1916) 48–51; *Mélanges de l'école française* 25 (1905) 179–80.

84. British School at Rome, *Reports* 5 (1904–5) 2.

Regia—a good opportunity to blow Boni's trumpet, and his own. At the end of his lecture he gave the audience a surprise:

> I should like to add that on Saturday morning I became the discoverer
> of one of the rarest antiquities it has ever fallen to my lot to meet
> with—a perfect stone inscription of a sacred grove, and I have brought
> it here for you to see . . .

The inscription was on a piece of white marble about 21 cm square and 3 cm thick, and read LVCV / SANCTV, in letters 45 mm high. It was found on the south side of the S. Stefano complex, near a small rectangular building with three niches, dubbed by Baddeley the '*sacrarium*'.[85]

Baddeley made the most of his find. He exhibited it at the British School on 3 April, with a talk on 'Remains attributable to a temple in the Colle di S. Stefano', and at the German Institute on 7 April, when Huelsen and Petersen held a seminar about it. And he wrote a full account of the S. Stefano villa, its remains and its inscriptions, with help from Ashby on the documentary evidence. The ownership of the villa was proved by the inscriptions found in 1899, as Lanciani had seen at the time. Baddeley gave him credit (surprisingly, perhaps), but succeeded in garbling the result. Admittedly, it is not easy to sort out fragmentary inscriptions of polyonymous Trajanic senators, but Baddeley evidently couldn't distinguish between Plancius Varus and Plautius Verus, nor between Plancii Vari and Vibii Vari. So when his pamphlet appeared in September 1906 (privately printed in Gloucester), the country house of C. Iulius Plancius Varus Cornutus was announced on the title page as the *Villa of the Vibii Vari*.[86]

From the end of April 1905 (when he accompanied Ashby to M. Circeo) to the end of February 1907 (when he addressed the Archaeological Society on Boni's new excavations in Trajan's Forum),

---

85. *Journal of the BAASR* 3.7 (1904–5) 376–83; Baddeley, *Villa of the Vibii Vari, near Tivoli, at Colli di S. Stefano* (Gloucester 1906) 5 etc.; *Inscriptiones Italiae* IV 72. Baddeley presented the stone to the British School.

86. See R. Syme, *Historia* 18 (1969) 365f. = *Roman Papers* (Oxford 1979) 2.787f., on Plancius Varus. The error persisted: see Lanciani, *Wanderings in the Roman Campagna* (London 1909) 160; Z. Mari in *Thomas Ashby . . .* (n. 26 above) 55.

nothing is known of Baddeley's movements. He may well have spent some time in North America; but his main preoccupation was certainly the excavation of Hailes Abbey, which resumed in 1906 after a six-year hiatus.

Baddeley's final contribution to archaeology in the city of Rome came in February or March 1907, when the American owner of the Villa Sciarra on the Janiculum invited him to inspect some inscriptions and reliefs that had been revealed the previous summer when a new house for the gardener was being built. It was the 'shrine of the Syrian gods' at the grove of Furrina. Baddeley brought Huelsen to see it, and also Paul Gauckler, ex-director of antiquities in Tunis, who happened to be in Rome. Huelsen produced a text of the Greek metrical inscription; Gauckler gave a paper to the Académie des Inscriptions et Belles Lettres in Paris; Baddeley wrote to *The Times* and *The Athenaeum*. (Gauckler began serious excavations, and in February 1909 uncovered a superb collection of statues that had been concealed in antiquity beneath the sanctuary floor. At that point Baddeley proposed that he should be involved as well, but nothing came of it.)[87]

1907–1945

Baddeley had joined the Bristol and Gloucestershire Archaeological Society in 1897, soon after making his home at Painswick, and 1898 saw the first of his very numerous publications in the Society's *Transactions*. A few weeks after giving the English-speaking world notice of the Janiculum discoveries, he was lecturing to the Society at Chedworth Roman villa; and on 16 July 1907 he was elected President. His presidential address, after the annual dinner, was on 'The Modern Status of Archaeology, and the Hopes of Archaeology in Relation to certain Dark Periods in Britain'; the following morning,

> at 9.30, the members started in several brakes on what proved a delightful and interesting excursion in brilliant summer weather, under the leadership of the President (Mr St Clair Baddeley), who was a truly admirable guide, his inexhaustible stores of antiquarian knowledge being freely drawn upon at each halting-place for the instruction of the party, there being no department of archaeological research on which he had not something of interest and value to say.

---

87. *Times* 15 March 1907 p. 15; *Athenaeum* 4145 (6 April 1907) 417f.

And in August he wrote a long letter to *The Times* reporting the Society's excavation at Hailes Abbey, with which he and Canon Bazeley had been involved since 1899.[88]

Baddeley was fifty years old. Ten years had passed since he had turned from the history of Angevin Naples to the antiquities of Rome. Now, his reputation greatly enhanced, he turned again, to the local history of the Cotswolds.

He did still sometimes visit Rome: in 1909 he met Rudyard Kipling at dinner at the British Embassy, and took him to the Forum to be introduced to Boni; in 1911 he even gave a lecture to the Archaeological Society, though it was not printed in their *Journal*. And when he went to America for seven weeks in the autumn of 1910, it was almost certainly to lecture about the Forum. But his last publication on the subject was a letter to *The Times* in January 1908, attacking the municipality of Rome for vandalism in their treatment of the Aurelian wall.

He had been working steadily at Gloucestershire history during the summers. The book on Painswick Church came out in 1902. In 1907, during Baddeley's year of office as President of the B.G.A.S., appeared the more substantial history of Painswick itself, 'written during leisure hours won from other labours (which have not been unhelpful to it)', and a year later the companion volume on Hailes Abbey, with acknowledgments to G. McNeil Rushforth, now retired from the British School to Malvern. (In fact, we happen to know that Rushforth wrote the anonymous review of the book in the *English Historical Review*.)[89] *The Place-Names of Gloucestershire* followed in 1913, a book of poems *From Cotteswold and Beyond* in 1922, and *The History of Cirencester* in 1924.

It was also in 1924 that the Baddeleys were in Rome again, to visit Boni. Baddeley was sixty-eight, Boni sixty-five. One would like to know what they said about Lanciani, honoured by George V the previous year as Knight Commander of the Royal Victorian Order.[90] Edmund

88. *Transactions of the BGAS* 30 (1907) 13–17, 37f., 49–75; *Times* 30 Aug. 1907 p. 10.
89. *EHR* 24 (1909) 414, on Baddeley, op. cit. (n. 48 above). Rushforth's notes for the review survive in his copy of the book (Exeter University Library).
90. Ashby, op. cit. (n. 17 above) 124: Lanciani, then 77, had been Queen Mary's guide during the royal visit.

Baddeley, whom Boni had known as a little boy, was now a pilot; at the time of the visit he was flying to India.

A year later, Boni was dead; Baddeley supplied letters and reminiscences to his biographer, Eva Tea. Lanciani died in 1929, Ashby in 1931. Edmund too died in 1931, tragically killed in a flying accident. Baddeley lived on with Helen at Castle Hale, a respected local dignitary (Plate VIIb).

In June 1933, at the age of seventy-eight, he was given an honorary Doctorate of Letters by the University of St Andrews, thus achieving at last the academic recognition he had sought so long. It was the end of his career; he wrote no more for publication. He died on 14 February 1945, in his 89th year, leaving his diaries and papers in two tin boxes to be opened twenty years after his death.[91]

Baddeley wrote an enormous amount, most of it ephemeral. A private comment on the *Cotteswold Shrine* book, made by one scholar to another, is all too revealing of the quality of his historical work:[92]

> The book on Hailes reached me a few days ago, and I have been looking into it. What a desultory book it is, and how often it repeats the same statement!

His energy, his memory, and his power of assimilation meant that Baddeley knew a great deal about a great many subjects, but one suspects that most of it was superficial. His learning was spread wide but thin. On the other hand, it is clear that he was a brilliant communicator. There is plenty of evidence to support his obituarist's observation that

> as years passed his mind was filled with an inexhaustible store of knowledge, so vividly presented in his talk that it was often with a shock that his hearers found themselves at the end of the day travelling in a motor-car and not in a Roman chariot or a medieval wool cart.

---

91. Gloucester MSS check-list.
92. R.L. Poole (editor of *EHR*) to G. McN. Rushforth, 13 Dec. 1908 (Rushforth papers, Exeter University Library).

In print, too, what he was best at was the vivid imaginative reconstruction.[93] Two generations later, he would surely have done well in television.

What sticks in the mind after reading Baddeley is his observation of places and of people. The sounds and colours of the Campagna, for instance:[94]

> Exquisite day on the lovely Campagna. Twitter of finches in flight, tall daisies swaying among skeleton buglossory . . . Monte Cavo mantled purple. Frascati chrome. Mackerel sky, flash of red sunset.

Or the table-talk of a disdainful artist:[95]

> 'Rome is a "jaune ville de stucco", a provincial French town. Archaeology is of no account: for archaeology is not life. No ruin counts. Things must be reckoned as they are, not as they were or might have been. England is the home of mediocrity . . .'

So too for the history of archaeology, what he offers is personal details (Lanciani in his silk hat, Baccelli and Bernabei speaking with their eyes), and the atmosphere of places, as in this glimpse of the Forum as an archaeological site:[96]

> As there has been no rain here for many days, the dust in the Forum deepens, and as the toiling horses drag their blue wheeled carts, heavily laden with soil from the excavations, up towards the Arch of Titus, clouds of it arise at every step . . .

Baddeley's importance is as a witness, not a participant. He himself was no more than a pretentious amateur, but his testimony illuminates the life and work of greater men.

---

93. *Times* 1 March 1945 p. 8; cf. *Times Lit. Supp.* 147 (4 Nov. 1908) 340 on *Rome and its Story* (n. 64 above), praising the freshness, force and vitality of Baddeley's descriptions.
94. Gloucester MSS, notebook 129 (8 Dec. 1898).
95. Gloucester MSS, notebook 21 (21 Feb. 1899, James McNeill Whistler).
96. *Globe* 10 July 1899 p. 4.

8

REDISCOVERING A BENEFACTOR

I give the following specific bequests: to the University College of the South West, Exeter, framed watercolour drawing of the Parthenon at Athens by William Page. Also all the books forming my library (except books of account and any books otherwise bequeathed by this my Will or any Codicil thereto), my Executors having absolute power and discretion to decide which of my books come under the above description . . .

Oxford

Gordon McNeil Rushforth (Plate VIIc) was born on 6 September 1862, at 83 Oxford Terrace, Paddington (W.2), to Daniel Rushforth and his wife Mary.[1] On the birth certificate, Daniel Rushforth is described as a button-maker; twelve years later, when he sent his eldest son to Merchant Taylors' School, he was a manufacturing chemist, and his address was 4 The Grove, Ealing. There were two other sons, Collingwood and Francis, and at least one daughter, Janet; all the children bore their mother's maiden name of McNeil.

Rushforth was at Merchant Taylors' from 1874 to 1881. Among his books are a matching set of Grote's *History of Greece* (12 volumes), Merivale's *History of the Romans under the Empire* (8 volumes),

---

1. The main source for his life is the *Times* obituary, 31 March 1938; no entry in the *DNB* or even *Who's Who*. Obituaries also in *Antiquaries Journal* 18 (1938) 335, *Transactions of the Bristol and Gloucester Archaeological Society* 59 (1938) 344–50, and *Journal of the British Society of Master Glass-Painters* 7.3 (October 1938) 150–1.

Mahaffy's *History of Classical Greek Literature* (2 volumes), and Cruttwell's *History of Roman Literature*, all with the Merchant Taylor's Company arms—a very handsome start for any boy's classical library. What he won them for we do not know, but according to the school records he carried off the Headmaster's Prize for Hebrew in 1880; and his copy of Dindorf's *Poetae Scaenici Graeci* contains the citation 'for proficiency in Latin Verse' the same year. Among his other school prizes were Watson's edition of Cicero's *Select Letters*, Sellar's *Roman Poets of the Republic* and Lewis Campbell's two-volume *Sophocles*—the last two titles bearing, in addition to the coat of arms, the legend 'Gilpin Prize 1881'. The Gilpin Prize was 'for the boy of the best conduct during the year, selected by the Headmaster'.

1881 was the year Rushforth went up on an Open Scholarship to St John's College, Oxford. He took a First in Classical Moderations in 1883, and a Second in his *Lit. Hum.* Schools in 1885. I imagine it was the philosophy papers in 'Greats' that brought him down a class (there are very few philosophical works among his surviving books); in ancient history, as the sequel shows, he was certainly well informed. After his degree he studied for the Bar, obtaining a studentship at the Inner Temple in 1887 and becoming Barrister-at-Law in 1889. But he evidently preferred scholarship to the law, and returned to Oxford. A local 'Who's Who' lists him under St John's as a 'resident member of Congregation' in the early nineties. Already in 1891 he was publishing in the *Classical Review* on matters concerned with Roman history.[2]

It was a time of great energy and achievement in Oxford classical studies, and nowhere was the energy more manifest than in Roman history, where the influence of Mommsen and the German school was being fruitfully absorbed. The main figure in the revolution of Roman history in Oxford was H.F. Pelham (1846–1907), Classical Fellow of Exeter College since 1870, who in 1889 was appointed Camden Professor of Ancient History. Among the brilliant young men who came to Oxford to teach Roman history in the early years of Pelham's reign were F.J. Haverfield, H. (later Sir Henry) Stuart Jones, and G. Mc.N. Rushforth.

Of all Mommsen's great achievements, one of the very greatest was the

---

2. J. Foster, *Oxford Men and their Colleges* (London and Oxford 1893) 491. See pp. 233–37 below for Rushforth's bibliography.

Corpus Inscriptionum Latinarum. Begun in 1863, it was now approaching completion, with the first supplementary volumes already appearing. Collections of selected inscriptions did exist—Orelli's two volumes of 1828, with a third volume by Henzen in 1856, and Wilmann's *Exempla inscriptionum Latinarum* (Berlin 1873), which now held the field—but there was a real need for an up-to-date selection of historically significant inscriptions, with a commentary that brought to bear on them all the advances in epigraphy and constitutional history that Mommsen and his followers had made. That was what Rushforth set himself to produce.

Latin Historical Inscriptions illustrating the History of the Early Empire was published by the Oxford University Press in 1893. It contained texts of, and commentary on, 100 inscriptions (including coins) chosen to illustrate the following subjects: Part I (Augustus): the victory of Octavian and the foundation of the Principate, the organisation of the provinces, the organisation of Rome and Italy, the imperial family, the worship of the emperor; Part II (Tiberius to Vespasian): history of the emperors and of persons connected with them, Rome and Italy, the Aerarium and the Fiscus, and the frontiers and provinces. It immediately became a standard work; 37 years later, when it was reissued in a second edition, the reviewer in the *Journal of Roman Studies* could still call it 'an excellent and necessary work'[3]—and indeed it remains of value even today.

The origin of the book is made clear by the author's handsome acknowledgement 'to Professor Pelham, without whose encouragement and help this collection would never have appeared. He has taken the keenest interest in the work in all its stages, and when I say that everything that I have written has had the benefit of his revision it will be understood how much my book owes to him.' Rushforth was always a self-effacing man. But whatever the contribution made by Pelham (and Haverfield, and the other scholars whose assistance is acknowledged), *Latin Historical Inscriptions* was still a substantial achievement for a man of only thirty.

The preface is dated 2 February 1893. Nine days earlier he had been appointed College Lecturer at Oriel. In 1897 he became Classical Tutor. He was also Vice-Principal of St Mary Hall, which was next to Oriel and later (1902) absorbed into it.

---

3. H. Mattingly, *JRS* 20 (1930) 97.

Rushforth's tastes were by no means restricted to the ancient world. Two of the books from his library that happen to have dated flyleaf inscriptions from this period are *The Visitation of Herefordshire made by Robert Cook, Clarencieux, in 1569*, ed. Frederic William Weaver M.A., privately printed Exeter 1886, 'with F.W. Weaver's best wishes, Evercreech, 22nd October 1886'; and *The Great Age of Italian Painting*, a series of lectures by S.G.C. Middlemore, London 1889: 'G.Mc.N. Rushforth from H.H. Middlemore Bartleet, Oct. 8th 1894'. (Weaver was Vicar of Milton Clevedon in Somerset; he became a Fellow of the Society of Antiquaries in 1900, and was for long the Somerset editor of the *Somerset and Dorset Notes and Queries*. Bartleet was a younger man, just ordained, Curate of St Martin's, Scarborough; thirty years later he became Rushforth's neighbour as Vicar of Great Malvern, 1924–1946.) Local history and the fine arts—these were later to be among Rushforth's main preoccupations, and it is interesting to see how early they became a part of his life.

He was no mere dilettante in these matters, especially on the subject of Italian painting. In 1900 he published in Bell's 'Great Masters' series a book on Carlo Crivelli, which combined a life of that fifteenth-century Venetian artist with a scholarly catalogue of his surviving works. Moreover, Rushforth was himself a serious collector. In 1894, he had bought for his rooms at St Mary Hall a Madonna, attributed to another fifteenth-century Venetian painter, Bartolommeo Vivarini, which is now the centre-piece of the restored altar in the Henry VII Chapel in Westminster Abbey.[4]

This combination of classical learning and expertise in Italian art made him a natural choice for his next position.

Rome

On 25 October 1899 a meeting was held in the rooms of the Royal Asiatic Society, 22 Albemarle Street, W.1. In the chair was H.F. Pelham, now

---

4. J. Perkins, *Westminster Abbey: its Worship and Ornaments* (Oxford and London 1940) 209. The painting had passed at some date into the possession of the Rt. Hon. Viscount Lee of Fareham, who presented it to the Dean and Chapter when the altar was being restored in 1932–5.

President of Trinity as well as Camden Professor. The others present, in the order given in the minutes,[5] were:

Prof. Percy Gardner (1846–1937), ex-Disney Professor of Archaeology in the University of Cambridge, now Lincoln and Merton Professor of Classical Archaeology in the University of Oxford;

Prof. W.C.F. Anderson, Classical archaeologist;

Dr Clifford Allbutt F.R.S. (1836–1925), Regius Professor of Physic in the University of Cambridge;

Mr G.W. Prothero (1848–1922), ex-Professor of Modern History in the University of Edinburgh, now editor of the *Quarterly Review*;

Mr Somers Clarke (1841–1926), architect;

Mr W. St Clair Baddeley (1856–1945), archaeologist;

Mr George A. Macmillan (1855–1936), director of Macmillan's publishing house, Chairman of the Managing Committee of the British School at Athens;

Mr J.W. Mackail (1859–1945), ex-Fellow of Balliol, now Examiner to the Board of Education (later Oxford Professor of Poetry, 1906; Professor of Ancient Literature in the Royal Academy, 1924; O.M., 1935);

Mr A.H. Smith (1860–1941), of the Department of Greek and Roman Antiquities in the British Museum, Librarian of the Hellenic Society;

Mr J.W. Headlam (1866–1908), Classical Fellow of King's College Cambridge;

Mr W. Loring (1865–1915) archaeologist.

The meeting was the result of an initiative by the Committee of the British School at Athens a fortnight earlier, to set up a British School at Rome 'to promote the study of Roman and Graeco-Roman archaeology in all its departments.' A circular was drafted to appeal for funds, with the following preamble:

The British School at Athens has now been in existence for thirteen years, and in spite of its comparatively slender resources, it has won for itself an honourable place by the side of the older and wealthier Schools of France and Germany.

---

5. Except where otherwise stated, the material for this section is taken from the first Minute Book of the Executive Committee of the British School at Rome, in the British School archives at Tuke Building, Regents College, London, N.W.1.

But a British School at Rome has still to be established. Germany, France, Austria, and now the United States, all possess more or less well-equipped institutions; Great Britain, almost alone among the great European States, is unrepresented.

The time has surely come when this omission should be supplied. For many years past excellent work has been done in Rome by British scholars, archaeologists, topographers, historians, and students of art. Every winter season finds British students at work there in one line of study or another, while the number of educated travellers who visit Rome steadily increases.

What is needed in Rome is what is now provided at Athens, a recognised British centre of study and research, which should offer to British students the advantages which German, French, and American students already enjoy . . .

. . . in some respects the work of a School at Rome would be more many-sided than is possible at Athens. It would be less predominantly classical and archaeological, and its students would be found in the galleries, libraries, and churches, as well as in the museums, on the Palatine, and in the Forum. A School at Rome would also be a natural centre from which work could be directed and organised at Naples, Florence, Venice, and elsewhere in Italy.

It is not therefore only to those who are interested in classical history or archaeology that the proposed School should be of service, but equally to students of Christian Antiquities, of Medieval History, of Palaeography, and of Italian Art.

What had no doubt given the project its impetus and urgency was the dramatic success of Giacomo Boni's excavations in the Forum. He had started only ten months earlier, at the very end of 1898, and already he had revealed the 'lapis niger' complex, the Volcanal, the 'Basilica Aemilia' and the Regia. Boni's friend St Clair Baddeley, one of those present at the October meeting, had returned to England in July, but kept in close touch with progress. That very month he had received a letter from Boni: 'I am now cutting off the electric tram so as to excavate the Comitium, as you hoped would be done. The Domus Publica becomes more and more interesting, revealing new rooms with very beautiful pavements.'[6] A

---

6. Quoted in W. St Clair Baddeley, *Recent Discoveries in the Forum 1898–1904, by an eye-witness* (London 1904) 17; see pp. 121–35 above.

new age in Roman archaeology had dawned, and it was a scandal that Great Britain was not officially represented there.

An Executive Committee was set up: Pelham, Gardner, Prothero, Macmillan and Loring from those present at the meeting; Gardner's brother-in-law J.S. Reid (1846–1926), Fellow of Caius and Professor of Ancient History at Cambridge; Charles Waldstein (1856–1927), Reader in Classical Archaeology and Slade Professor of Fine Art at Cambridge; and F.J. Haverfield (1860–1919), Senior Student of Christ Church Oxford, who was soon to succeed Pelham as Camden Professor. After some delays because of the war in South Africa, the appeal was successfully launched, and when the Executive Committee met for the fifth time, on 8 March 1900, it was resolved to start the School the following November. 'In view of this Prof. Pelham was authorised to write to Mr G. Mc.Neil Rushforth M.A. of Oriel College, Oxford, and offer him the post of Director at a salary of not less than £200 a year.'

Rushforth accepted. He was present at the Committee's next meetings on 24 May, when he undertook to draw up a list of books to be purchased for the School's library, and on 9 November, when he was authorised to secure two or three rooms in Rome 'for the temporary use of the School'.

What he found was a suite on the second floor of the Palazzo Odescalchi in the Piazza Santi Apostoli. It had been built in the 1660s as the Palazzo Chigi and passed to the Odescalchi in 1694. The plan and interior were by Carlo Maderna, the facade—lengthened and spoiled in 1745—by Bernini. In 1885 the palace had suffered a serious fire, but the repairs were now complete and the apartments Rushforth found were eminently suitable. On 10 January 1901 the Committee authorised him to take the lease for three years, at a rent of 250 lire per month. In the event, the British School was housed there for fourteen years, until in July 1915 it moved to its present home in the Valle Giulia.[7]

Rushforth was doing more in Rome than just house-hunting. Early in 1900, Boni had had the church of S. Maria Liberatrice (behind the temple of Castor in the Forum) demolished, to reveal the sixth-century basilica of S. Maria Antiqua that had been buried beneath it. St Clair Baddeley, back in Rome again, had reported the demolition and subsequent

---

7. T. Ashby, 'The Palazzo Odescalchi', *PBSR* 8 (1916) 55–90, and 9 (1920) 67–74; T.P. Wiseman, *A Short History of the British School at Rome* (London 1990) 5–14.

excavations in the *Globe* in February, March and April; one wonders how much his articles had influenced Rushforth in his acceptance of the Directorship at that very time. Certainly the newly revealed frescoes of S. Maria Antiqua would be likely to excite both his historical and his artistic enthusiasms.

Rushforth met Boni 'in a select company which used to gather in the hospitable rooms of Mr Wickham Steed', Rome correspondent of the *Times* from 1897 to 1902. The two men evidently got on well, and it was with Boni's helpful co-operation that Rushforth applied himself to the detailed study of S. Maria Antiqua and its wall-paintings.[8] Already by March 1901 he had suggested the publication of a monograph on the subject to the Executive Committee in London. Approval was given: a 'scientific journal' had been part of the idea of the School from the very beginning, and at the Committee's meeting on 27 June 1901 the *Papers of the British School at Rome* were born. The first number was to contain Rushforth on S. Maria Antiqua, and Ashby on Roman roads in the Campagna.

A brief word is necessary on Thomas Ashby (1874–1931). He had been sixteen when his family settled in Rome, and after a brilliant Oxford career he devoted himself to the study of the city and its surrounding countryside. In a sense, the British School was founded just in time to benefit from his talents. In 1901 he was the School's first student; in 1902 its Honorary Librarian; in 1903 its Assistant Director; and from 1906 to 1925 its Director. His contribution to *PBSR* I was the first in a long and distinguished series on the topography of the Roman Campagna, resulting eventually in a classic synthesis (*The Roman Campagna in Classical Times*, 1927) which, together with the magnificent *Aqueducts of Ancient Rome*, posthumously published in 1935, will be his lasting memorial.

Ashby's fame is secure.[9] But it is only just to point out that his 160 pages in the first *Papers* were the result of work already well advanced; Rushforth's 123 pages on S. Maria Antiqua became the standard account of a major monument that had been discovered only two years before.

---

8. Rushforth, *Antiquaries Journal* 5 (1925) 442f., and *PBSR* 1 (1902) 1 n. 1.
9. See now *Thomas Ashby: un archeologo fotografa la Campagna romana tra '800 e '900* (Rome 1986), and *Archeologia a Roma nelle fotografie di Thomas Ashby 1891–1930* (Naples 1989), both with detailed bibliographies.

The first Director's inaugural publication in the new journal was a remarkable piece of work.

In other ways, too, he was giving good service. 'With his wide range of learning and sympathies, his distinguished diplomatic manners, and his linguistic abilities, Rushforth did excellent work in helping the School to take its place beside older institutions of the same kind in Rome, and establishing cordial relations with them.' Thus the *Times* obituarist, whose verdict is borne out by the report of the Committee to the Annual General Meeting of subscribers in 1903: it was, they said, 'largely owing to Mr Rushforth's scholarship, tact, and ready courtesy that the School had won the position it held in Rome, and especially in the estimation of the other foreign schools.' (His touch was evidently sure in domestic matters as well: on 16 January 1902 the Committee approved a proposal by the Director to employ the son of the landlord's coachman as a second servant.)

But not everything was well. On 29 May 1902, he wrote to the Committee about the terms of his tenure of the Directorship. The Committee felt that he was being unreasonable, and at Pelham's urging he withdrew from his position, 'except as regards Rule XX, requiring a fixed term of residence in Rome; as to which he felt some difficulty, his health being indifferent, and no such rule having been in existence when he accepted the Directorship.'

Rushforth's appointment in 1900 had been welcome to him, his obituarist tells us, 'as the climate of Oxford was beginning to tell on his health.' A move to Rome might have seemed a good idea from that point of view, but he should perhaps have known better. Augustus Hare's famous guidebook *Walks in Rome*, already in its 14th edition by 1900, contained a conspicuous warning in its introduction:

> Nothing can be more mistaken than the impression that those who go to Italy are sure to find there a mild and congenial temperature. The climate of Rome . . . is not to be trifled with, and violent transitions from the hot sunshine to the cold shade of the street often prove fatal. 'No one but dogs and Englishmen', say the Romans, 'ever walk in the sun'.
>
> The *malaria*, which is so much dreaded by the natives, generally lies dormant during the winter months, and seldom affects strangers, unless they live near recent excavations or are inordinately imprudent in setting out in the sunset. With the heats of the late summer this insidious ague-fever is apt to follow on the slightest exertion, and

particularly to overwhelm those who are employed in field-labour.
From June to November the Villa Borghese and the Villa Doria are
uninhabitable, and the more deserted hills—the Coelian, the Aventine,
and a great part of the Esquiline—are a constant prey to fever.

If the 'inordinate imprudence' of setting out at sunset seems over-stated,
remember Henry James's *Daisy Miller* (1878), in which the eponymous
heroine dies of a romantic midnight visit to the Colosseum. The risk was
real.

At any rate, Rushforth's health was causing him anxiety. The Committee reassured him of its sympathy and inserted a saving clause into the
offending Rule XX. But it was not enough. On 8 November 1902 the
Committee was informed that the Director, on the advice of his doctor,
wished to relinquish his post on 25 March 1903—just three years after his
appointment. In fact, on doctor's orders, Rushforth left Rome a little
before that date, leaving Ashby in charge as Acting Director until the
arrival of his successor (H. Stuart Jones, Classical Fellow of Pelham's
college, Trinity). It was an untimely end to a notably successful
Directorship.

Malvern

Rushforth was still only forty. As the Vivarini Madonna shows, he was a
man of independent means; his father's business must have done well
and he had no wife and children to support. With no need to work for
his living, and every reason to choose a healthy atmosphere to live in, he
settled at Malvern, in a house on the hill called Riddlesden which was to
be his home for the rest of his life. There he devoted his ample time to
the pursuit of scholarship, an 'amateur' in the best sense of that much-
abused term, undistracted by preoccupations of teaching or
administration, and entirely free from that 'demarcation' mentality that
leads professional academics to pigeon-hole themselves as classicists,
medievalists, archaeologists, art-historians, and so on. Rushforth was all
those things at once, and more besides.

He had recently been elected a Fellow of the Society of Antiquaries.
(He and Ashby were admitted on the same day, 6 June 1901, when a
paper was being read on the *lapis niger* inscription recently discovered
by Boni.) The pride and pleasure he took in his election may be seen
from his constant use thereafter of the letters 'F.S.A.' after his name, and
from his contributions to the Society's proceedings in later years. In May

and June 1910, the Society held an exhibition of English medieval alabaster work in its rooms in Burlington House, Piccadilly; Rushforth lent a fifteenth-century alabaster table, and kept the organiser's thank-you letter by him for three years, until he could slip it into his copy of the Catalogue, published in 1913, where it is still to be found.

One of his neighbours at Malvern was a collector on a much grander scale, C.W. Dyson Perrins (1864–1958), whose father had been one of the original partners in the Lea and Perrins Worcester Sauce firm. Perrins was at this time building up his magnificent library of manuscripts and printed books (the manuscripts alone fetched over a million pounds when they were sold after his death), and in 1906 acquired a sixteenth-century collection of views of Rome, with manuscript text. Thomas Ashby, now Director of the British School, examined the work in Perrins's library in the summer of that year, and his old friend Rushforth helped him to decipher the fragmentary text. When Ashby's brilliant edition of the work was sumptuously published by the Roxburghe Club in 1916,[10] Rushforth received a copy 'with grateful acknowledgements from Dyson Perrins, March 25 1917'.

'Rushforth', his obituarist rightly observed, 'was one of those scholars of whom it has been said that their epitaphs are inscribed in the prefaces to their friends' books. He would have wished it so, for his extreme modesty was accompanied by a total freedom from any trace of petty jealousy or professional spitefulness.' The fly-leaves of the books in his own library certainly bear out that judgement.

For instance, two offprints from the *Numismatic Chronicle*, 1905 and 1908. On the first, 'G. Mc.N. Rushforth F.S.A. with kind regards from John Evans'—i.e. Sir John Evans, K.C.B., D.C.L., Ll.D., Sc.D., F.R.S. (1823–1908), President of the Royal Numismatic Society, ex-President of the British Association, the Geological Society, the Egypt Exploration Fund and the Society of Antiquaries, and for twenty years Treasurer of the Royal Society. On the second, two inscriptions in Rushforth's own sloping hand: 'Read before the Roy: Num: Soc: Lond: April 23 1908', and, at the top of the title page, 'In memory of a friend'. Evans had died on 31 May 1908.

---

10. T. Ashby (ed.), *Topographical Study in Rome in 1581: a Series of Views with a Fragmentary Text by Etienne du Pérac in the Library of C.W. Dyson Perrins Esq.* (London 1916): see p. 30f. for Rushforth's help.

The architectural works of Gian Teresio Rivoira (1849–1919) provide a more spectacular example. Rivoira was still a civil servant in the Italian Department of Posts and Telegraphs when Rushforth went to Rome in 1900. When the first volume of *Le origini dell'architettura lombarda* appeared the following year, he sent him a copy with the inscription 'omaggio dell'autore al chiarissimo Prof. Rushforth'. Volume 2 (1907) bore the less formal dedication 'all'amico Rushforth, G.T. Rivoira'. Rushforth translated the whole work, and Rivoira's *Lombardic Architecture* was published by Heinemann in 1910 (rev. ed. Oxford U.P. 1933). Meanwhile Rivoira had been travelling in the Middle East. In May 1914 his *Architettura musulmana* was published, and a copy came to Malvern 'a G. McN. Rushforth, in segno di amicizia, G.T. Rivoira'. Again, Rushforth did the English version. But for the war, it would have appeared at almost the same time (author and translator evidently worked in collaboration); in the end, *Moslem Architecture, its Origins and Development* was published by O.U.P. in 1918. Rivoira died in the influenza epidemic of 1919, but he had just completed his *Architettura romana*, which was published posthumously two years later. Rushforth received no. 8 in a numbered edition of 650 copies. Yet again the English translation was by his hand, with help—scrupulously acknowledged—from Ashby; and when the Oxford press published *Roman Architecture and its Principles of Construction* in 1925, it included a six-page 'biographical note' on Rivoira by Rushforth himself. In memory of a friend . . .

Sir John Evans and Commendatore Rivoira were great men, famous in the world. J.D. Le Couteur (1883–1925) was an obscure scholar, known only to a few; but his story too illustrates Rushforth's *pietas* and gift for friendship. Le Couteur lived for a while in Malvern, and was involved in the re-leading of the medieval windows of the Priory Church (of which more later) in 1910. That, presumably, was when he met Rushforth, twenty years his senior, to whom he sent in 1911, 'with the author's compliments', an offprint on the great north window of Canterbury cathedral. After the Great War he settled at Winchester, and in 1920 published *Ancient Glass in Winchester*, with Rushforth's name among the acknowledgements. But his career was cut untimely short; he died at 42, in August 1925. Rushforth's copy of his book contains the report of his funeral from the *Hampshire Observer*. The following year Le Couteur's posthumous *English Medieval Stained Glass* was published by the S.P.C.K., with a four-page 'biographical note' by Rushforth, who had revised the text and prepared it for the press.

Rushforth's own work in the pre-war period is inconspicuous—not surprisingly, considering the labour that must have been involved in the Rivoira translations. I know only of two short articles in the *Burlington Magazine* in 1911, and his first contribution to the Antiquaries (22 January 1914), on the iconography of the windows in Leominster church, which is the first sign of the special interest which was to engross him in later years. The Great War itself probably made little difference to a gentleman scholar of uncertain health, already in his fifties, with no sons or nephews to make him fear the casualty-lists. His main preoccupation, as we shall see, was with the Malvern Priory church windows, but in 1917 he was summoned back to the study of Roman topography.

In that year Dr M.R. James (1862–1936), Provost of King's College Cambridge, discovered a thirteenth-century manuscript in St Catherine's College Library containing a hitherto unknown work 'On the Marvels of the City of Rome' (*narracio de mirabilibus urbis Romae*) by one Magister Gregorius.[11] James, himself a very distinguished scholar, published it in the *English Historical Review*, but was perhaps too preoccupied by his appointment as Provost of Eton in 1918 to explore the full significance of the work. Rushforth, acknowledging the help of Ashby, Stuart Jones, St Clair Baddeley and Mrs Strong (Ashby's Assistant Director at the British School), produced within two years a detailed commentary and revised text—45 pages of the *Journal of Roman Studies* that beautifully exemplify his obituarist's judgement on his work: 'characterized by exact information, perfect finish, and a lucid style'. (Seventeen years later a German scholar called Paul Borchardt published a small follow-up article in the *JRS*: Rushforth, characteristically, had not only given advice but translated the text into English.)

After the war, in the last twenty years of his life (he died at 76), Rushforth published a good deal, mostly in the *Antiquaries Journal* and in the *Transactions* of the Bristol and Gloucester Archaeological Society, which he had joined in 1920. He was at once invited on to the Council of the B.G.A.S. (just as he had been elected to the Council of the Antiquaries in 1919), and he served twice as the Society's President in 1927 and 1928. One of the books in his library, presented by the Rev.

---

11. See now *Master Gregorius: The Marvels of Rome* (Pontifical Institute of Mediaeval Studies, Toronto 1987), translated with introduction and commentary by John Osborne.

L.H. Dahl, bears the inscription: 'From the author. In gratitude for much information imparted during your two years' Presidency of the Glouc. Arch. Society. Stapleton Rectory, Bristol. Sept. 24 1929'.

It is through another clerical member of the B.G.A.S., the Rev. E.P. Baker, that we get a precious glimpse of Rushforth in action, and some idea of the respectful affection he inspired:[12]

> We shall not easily forget the spare, frail figure that stood beneath many a Gloucestershire chancel arch to address the Society, the thin high-pitched voice, the quick sharp gestures of head and hand lending emphasis to his words . . . There was something in his manner and presence, a zest, an acumen, together with a practised eye and well-trained intellect that brought an air of distinction to any gathering of which he was a member.
>
> He insisted that others more expert than himself should expound the purely architectural features of a church—he was too unassuming to take into account his own immense knowledge of the subject. His contribution, as he saw it, was to record the story that lay behind the monuments of brick and stone, for it was the human aspect of our studies that absorbed him. This explains his invariable habit of commenting upon the mural tablets of a church, the family trees which littered the pages of his notebook, the pedigrees he delighted to embody in his discourse . . . His was no dry-as-dust interest in pedigree as an end in itself. It expressed and clarified for him the human element in his story. To illustrate the theme he would draw upon all the evidence the church afforded—brasses, fragments of painted glass, effigies, inscriptions and so on, weaving them as far as possible into a historical pattern, always with the purpose of 'making sense of it', as he would say. He sought to convey a sense of action that characterizes the pageant of history, setting the events and traditions of each locality in the wider perspective of national life. Scarcely a church that he visited with the Society was not the occasion for some new discovery, some fresh observation due to Rushforth.

Baker's last comment is borne out—and not only for Gloucestershire—by the titles of some of Rushforth's papers: 'A Sketch of the History of Malvern' (1920); 'An Indulgence Inscription in Clapton Church, Gloucestershire' (1923); 'Medieval Tiles in the Church of Llangattock-nigh-Usk' (1924); 'The Burial of Lancastrian Notables in Tewkesbury

---

12. *Trans. BGAS* 59 (1938) 348–9.

Abbey after the Battle, A.D. 1471' (1925); 'Tewkesbury Abbey: the Wakeman Cenotaph and the starved Monk' (1925); 'Lord Cromwell's Rebus in Tattershall Castle' (1926); 'The Kirkham Monument in Paignton Church, Devon' (1927); 'Herefordshire' (Presidential Address, 1927); 'The Story of Dauntsey' (1928); 'Warkworth' (1930); 'A Fourteenth-century Tomb from Little Malvern Priory Church' (1931); 'The Arms of St Augustine's Abbey and of St Mark's or the Gaunts' Hospital, Bristol' (1932).

Besides all this, there were contributions (on art) to the *Legacy of Rome* and *Medieval England* volumes, revised editions of his *Latin Historical Inscriptions* (urged on him by the new Camden Professor, J.G.C. Anderson)[13] and of Rivoira's *Lombardic Architecture*—and, above all, there was his work on English medieval stained glass. For that, which was arguably his most important scholarly achievement, we have to go right back to his early years in Malvern.

At that time, the St Anne's Chapel of the Great Malvern Priory Church was being restored. In 1910, the chapel windows and the clerestory windows above, on the south side of the choir, were re-leaded, and the opportunity was taken to restore them to their original order and banish the 18th- and 19th-century intrusions. The Vicar of Malvern, A.C. Deane (1870–1946), called on the advice of M.R. James, Provost of King's— whom we have already met in the context of Magister Gregorius' *narracio de mirabilibus*. Rushforth was very interested, and planned a monograph on the ancient glass in the Priory.

In 1913 Deane published a history of the church in Bell's 'Cathedral Series'. He then moved to the Vicarage of Hampstead (on the progress that was to make him eventually Chaplain to King George V), but on 7 March 1914 sent Rushforth a copy, with the following letter:

My dear Rushforth,
    I have had a few copies of the Priory book specially bound, and it's a great pleasure to send one for your acceptance. You know how

---

13. Preface to the second edition (Oxford 1930) viii: 'For almost the whole of this new matter I am indebted to Professor J.G.C. Anderson and Mr H.M. Last, who may be said to have fathered this reissue in the same way that the later Professor Pelham and Mr (as he then was) Haverfield did its original form; but, as before, the share of the Camden Professor has been the largest.'

grateful I am for all your ungrudging help. I hope it will not be very long before you are able to send to press your work on the windows.

With best remembrances from us both,

Yours sincerely,

Anthony C. Deane

In fact, Rushforth's book would not see the light for more than twenty years. Canon Deane's successor had the rest of the windows of the Priory church re-leaded; under Rushforth's supervision (in succession to James), the restoration and re-ordering that had been done in St Anne's Chapel was repeated, between 1915 and 1919, for the whole church. The monograph was going to become a major work: 'daily contact with the glass during the releading greatly increased my knowledge, and I felt that it was my duty to preserve the results which I had gained in some permanent form.'[14]

A series of photographs of the dismantled windows was taken by Sydney A. Pitcher, of College Court, Gloucester, who was (or became) a close friend of Rushforth. Pitcher published the photographs in six folios (1916–1927), 'with descriptive notes by G. Mc.N. Rushforth F.S.A.'. Meanwhile Rushforth himself was already producing important historical and iconographical accounts of medieval stained glass elsewhere in England. Between 1914 and 1938, the bibliography lists more than twenty such studies, from the great cathedrals of Gloucester and Exeter down to village churches like Birtsmorton and Nettlecombe.[15]

It was in 1936 that the Clarendon Press at last brought out *Medieval Christian Imagery, as illustrated by the painted windows of Great Malvern Priory Church Worcestershire*. It is a magnificent achievement: 'Mr Rushforth', said the *Times Literary Supplement*, 'has lifted the subject on to another plane, and by close study of a single church, illustrated by the widest reading and knowledge of other examples, has produced a truly monumental work.'[16] Rushforth was seventy-three. In a sense, it really was his monument.

---

14. Rushforth, *Medieval Christian Imagery* (Oxford 1936) 18–20; A.C. Deane, *A Short Account of Great Malvern Priory Church* (London 1914) vii, 31, and *Time Remembered* (London 1945) 130–3; L.A. Hamand, *The Ancient Windows of Great Malvern Priory Church* (St Albans 1947) vii-viii.

15. See pp. 233–7 below.

16. *TLS* 1774 (1 February 1936) 87; cf. F.J.E. Raby, *Ant. Journal* 16 (1936) 330, 'a book such as Mr Rushforth has given us here is virtually beyond criticism.'

In 1935, All Souls College had asked him to study the surviving medieval glass in the ante-chapel. Sydney Pitcher (who had illustrated the Malvern book) again produced a series of photographs. Rushforth began the work, but was never able to complete it.[17]

Exmouth

Of Rushforth's two brothers, Francis became a solicitor and Collingwood a clergyman. The latter had retired in 1916 from his living at Great Staughton, Huntingdonshire, and settled at Elmhurst, Hartley Road, Exmouth, where he evidently lived with their sister, Janet, until his death in March 1933. At any rate, Janet McNeil Rushforth was certainly living at that address in 1936; her eldest brother was in the habit of going there for Christmas and staying for the winter months.

He knew Devon well. Already in 1927 he had published a study of the fifteenth-century tombs of Paignton church for the Exeter Diocesan Architectural and Archaeological Society; a note on a lily-crucifix and an unidentified saint in Kenn church appeared in the *Antiquaries Journal* the same year; in 1929 his study of the iconography of the Seven Sacraments included the medieval glass in the churches of Cadbury and Doddiscombeleigh; and in 1933 he had discussed Exeter's St Sidwell and the great east window of the Cathedral.[18] As one would expect, he was on good terms with the scholarly clerics of the Exeter Cathedral Chapter. Prebendary J.F. Chanter, Treasurer of the Cathedral and Honorary Archivist of the Diocese and Chapter, gave Rushforth an inscribed copy of his book *The Bishop's Palace at Exeter and its Story* (S.P.C.K. 1932), and it was in the *Transactions* of the Exeter Diocesan Society that Rushforth published his last substantial work, forty pages on the medieval glass at St Neot in Cornwall.

He was also in touch with John Murray, the energetic Principal of the University College of the South West. Murray was busy organising the start of the transfer of the College from its quarters in Gandy Street, in the middle of Exeter, out to the Streatham Estate where its successor, the University of Exeter, now stands. Murray was Acting Head of the

---

17. F.E. Hutchinson, *Medieval Glass at All Souls College* (London 1949) 7.
18. Rushforth was first invited to study the Exeter glass in 1921: see Chris Brooks and David Evans, *The Great East Window of Exeter Cathedral* (Exeter 1988) 72–4.

College's Classics Department from 1933 to 1938; his main preoccupation, however, was not teaching but raising funds. A new library—the
Roborough—was being planned for the new site, and books to equip it
were one of the College's main needs. (Among his correspondence about
the Roborough, incidentally, is a letter of January 1938 from Vincent
Harris, the architect, in which he points out to Murray that if the new
library is lit with table lights, 'there will be difficulty in using it for
dancing'.)

The records of the University College were destroyed in the 'Exeter
blitz' of 1942, but Murray's own papers survive in the University of
Exeter's archives.[19] They include an exchange of letters with Rushforth
in December 1936, which suggests that the two men were already on
good terms. The letters are revealing of both their characters:

6.12.36

My dear Principal,

I am intending to come to Exmouth just before Christmas for my
usual winter stay, and, partly in order to relieve my shelves, should like
to bring with me some books for your college Library. I enclose a list
of items which I am not likely to want again, and you may think worth
having. I could add, if necessary, various commentaries on Aristotle's
Ethics.

Hoping that you and your affairs are flourishing, I am,
Yours sincerely,
G.Mc.N. Rushforth.

8.12.36

My dear Rushforth,

Thank you for your letter and for the offer of books which you
would bring with you to Devon. They will be very welcome. Will you
please bring the Commentaries on Aristotle too.

I should like to know which day you would drop them here, and
how long you will be in these parts. Perhaps you would give me the
pleasure of putting you up for a night or two. Term ends on Saturday
week, and on 30th December I am leaving here for Uganda on a
Colonial Office Commission, but till then I expect to be here. I am all
alone with room to spare, my wife having just arrived at Johannesburg
on a visit to my stepdaughter married there.

The College is indeed flourishing: numbers 50 up on last year: all
Halls full and overfull: the UGC grant up from £14,500 to £15,000. But

---

19. University of Exeter archive, Principal's Papers, Box B, file 27.

we are likely to have to vacate Gandy Street and heavy capital is needed for rehousing at Streatham, and we must try to build a Library besides extending a women's Hall and building one for men. The capital account is anything but prosperous.

But growth is the great thing. Why, yesterday five Turks arrived, two of them with no English whatever, though some French. In this emergency I am using a Turk from Cyprus, a Government Scholar, to teach his collinguals their first English. We do very well in the Levant. The Egyptian Government was due to send us four freshmen scholars this term, and sent twelve—first-fruits of the Treaty, I suppose.

Do you think anything can be done with Perrins about helping our Library? A few of his odd thousands would help enormously.

With kind regards,

Yours sincerely,

John Murray.

The foundation stone of the Roborough Library was laid by the Duke of Gloucester on 20 October 1937. Rushforth had been invited, but wrote to Murray on 17 October:

My dear Principal,

Thank you for your very kind letter and invitation. It is with the deepest regret that I have to decline it, for I should have felt greatly honoured by the opportunity of meeting HRH under such circumstances, and for the recognition of my modest benefaction to the College. But in my present condition it is impossible, for the fact is that, though I had no reason to mention it to you before, early in this year I was found to be suffering from heart weakness, and till recently I had to lie low and keep very quiet, so that it was only lately that I could return to Malvern. Though my doctor has considerably improved my condition, at my time of life I cannot expect to resume my former activities, and must be content for the future to be a looker on. Fortunately, I can keep up my old interests, and I am fully occupied.

If all goes well I am intending to return to Exmouth for the winter, and shall hope to see you then, to talk over with you various matters connected with my books. I take this opportunity of saying that I leave the College at perfect liberty to deal with them as seems best.

I shall look forward to reading the account of your ceremony on the 20th, and with every good wish for the future of the College, I am

Yours sincerely,

G. Mc.N. Rushforth.

Already, on 21 August, Rushforth had made his will. He left Riddlesden to his servant, Charles Leonard Goodyear, and all his manuscripts and papers concerning the Priory Church to the Library Authority, Malvern Urban District. Of his art collection, he left to the Society of Antiquaries an Italian panel painting of the Crucifix rising out of the recumbent figure of the Virgin, and a small framed Byzantine painting of John the Baptist with wings like an angel; and to the Ashmolean, Richard Westall's watercolour 'Boreas and Oreithyia' and two oil sketches by Benedetto di Castiglione. In order to increase the residue of the estate (eventually valued at £16,000 net) which was to be invested as a trust fund for his sister and surviving brother, Rushforth instructed his executors to sell the following items:

> 'Ships in a calm sea', oil-painting by Dubbels;
> 'Storm on coast, ships driving ashore', oil painting by Turner;
> 'Beauty controlled by Prudence and crowned by Merit', oil painting by Angelica Kauffmann;
> 'Landscape, ruined temple above a cascade', oil painting by Hubert Robert;
> 'Virgin and Child', oil painting, school of Perugino;
> 'Lausanne', water-colour by John Glover Crystal;
> intaglio by Giovanni Bernardi (on which Rushforth had published a note in the *Burlington Magazine* in 1937).

All his other pictures, plate, china, etc, went to a cousin, who was also to inherit the income from the trust fund after the deaths of Francis and Janet McNeil Rushforth, with the request that he would 'adopt and prefix the surname of Rushforth to his present surname'.

His books, and the water-colour of the Parthenon that now hangs in the Thornton West suite of Reed Hall, were left to the University College of the South West. He intended to draw up a catalogue of the books for the guidance of his executors, but if he did so, and it ever came to Exeter, it must have been lost in the 1942 destruction. The only record the present University Library has is a list, compiled in 1981 by Miss Sarah Newton, of the valuable items that were put in the Rare Books Room (81 titles) and the Reserve Collection (136). Of the Rushforth books on the open shelves I have identified about 460 titles, mainly in the Classics, Fine Art, History and Theology sections. There must be many more, for instance in English Literature, and no doubt French and Italian too— standard works of classic authors that such a library might be expected to contain (for instance, there is a set of Dickens first editions in the Rare Books Room)—but I have not been able to track them all down.

What is abundantly clear is that Rushforth's library included, among other things, an excellent coverage of Latin and Greek texts, mainly Teubners, including recondite items as well as 'classics' in the usual sense; a good collection of works on the topography and history of the city of Rome; many expensive illustrated catalogues of exhibitions of paintings, furniture and other *objets d'art*; and an extraordinarily wide range of works on English local history, genealogy, heraldry and secular and ecclesiastical architecture, which vividly illuminate the lost world of learned vicars and gentlemen scholars in which Rushforth spent so much of his life.

He died in Exmouth on 26 March 1938. Murray, wishing to commemorate his benefaction, asked the executors if they could provide a photograph of him to hang in the Roborough. They consulted Janet Rushforth; she in turn applied to her brother's old friend Sydney Pitcher, and enclosed his reply (dated 18 July 1938) with her letter to Murray. He was not surprised, he said, that the books were to go to the U.C.S.W.: 'Mr Rushforth had mentioned it to me about a year ago, and I thought his reasons for this very sound.'

We can guess what the reasons were. Another friend, the Rev. Baker, quotes a revealing phrase:[20]

> Even in the last months of his life, when health and strength were ebbing fast, he was devouring the latest books and periodicals that he might still 'continue to learn', and a yet deeper source of satisfaction, as he once admitted, was to realize that in personal intercourse and correspondence he could be of some avail in 'passing on the torch to others'.

By leaving his books to enrich the library of the U.C.S.W., and to stimulate the imagination of its students in generations to come, he was passing on the torch.

Sydney Pitcher duly produced a framed photograph for the Roborough. Alas, no record of it now remains. Worse, in the Exeter University Library catalogue a false expansion of Rushforth's first initial turned him into 'George' McNeil Rushforth. Modest and self-effacing

---

20. *Trans. BGAS* 59 (1938) 348.

though he was, he deserved better than that. The blame, perhaps, should go to the bomb-aimers of the Luftwaffe in 1942. Exeter did remember him, for a while at least: a Guide to the Roborough Library in the late fifties, by the then librarian L.J. Lloyd, refers to its 'small collection of rare editions and printed books, chiefly of Greek and Roman Literature, most of which are part of the collection bequeathed by the late G.McN.Rushforth.' After that, he was forgotten for twenty years.

In April 1981 the Classical Association held its annual conference in Exeter, and a small exhibition of some of the Rushforth books was put on in the University Library; the original version of this study was written for that occasion. Rediscovering Rushforth was a particular pleasure for the present writer, as an ex-Scholar of the British School at Rome. But in any case, he deserves commemoration. He lived in a world of privilege but was not corrupted by it; what he cared about was true scholarship and selfless loyalty to his friends. And he left his books to Exeter because he wanted to bring alive in us ('passing on the torch to others') that fascination with the living world of the past, and that love for the things of beauty that men have made, which had been the meaning of his own life.

9

TALKING TO VIRGIL

A mature scholar

In the early nineteen-thirties, readers of the learned journals in both Britain and the United States became aware of the work of a classical scholar called W.F.J. Knight, writing from Bloxham School in Oxfordshire. The articles were not only numerous, erudite, and very wide-ranging; they were also, in more ways than one, distinctly original.[1]

Their most striking feature was what we might nowadays call lateral thinking. Knight was evidently not just a learned classicist: he understood many other things too, and exploited them to good effect. In his very first publication, a brief note on the 'labyrinth' passage in *Aeneid* VI 24–35, he applied to Virgil the insights of Shakespearean scholarship

---

Abbreviations

CLA: G. Wilson Knight, *Caroline: Life and After-Life* (unpublished typescript, Exeter University Library)

JKB: G. Wilson Knight, *Jackson Knight: A Biography* (Alden Press, Oxford 1975)

Note: I spell the poet's name 'Virgil' in English; Jackson Knight normally (but not quite always) spelt it 'Vergil', as did T.J. Haarhoff. I hope the reader will not find the inconsistency distracting.

1. The full bibliography is in *JKB* 495–506. Articles from the Bloxham period appeared in *Classical Review* 1929, 1930, 1932, 1933, 1934; *Classical Philology* 1930, 1931; *Latin Teaching* 1930; *Journal of Hellenic Studies* 1931, 1934; *Classical Quarterly* 1931, 1932; *Classical Journal* 1931, 1933; *Antiquity* 1932, 1933; *Transactions of the American Philological Association* 1932, 1935; *Classical Weekly* 1933, 1934; *Greece and Rome* 1935; *Folklore* 1935.

(Colin Still's book on *The Tempest*), and found it natural to refer in his footnotes not only to Norden and Conway on Virgil but also to W.B. Yeats on symbolism and William James on the disintegration of consciousness. More startlingly, his studies of the rhythm of Virgil's hexameters used the terminology of wireless telegraphy to illustrate the interaction of stress and metrical ictus—'homodyne' for where they coincide, 'heterodyne' for where they conflict. But the most far-reaching of all Knight's cross-disciplinary insights was his application of the ideas of anthropology to classical texts, in particular to the Virgilian themes of the Trojan Horse and the descent to the Underworld. His evident mastery of the subject enabled him to exploit new discoveries at once, like the chambered cairn of Bryn Celli Ddu with its maze-patterned stone; published in 1930, it formed the basis of Knight's tightly-argued interpretation of the *lusus Troiae* only two years later. A powerful and original mind was beginning to make itself known.

William Francis Jackson Knight was thirty-four when the first of these publications appeared. He had gone up to Oxford in 1914 with a scholarship to Hertford College, joined the Army a year later and served for three years in the signal service of the Royal Engineers. Invalided out in August 1918, with serious leg wounds and shell-shock, he returned to Oxford in 1920, graduated in 1922 with a Second in Greats, and taught for three years at Henley House, a 'crammer's' establishment, before going to Bloxham as Classics master in 1925, a month or so before his thirtieth birthday. As the training of a serious scholar, it sounds unimpressive. But that summary leaves out everything that was important about Jackson Knight.

He and his brother (G. Wilson Knight) were brought up in an atmosphere of ambition and aspiration wholly generated by their mother. 'The aim was, not merely to make good and draw level, but to surpass.'[2] Their relationship with her became even closer and more intense after her separation from their father in 1918, and the financial disasters that accompanied the separation added urgency to their will to succeed.

Much later, after her death in 1950, her younger son did his best to define Caroline Knight's dominating and tormented personality.[3]

---

2. *JKB* 39. All information not otherwise referenced will be found in the biography, which has an excellent index.

3. *CLA* 4–6.

As I look back on it, the personality I and my brother remember as 'Mother' grows more, not less, mysterious. It would be a severe error to read into this three-cornered relationship no more than the obvious parental and filial emotions, though these had, originally at least, played their part. There was, nevertheless, little conventional or normal about any of it, and I know no ordinary words to define the forces at play. After all, the determining factor was Caroline's personality, and there was nothing normal about that. During these years she not only suffered in turn almost every physical ailment conceivable, but was also afflicted by a certain terrible mental unrest or 'neurosis'. From our childhood onwards, she had set the pace of our family life with a burning idealism; but somehow from beneath this, as its anti-self, was thrown up, during our schooldays, a dark torment which never thereafter left her, and certainly helped to precipitate the marriage-break; if indeed it was not somehow caused by marital disturbance. But none of this prevented her from exercising, until near the end, a ceaseless physical activity and an indomitable mental power, together with a remarkable flair for leadership. There were years of battling, with ambitions, with work, with many moves. Entwined with the story were tensions and devotions that cannot here be discussed, but little obvious sentimentality, and no easy emotions of any sort; rather, deeply founded instincts and loyalties tugging, wrenching, conflicting, demanding; and yet, in general, a pushing always on and up. Such was the thirty years' whirlwind in which we were caught.

In the first book of the *Aeneid*, the hero describes how he began his journey from Troy, following his allotted destiny and shown the way by his goddess mother (I 382): 'matre dea monstrante viam data fata secutus', a wonderfully 'heterodyned' line. Jackson Knight's first book, published in 1932, was dedicated *matri monstranti viam*.

The preface of *Vergil's Troy* gives a hint of how the shell-shocked signals officer had become the mature scholar capable of so elegantly erudite a work:[4]

> For the kindest of advice and criticism during my investigations I am deeply grateful to Professor J.L. Myres, who has freely and repeatedly afforded me the advantage of conversations with him, to Professor H.J.

---

4. *Vergil's Troy* (Oxford 1932) vii–viii = *Vergil: Epic and Anthropology* (London 1967) 17.

Rose, and to Mr J.D. Denniston; and for generous encouragement . . .
to Professor R.S. Conway. To these scholars I owe much more than this
small book can clearly show.

Henley House and Bloxham School were close to Oxford, where Myres
was Wykeham Professor of Ancient History and Denniston a Fellow of
Hertford. (Rose was at St Andrews, Conway at Manchester.) Jackson
Knight was always extrovert and gregarious, a compulsive conversation-
alist and correspondent, and a man of dynamic energy. So while he was
earning his living coaching 'averagely barbarous Old Harrovians', and
then knocking the Bloxham School OTC into shape,[5] he was reading
intensively and discussing what he read with a wide range of scholarly
contacts.

It is not surprising that first in the list of acknowledgements was Myres,
whose Sather Lectures *Who Were the Greeks?* were published in 1930.
This great synthesis is justly described by Dorothea Gray as 'a
magnificent narrative, bold in conception and worked out in minute
detail. The Greek heroic age is superimposed on the archaeological
record, to take its place in the documented history of its neighbours.'
Vergil's Troy is a more modest work, but Myres' aims and methods have
left their mark on it, as has the intellectual stimulus of his conversation.[6]

But another influence was equally strong:

> Lastly, I am greatly indebted to my brother G. Wilson Knight, whose
> thought has continually influenced my views, and whose suggestions
> have helped my work.

Wilson Knight's splendid sequence of Shakespearean interpretations had
already begun, with *The Wheel of Fire* in 1930 and *The Imperial Theme* in
1931. His technique was the opposite of Myres', rejecting the 'temporal'
dimension of source-criticism and historical context for the 'spatial'
approach to the text as composed of symbolic and metaphoric struc-

---

5. *JKB* 86 (Alan Sims' phrase), 102–113.
6. Dorothea Gray in Sir John Myres, *Homer and his Critics* (London 1958) 235.
   Cf. T.J. Dunbabin, *Proc. Brit. Acad.* 41 (1955) 365: '[Myres] was generous,
   particularly to young men at the outset of their careers, who would come
   away from a long session with enough ideas for a book.'

tures.[7] The tension between these two modes of thought, the scholarly and the imaginative, is very clear in the introduction to *Vergil's Troy*:[8]

> However long and deep may have been the thinking with which the poetic act has been prepared or reinforced, great poetry is not made by mechanical combination only, and even when elements, which seem to have been contributed by prosaic faculties of invention and design, have been examined in abstraction from the poetic whole, the very difficulties and discussions which arise show that some of the self-dependent and self-evident truth of great art has gone.
>
> The tragic and epic unity of the Second *Aeneid* offers little to this critique by abstraction, and invokes, instead, the judgement of receptivity and contemplation. There is less temptation to discuss parts or single members of the poetic organism, as if the material taken for criticism were not poetry at all. *This does not mean that there are not questions in this book to be asked and diffidently answered by careful investigation.* There are many: concerning the right place which a detail should hold in the main poetic unity; the forms of old myths and old beliefs which Vergil has inherited and transmuted; and the method by which the intellect of Vergil worked, in the service of his sovereign vision. But the vision itself must remain sovereign and unforgotten, for it alone gives full reality to everything that it has comprised.

Jackson Knight's three examples of the 'questions to be asked and diffidently answered' define a large part of his life's work.

He begins the book with a chapter entitled 'The Poetry'. Jackson Knight had a superb ear for the rhythms and sound effects of the Virgilian hexameter, and I think it could well be argued that his exposition of them is his most permanently significant achievement. Particularly acute was his detection and definition of the way Virgil distributes 'homodyned' and 'heterodyned' lines into movements and patterns which are integral to the total poetic effect. (The first sentence of the *Aeneid* offers a simple example of how 'thought and rhythm are harmonised' in what he called a 'released movement': six lines with conflict of stress and ictus after the caesura, followed by a seventh—the last in the period—in which they coincide.) At Denniston's suggestion, Jackson Knight later expanded his

7. *JKB* 120, 162f. See John E. Van Domelen, *Tarzan of Athens: a Biographical study of G. Wilson Knight* (Bristol 1987), ch. 3.
8. Op. cit. (n. 4) 1–2 = 19–20. My italics.

discussion of this into a separate monograph, which appeared in 1939.[9] Soon after that, the whole treatment of the poetry of *Aeneid* II was extended to cover the complete works in the long and brilliant fifth chapter of *Roman Vergil*, which T.S. Eliot rightly identified as the best part of that admirable book.[10]

I anticipate the chronology in order to emphasise the *success* of this part of Jackson Knight's work. Less original, but also of real scholarly value, are the two following chapters in *Vergil's Troy*, 'The Epic Tragedy' and 'The Legends' (particularly the latter, an excellent account of the traditions on the fall of Troy). But purely literary matters were not what excited him most. Of greater interest for his own story are the ideas that did *not* succeed.

'The Events' is the confident title of the final chapter of *Vergil's Troy*. Jackson Knight is quite sure that the Trojan War is historical: 'it is likely that the siege of Troy actually lasted about two years, not ten . . . Helen may actually have been the immediate cause of the war, for she was a queen of the older stock, and the Achaeans may have ruled by her right . . . The Trojans were, in fact, defeated, not in cavalry action, but in a contest of horse-magic . . .'[11] And so on. His basic concept, that the wooden horse was a means of breaking the defensive magic of the city wall, is a brilliant one; but if that *is* what lies behind the story, it does not thereby follow that real Achaeans really used it in a real war at a real time. According to Jackson Knight, even the details can be recovered:[12]

> Helenus or some other Trojan told the Achaeans how the magical defence could be defeated. In fact, one writer seems to have preserved the exact truth: Conon, who records that Helenus suggested the wooden horse.

Conon was a mythographer of the Augustan age. That his version was a true record of events twelve hundred years earlier, rather than the plausible embroidery of a Hellenistic *littérateur*, would strike most

---

9. *Vergil's Troy* (n.4 above) 17–24 = 31–36; *Accentual Symmetry in Vergil* (Oxford 1939), p. x for Denniston.

10. *JKB* 299; *Roman Vergil* (London 1944) 180–281 = (Harmondsworth 1966) 225–341.

11. *Vergil's Troy* 105f. = 103, 106 = 104 (following Myres), 133 = 123.

12. Ibid. 128 = 119.

classicists as improbable to the point of fantasy. For Jackson Knight, its likelihood did not even need arguing; it could simply be assumed.

What we have here is not mere naïve gullibility. Part of it is a characteristic recognisable in other scholars too, a reluctance to distinguish between evidence and speculation, or to test hypotheses against possible alternatives. One man particularly prone to this, whose work Jackson Knight cites with approval, was the biblical scholar and archaeologist Rendel Harris. In his book *Boanerges*, Harris gives a disarming account of his inability to break the habit:[13]

> As often as I repeated to myself the warning to beware of the idea that one had found a master-key in mythology, so often some fresh door or window would open under the stress of the particular key I was carrying; and it was necessary to go on with what one had begun, when the first stages of enquiry were so rich in results.

Without testing the evidence—*abasanistos*, as Thucydides has it—the danger is that one builds a house of cards, one speculation upon another.

But there is also a more specific point. Like Harris, Jackson Knight was widely read in anthropology; like Harris, he thought that the evidence of comparative mythology and folklore could be directly applied to particular historical situations. Hence the uncontrolled leap from the hypothesis about the meaning of the wooden horse story to a factual record of the Trojan War.

Wilson Knight records a moment when his brother was oppressed by doubts about the wooden horse theory. 'I recall insisting that one had only to hear of it to know that it was, in *some sense*, true.'[14] Exactly: but in *what* sense? Meanwhile, Wilson Knight goes on, 'more material of similar sort was swirling in his mind.'

One step into the mystery

Now that *Vergil's Troy* had established his scholarly credentials, Jackson Knight was applying for university posts. No doubt he hoped to emulate his brother, whose first book had moved him from Dean Close School,

---

13. J. Rendel Harris, *Boanerges* (Cambridge 1913) vii. Harris' biographer in the *DNB* quotes a colleague's judgement: 'it is a pity that he does not allow himself time to think of more than one theoretical possibility at once.'
14. *JKB* 162 (his italics).

Cheltenham, to the Chancellors' professorship of English at Trinity College in the University of Toronto. But Jackson found it much harder. He was an unusual sort of scholar, and an unusual sort of man. It is hard to guess what appointing committees made of this powerful but eccentric personality, 'a dapper, dandyish figure' startlingly combining an authoritative military manner with the famous high-pitched voice which Cecil Day-Lewis later described, immortally, as the sound of a demented seagull.[15]

'Titles meant much to him', says Wilson Knight—and all his life he missed them. He didn't get a decoration for his war service; he didn't get a First in Greats; he didn't get a Fellowship, or a D.Litt., or a Chair, any of which he would have loved. It was all very well for Maurice Bowra to write 'It is a scandal to British scholarship that Mr Knight is still only a schoolmaster'; Oxford, which knew him well, offered him nothing.[16] When the opening came, it was by a quite different route.

In 1930, he had published a short note in the *Classical Review* on a difficult passage in *Aeneid* VI (lines 567–9, the judgements of Rhadamanthus in Tartarus), which elicited in turn an even shorter note from Professor T.J. Haarhoff of the University of the Witwatersrand. It was probably that—appropriately, Virgil on the afterlife—that began their life-long correspondence. 'It is strange', said Haarhoff later, 'how two people separated by thousands of sea-miles can without meeting be drawn together . . . There was a spontaneous enthusiasm and understanding on both sides.'[17] In May 1934, Haarhoff sent Jackson Knight a copy of his book *Schools of Gaul*, with a flyleaf inscription:

> Amico nondum viso
> bene tamen cognito
> Vergiliano Vergilianus
> d.d.

The two men first met in 1935, when Haarhoff was Professor of Greek at Cardiff for a year. During that summer, Haarhoff also met John Murray, Principal of the University College of the South-West at Exeter. Murray was looking for an Assistant Lecturer in Classics; Haarhoff 'spoke to him

15. *JKB* 11; cf. 77, 108f. for the authoritative bearing.
16. *JKB* 121, 160 (titles), 163f. (Bowra).
17. *CR* 44 (1930) 5, 170f.; Haarhoff, *Proc. Virg. Soc.* 4 (1964–5) 74.

about J.K., who seemed rather overwhelmed by his scholastic duties at Bloxham School. I pleaded that if he were given a university post he could do much valuable work.' To this very junior job, at a salary of £250, Jackson Knight was appointed at the age of forty.[18] He thought it would be a stepping-stone to something better: 'I go in for everything', he wrote to Haarhoff from Exeter in 1936, 'because I can't afford not to; though it is ever so nice here.'[19]

The dowry Jackson Knight brought to Exeter was the almost completed text of a book called *Cumaean Gates*. The Oxford University Press had turned it down, and despite the immense—and genuine—erudition that had gone into it, one can see why. As so often, Wilson Knight's judgement is acute:[20]

> Close archaeological research was plunging him among the mysteries . . . Evidences were used as corroborations for what was intuitively known; indeed, *Cumaean Gates* often reads as a massing of corroborative evidence for a thesis never exactly defined . . . [It is] a work richer in compacted evidence than in clarity of argument.

Nevertheless, Blackwell accepted it for publication, and it became one of Jackson Knight's best known books—though more often admired, I think, than understood. Much later, reflecting on its evident appeal to creative artists, the author commented: 'Odd: it seems to be bad science but some sort of poetry.'[21]

The book itself defies synopsis; but its main theme had already been presented in an American journal, with the following summary:[22]

> The Sixth *Aeneid* corresponds with myths of the modern megalithic Malekulans of the New Hebrides, and with the *Epic of Gilgamish*. All have the same ritual pattern. This explains difficulties in Vergil, especially the functions of the picture of a labyrinth, seen on the temple gate at Cumae, and of the golden bough. Further, all three myths represent a similar conflation of older elements: the cave type of

---

18. Haarhoff, loc. cit.; *JKB* 166.
19. JK to TJH, 30 April 1936 (by courtesy of the Archivist, University of the Witwatersrand).
20. *JKB* 162, 181, 191.
21. *JKB* 433 (1964), on Michael Ayrton and David Jones.
22. *Trans. Am. Phil. Ass.* 66 (1935) 256–73.

myth, in which the dead go into a cave, and the ocean type, in which they cross water. This is clearly a very old pattern, which may have been reconstructed by Vergil's accurate imagination; among other possibilities, it may have been spread to Greece and Italy by the 'stone folk', associated with megalithic monuments.

Let us be clear about it: the parallels with *Aeneid* VI are from two thousand years before, in Mesopotamia, and two thousand years after, in the South Pacific. In which case, the historian asks, how can they be other than coincidental? For Jackson Knight, to ask that question was to misplace the onus of proof. 'I risk one assumption: that something should not be expected to come out of nothing—until it is proved to have done so.'[23]

He does, however, offer an answer. Or rather two answers, of very different kinds.

For the first, we must go back to October 1933, when Jackson Knight gave a paper on the meaning of the labyrinth to the Oxford branch of the Classical Association. He drew attention to an article on the subject by Hermann Güntert in the latest number of the *Sitzungsberichte der Heidelberger Akademie der Wissenschaften*, which derived 'labyrinth' from the root of *laas* and *lapis* ('stone'), and by plotting its supposed cognates, claimed to trace

> the diffusion over the mediterranean area and beyond of a racial stock which, coming from western Asia, furnished a foundation for many of the greater cultures of the ancient world, even including the megalithic. The word *labyrinth*, explained to mean 'place of stone', is characteristic of them; they were in fact 'stone-folk', and stone ring walls and 'labyrinths' are their typical remains.

The Mediterranean area *and beyond* . . . Jackson Knight's lateral thinking added this footnote in the published version of his paper:

> Much in Güntert's theory is impressively confirmed by observations of a modern megalithic people, the Malekulans . . . The Malekulans are emphatically 'stone-folk'.

---

23. *Greece and Rome* 6 (1937) 71, on the historicity of Aeneas.

For his Oxford audience, he was cautious about Güntert's 'very bold theory', which 'has obvious difficulties'. But it is clear that he believed it. In other places he takes it as proved, or mentions reservations only for form's sake.[24] One is irresistibly reminded of Rendel Harris' 'master-key in mythology'.

So, in *Cumaean Gates*, much depends on Güntert's 'bold but enlightening theory' about the diffusion of the stone-men: 'these people seem to be historical.'[25] They were megalith-builders, like the Malekulans, and they came from western Asia, which accounts for Gilgamish. But how did Virgil know about their myths? Perhaps via the Cyclopes:

> The name seems to have been applied to men of an ousted population here and there in Greece, of a lower civilisation than the true Greeks, and of a different physical type . . . Such survivals are argued for Britain, where it is thought that a stone-age folk lingered in small groups, helping to create the folklore of the fairies. Strangely, such a group is said to have existed at Cumae, where they were still more strangely called Cimmerians.

Most classicists would say there is nothing strange about it all. Strabo's reference to Cimmerians at Cumae derives from learned attempts to place the events of the *Odyssey* in the western Mediterranean: Homer says that Odysseus visited the dead in the misty land of the Cimmerians, so if Avernus and Cumae mark the entrance to the underworld, *ergo* there must be Cimmerians there. But for Jackson Knight these people were historical—and quasi-Cyclopes at that. Now, the Cyclopes make Aeneas' shield in Book VIII:

> The work of the Cyclopes in the world below may well mean that Vergil is giving what is partly their myth; that he is setting forth truth as old as the old men of stone, perhaps of the very same lineage as the surviving 'Cimmerians' of Cumae, from whom he may even have gained some secrets, which others did not know.

---

24. H. Güntert, in *SHAW* Phil.-Hist. Klasse (1932–3), 1. Abh.; Knight, *Folklore* 46 (1935) 98–121, quotations from pp. 112 (and no. 60), 117f.; *TAPA* 66 (1935) 270, *Greece and Rome* 6 (1937) 75.
25. *Cumaean Gates* (Oxford 1936) 10f. = *Vergil: Epic and Anthropology* (London 1967) 148f.; cf. 135 = 247f., 154 = 263.

It is only fair to point out that the paragraph concludes 'This, however, is only a possibility'.[26]

At that level of explanation, even the most sympathetic scholar must conclude that the theory is untenable.[27] But it was not that level that mattered most to Jackson Knight. His *other* answer to the question 'How did Virgil know?' explains the book's continuing appeal, and its author's own judgement of it as bad science, but some sort of poetry.

According to Jackson Knight's first statement of the theme, Virgil preserved the ancient memory 'by his poetic insight and by his knowledge of the inherent meaning of tradition'. In the preface to *Cumaean Gates*, the book is described as 'a short account of some of the old stored energies of heart and mind, that have gone to make a small part of Vergil's poetry'. The crucial words are 'inherent' and 'stored'. What we have here, made explicit on the first page of the first chapter, is Jung's collective unconscious.[28]

That idea is left in the background as Jackson Knight works through his dense anthropological material. But it reappears in a powerful paragraph in the final chapter, which reads to me as if it was originally intended as a peroration:

> Vergil's poetic meaning is concerned with old values and symbols which are eloquent below the threshold of full consciousness; he assimilates them, and renders them in his poem, in the full characteristically poetic manner, mysteriously conscious of the common racial past alive to his own individual apprehension. The collective mind had inherited something of evocative power from old facts of history that joined Italy to the very ancient east, and to its values, and religious thought. Some old streams of culture had come to Italy from the east, and perhaps many at many times. Antiquity had dimmed the outlines, but pent up symbolic power, which Vergil could release. Such is the truth of the *Aeneid*, spoken by a single man, to single but connected minds in the present and far future, but spoken through the living past, and out of it. That is why it is worth while to enquire into many things which Vergil himself could not consciously know, for they have helped him to make what he and we through him

26. Ibid. 38f. = 169f. (Strabo V 244, Homer *Od.* XI 13ff.), 41 = 171.
27. Raymond J. Clark, *Catabasis: Vergil and the Wisdom Tradition* (Amsterdam 1979), esp. 23–5, 148; p. 4 for Jackson Knight's inspiration.
28. *TAPA* 66 (1935) 272f.; *Cumaean Gates* (n. 25 above) vii, 1 = 137, 142.

can feel and see. These things have their richness from the years and
the countless spirits of men that have enlivened them. Among them are
the kinship with God and earth and king, the sacred city, and the
labyrinthine cave that means them all, reaching from the simplest form
to emotions that are still deep, and reverences that still are real.

That is not a scholar's argument. It is a believer's profession of faith.[29]

With Jung, Jackson Knight had taken one large step towards the
mystical. It looks as if, in the late stages of composing *Cumaean Gates*,
he was prepared to go further. In a last-minute appendix, he added
this:[30]

> The only possible alternative to something like the doctrines of Jung
> seems to be a theory of reincarnation. Remarkably strong arguments in
> favour of it have lately been put forward by the Hon. Ralph Shirley,
> *The Problem of Rebirth* (London 1936), *passim*. If he is right, Vergil
> states in the Sixth *Aeneid* what may almost be the literal truth.

We must remember that Theodore Haarhoff had spent the year 1935 in
Britain. He was a convinced spiritualist and a believer in reincarnation,
already exploring the phenomena of mediumship which were to engross
him in later years.[31] Given their friendship, and Haarhoff's part in
getting him his Exeter post, it is not surprising to find Jackson Knight
referring on the first page of *Cumaean Gates* to 'psychic experiences,
not all unconvincing . . .'.

For unbelievers, the mixture of the scholarly and mystical modes
makes *Cumaean Gates* an infuriating work. Those who prefer empirical
enquiry may also regret the way it has overshadowed his next book, the
less pretentious but arguably more deserving *Accentual Symmetry in
Vergil* (1939). However exciting the anthropological speculations may
have been, it is important to remember that Jackson Knight was also a
classical scholar, and a very good one.

He was working hard at Exeter, too hard for his own health. Two other
books were written in the years 1937–39. One of them was eventually

---

29. *Cumaean Gates* 158f. = 265f.; and cf. *JKB* 181.
30. *Ibid*. 183 = 286f., cf. 174 = 276 ('more wonderful still').
31. Experiences in 1931 and 1935: Haarhoff in V. Carleton Jones, *And the Sound
    of a Voice* (London 1953) 29; TJH to JK, 9 Sept. 1947 (Exeter University
    Library).

published as *Roman Vergil*; the other, *Homeric Poetry*, was left uncompleted. Both were for the general reader, commissioned rather than self-generated—and all the better for that. Jackson Knight himself thought the Homer book was dull. His brother, I think, had a better instinct: perhaps his best, and certainly 'his most harmonious and assured'. (It was published posthumously, with a pretentious new title and the unnatural addition of two later essays in Jackson Knight's worst style.) Here is a specimen passage—on the gods whom Homer doesn't laugh at—to show what he sounded like at the top of his form:[32]

> One of these deities is Poseidon. Like all Greeks, Homer found it hard to laugh at the power of the sea. He thrilled to its peril, and to its loveliness. But he did not laugh. Nor could he laugh at Apollo, god of the silver bow and wondrous lyre, for Apollo was in his own song, and he knew Apollo's might on him; and of Apollo was his song, Apollo who hit from afar, the lovely, the masterful, the dangerous, Apollo who could not save Hector, but who thrust Patroclus back from Troy wall. Then, lastly, Athena was not for Homer's laughter; Athena, the power in the world which answers man out of the impossible, if man can do for himself the possible, and a little more . . .

An unquiet mind

'The greatest things have many times been done by men under the shadows.' Jackson Knight was referring to the age of heroes when he wrote that in *Homeric Poetry*. But it is hard to believe that he was not also partly thinking of himself. Certainly the phrase is all too apt for his own condition from about 1938 onwards. Wilson Knight provides ample evidence in a long and fascinating section of the biography.[33] But even without that, style alone shows that something serious was amiss.

Jackson Knight always liked to place his work in an intellectual context. The first sentence of his first published paper begins 'It has been thought . . .', and the mannerism constantly recurs: 'Commentators have generally seen . . .', 'Productive work has lately been done . . .', 'Several writers lately have shown . . .', and so on.[34] Where the article is a contribution to a scholarly debate on a particular point, that is a natural,

---

32. *JKB* 211f.; *Many-Minded Homer: an Introduction* (London 1968) 115.
33. *Many-Minded Homer* 57; *JKB* 206–49.
34. *Class. Rev.* 43 (1929) 212, 46 (1932) 55; *Greece and Rome* 5 (1935) 29, 6 (1937) 70; etc.

even an inevitable, way to begin. But Jackson Knight does it also in a much wider context. The preface to *Vergil's Troy* refers rather vaguely to 'questions which there is at present a strong tendency to ask'. Even more portentously, *Cumaean Gates* begins: 'The strange participation of present in past or past in present has lately been winning a new notice and importance . . .'.

I think this is more than mere throat-clearing. We have already seen how quickly he could respond to very recent publications, building some new insight immediately into a major theoretical structure of his own; Güntert's notion of the diffusion of the 'stone-men' is only one example out of many. He always wrote fast, and under pressure. Every publication really *was* of a particular moment, sparked off by particular ideas and combinations of ideas from his wide and avid reading. But that way of working has its dangers. If your interests are as wide as Jackson Knight's, and you try to read everything, and everything you read has to be taken on board, then even a mind as capacious and flexible as his will reach its limit. That moment came in 1938.

In the *Journal of Hellenic Studies* that year, Jackson Knight published an article entitled 'Zeus in the *Prometheia*'. It has no footnotes; all the references are incorporated into the text, and all their authors given their full titles, in a way which makes it practically unreadable. It is the first example of something that becomes all too familiar, a compulsively name-dropping style which Wilson Knight, a few years later, brilliantly likened to a private soldier walking down Piccadilly in wartime, constantly saluting to right and left.[35]

Here is a characteristic example, from a 1940 article on Virgil's 'integration' of his source material:

> Integration is indeed exceedingly complicated, like the diagram published by Dr I.A. Richards to indicate aesthetic perception. Associations of sound and rhythm, no less than of thought or visual image, connect elements and offer them to the poet's conscious use. Father F.-X.M.J. Roiron explained Vergil's *imagination auditive* in this way; his work ought to have been set beside investigations of other parts of the field more often . . . Dr C.M. Bowra and Dr Cyril Bailey have shewn the kind of change Vergil makes in using old phrases to create new; and Mr John Sparrow has proved that Vergil used his own former work as he used the work of other poets.

---

35. *JKB* 384, on *Poetic Inspiration* (1946).

'Integration' is precisely what Jackson Knight here fails to achieve. Each name represents a particular idea or insight; but just playing them out like counters in succession does not make them add up to anything new. And there was worse to come, for some of the talismanic names had no significance for anyone but him. Later in the same article we get this, on Greek lyric:

> The tradition is social, not literary; but of course it soon becomes literary, as when Alcman's sleep motive is rehandled by Vergil, Statius, Goethe, G.H. Crow, and Miss V.J. Williams . . .

Who? No reference or explanation is offered. The bathos is sublime, but not intentional.[36]

As we shall see, Jackson Knight told Haarhoff in 1942 that he had hardly read anything for four years. Hardly read anything scholarly, that is; for the bibliography reveals no fewer than 57 book reviews in the *Western Morning News* between March 1938 and August 1939. That powerful mind was spinning, if not out of control, then perilously close to it. A few articles still appeared, but not for long. The last thing he ever published in a major classical journal was another Aeschylean piece in the *Journal of Hellenic Studies*. The style is almost self-parody: 'We have been noticing lately that morals depend on belief . . .'.[37]

What was it that happened in 1938? Part of it was emotional, what our cruder generation would call a mid-life crisis. At forty-two, he was seriously and idealistically in love with a girl twenty-five years his junior. In August 1938 he proposed and was refused. But that was not the whole of it. As he wrote to her later in the year, there were other disappointments, 'e.g. in my writing and advancement (very bitter) . . . My troubles are over work, writing, money, wounds.'[38]

Does the last item refer to the legs, or the shell-shock? For years he had suffered from insomnia, and the evidence suggests that just at this time it was particularly acute. In April 1939 he describes himself as

> more and more tired and aching, no better for staying in bed for a day and then a week later another day, too stupid and headachy for work . . . I do have this strange not-understood exhaustion-illness.

---

36 *Vergilius* 5 (1940) 11, 12.
37. *JHS* 63 (1943) 15.
38. *JKB* 218, 219 (to Jean Howard).

Wilson Knight reports him as acutely anxious about the approaching war; it was not just the general worry, but a real anxiety neurosis, as if he were responsible for everyone.[39] He held the rank of Major, and hoped for military employment, for example in Intelligence. But that fell through; in December 1939 the Medical Board found him 'fit for restricted duties at home only', and later he had to abandon even those.

In May 1939 the publisher who had commissioned *Homeric Poetry* cancelled the agreement; *Roman Vergil* was accepted instead, but that arrangement too was cancelled in 1940. Wilson Knight, meanwhile, had just published *The Burning Oracle*, his fifth volume of criticism; there had also been an autobiographical work, and fame of another sort from the stage. He says, and we must believe him, that jealousy was not the cause of Jackson's unprecedented emotional outburst against him, which happened in the summer of either 1939 or 1940. But disappointment must surely have added to the mental strain. It may be significant that that momentary breach of fraternal harmony took place at the Cheltenham hotel where their mother was living; the intensity of their three-cornered relationship means that Mrs Knight's own breakdown, in the winter of 1939–40, may be taken as further evidence of the pressures on her elder son.[40]

The crisis continued. In the summer of 1941 Jackson Knight was getting psychological help, not only from an Exeter specialist but also from his friend John Layard, who refers in a letter to 'the repressed furies and disgusts from which you suffer'. Perhaps it was literally the Furies, with a capital. In an essay a few years later on 'the classics and psychology', Jackson Knight insisted on their reality:

> The Furies, however, cannot be left aside . . . We must love them, as the Ancient Mariner loved the water-snakes; and take them to their home in the cave where of course it must be, a depth of motherhood . . . the cave, which many of us know well in dreams as the symbol of the deeper less conscious parts of the mind. The Furies are to stay there. We should keep these dark things in us, horrible as they may be . . .

---

39. *JKB* 219 (quotation), 225, 227, 240–2.
40. *JKB* 240; 231–2.

And from the horrors of the night he could escape only into a 'headachy, feverish, tottering daze'.[41]

That last phrase comes from a letter of 11 April 1942. A fortnight later Exeter was blitzed, in revenge for the bombing of Lübeck, and again on the night of 3–4 May, in an incendiary attack which destroyed half the city. That *real* horror did Jackson Knight a lot of good. He referred to it later, transparently in the third person:[42]

> Another man was neurotically ill until he saw the fires of a blitz in a provincial city. They made him much better. His psychotherapist explained to me that the experience externalized the fires within him, and put them in relation to him where they should be.

Haarhoff cabled from Johannesburg when he heard the news, and Jackson Knight's reply reveals another reason for the improvement:[43]

> I've been to Oxford for a day and Cambridge for the Class. Ass. where I spoke on Greek for the Amateur, and T.S. Eliot, met for the first time, said to me (on his own) 'I *like* your Vergil'; this is my book that I was so depressed about, sent afterwards on my brother Dick's suggestion, to Faber; who've now written saying they are inclined to print it, though I must wait a little longer. Isn't this nice? So I feel better.

(Faber eventually published *Roman Vergil* in 1944.) He goes on:

> Richardson (Cardiff) in a paper at Cambridge, and Colin Hardie (Magdalen) in conversation with Denniston, and A.B. Cook, walking up and introducing himself to me at Cambridge in the nicest way, have all expressed, lately, approval of *Cumaean Gates*. Isn't that pleasant for me? It makes things better, though it's all wrong to get fed up the way I do, and to think so much of other people's opinion.

---

41. *JKB* 242, 246 (cf. 212, 'horrors'); *Comparative Literature Studies* 21/22 (1946) 18.
42. *Comp. Lit. Stud.* 21/22 (1946) 20. See Đavid Rees' prize-winning children's novel *The Exeter Blitz* (London 1978).
43. JK to TJH, 16 May 1942 and 25 October 1942 (by courtesy of the Archivist, University of the Witwatersrand).

Similarly in October:

> I'm reading a bit now—I hardly read at all the last four years . . . My
> book's proofs are coming. T.S. Eliot is charming to me about it. He
> seems so pleased . . . I am reviving slowly, and I hope presently to
> recover the power of *thinking*. I'd lost it, you know—never any brain-
> waves—but it comes back if you wait.

The 'brainwaves' did not come back; Jackson Knight never again wrote
a book like *Vergil's Troy* or *Cumaean Gates*. But at least he was thinking
again.

He was thinking, as always, about Virgil. In 1943, he was one of the
founders of the Virgil Society; in 1945, he started his own branch of it at
Exmouth, where he and his mother were now living; for these audiences,
and others, he wrote and lectured constantly. His main achievement in
this period was a 56-page booklet entitled *Poetic Inspiration: an
Approach to Virgil*, privately printed at Exmouth in 1946. This is the
work which Wilson Knight likened to the saluting private in Piccadilly,
and it is indeed, explicitly, a collage: 'my main concern is to quote, from
thoughtful writers, statements of some general facts, elusive, but cardinal
for the greatest poems . . . Argument about them can wait.' But there *is*
an argument, and it is a very significant one.

First, poetic inspiration is like the inspired wisdom of seers and
shamans: like them, poets 'make use of a special mood or state in which
they are aware of important things normally concealed from human
knowledge.' But where does the material originate? 'To understand the
source of poetry at all, the treatment of it by Dr C.G. Jung . . . is indis-
pensable.' The collective unconscious is the answer. Jung 'has proved
that it, or something very like it, exists;' and even if he had not,
something of the sort would in any case have had to be postulated. Put
that next to Shelley's *Defence of Poetry*, and you see that the poet has
access to a different world or order of existence:

> It may be wisely called the collective unconscious or fundamental
> being or a world beyond death or a world outside of time. All the ways
> of describing it are instructive and help to endorse its reality. The main
> point is that such a place or world or order exists, and poetry is about
> it as well as about everyday things.

What sort of other world? *Cumaean Gates* had brought him half-way to the startling equation he now makes, and his own illness had added something too. He goes on:

> Now the other world, the psychic world, is validly reported to contain terrors and horrors. Poetry therefore should shew us what we do not like. So it does; but somehow so that we enjoy the experience. It seems to carry us past the terrors and horrors so that we enjoy the Heaven beyond Hell and Purgatory even before we get there.

One of Jackson Knight's favourite quotations at this time was from Vita Sackville-West's poem *The Land*:

> Here the long sense of classic measure cures
> The spirit weary of its difficult pain . . .

If poetic inspiration is access to the psychic world, the great tradition can be therapy for the spirit that deserves it.[44]

And what of Virgil? He went 'farther than others into the deep. In these deep realms of thought are the collective memories of all humanity, perhaps even of pre-human existence.' Characteristically, Jackson Knight fuses the empirical evidence of the poet's art with a mystic vision:

> The sound and rhythm and even grammar of Virgil are all signs that he was concentrating and compressing vast resources from all the long reach of time. The compression of them came to flash-points of creative discernment. Virgil could see the spirit-world, and, beyond the horrors, the 'purposefulness outreaching human ends' . . . It is not, I think, presumptuous, even though we know so little, and even without the research which the question really demands, to see in the poetry of Virgil true signs that it came from the deep mind, and has the authority of vision.

Naturally he is thinking of *Aeneid* VI, where the underworld scene is 'not fancy, but revelation of vision in symbol'. But that is not all. Several

---

44. *Poetic Inspiration* (Exmouth 1946) 3, 13, 29, 32, 39. Sackville-West quotation: *Virgil Society Lecture Summaries* 12 (25 Oct. 1945) 4; *Exe* 3 (U.C.S.W., Winter 1948) 3; *Rivista di cultura classica e medioevale* 2 (1960) 203, a talk given in September 1950. (Jackson Knight always misquoted it as 'the spirit *worthy* of . . .'.)

passages in the poem 'agree closely with typical forms of dreams, and some, as in the sixth and the seventh books, have the mark of clairvoyance into a daemonic world.' Book VII is dominated by the terrifying figure of Allecto, Fury of Hell, bringer of madness. She comes to Turnus in his nightmare, with her whip and her blazing torch and her eyes of fire: *Respice ad haec! adsum dirarum ab sede sororum* . . . When Jackson Knight concludes that Virgil 'had personal access to visionary experience', it is not for the sane and balanced among us to say that he was wrong.[45]

Haarhoff and Mrs Lloyd

In the summer of 1946 Theodore Haarhoff was in London. His psychic experiences had continued, and now included personal communication with the Ionian philosopher Heraclitus. As he was packing to return to South Africa, he wrote to Jackson Knight in terms which show clearly that such matters were a familiar subject of private discussion between the two of them.[46] The letter is the first in a sequence of about 140, covering 27 years, which survives among the Jackson Knight papers in the Exeter University Library.

Haarhoff enjoyed reading *Poetic Inspiration*:[47]

> [I went] to Cape Town to examine and took your inspirational essay
> with me. It proved a delightful companion and I thank you warmly for
> it and congratulate you as warmly. I feel we shall speak more plainly of
> inspiration in the near future. When Jung's papers are published the
> truth will appear more nakedly.

He hoped to win a convert; but he had a formidable opponent in Mrs Knight, whose attitude to spiritualism was one of amused scepticism. St Thomas, she said, was her patron saint.[48]

---

45. Virg. *Aen.* VII 454; *Poetic Inspiration* 49, 50, 53, 55. *JKB* 347 for his fear of Hell.
46. TJH to JK, 24 July 1946. Heraclitus (1943): Haarhoff in *Two Worlds*, 4 April 1953; cf. Carleton Jones, loc. cit. (n. 31 above) for another 1943 experience.
47. TJH to JK, date missing but probably late 1946. The first few words are lost.
48. *CLA* 35, 115; *JKB* 243, 340.

In May 1947, Haarhoff writes:

> My dear friend Mrs Lloyd, the medium, better than any I found in
> London, is going to England this week. It would be wonderful if you
> could have a sitting with her. Her guide knows about you.

Mrs Margaret Lloyd was a person of some consequence in psychic
matters, described by one who should know as 'probably the most out-
standing trance medium in the southern hemisphere'.[49] Haarhoff himself
wrote of her a few years later:

> She is the founder and leader of a circle for psychic investigation which
> has an unbroken record of 36 years . . . It is a serious circle to which
> several University people, trained in scientific methods, have
> belonged. It does more than investigate principles, but that is an
> important part of its work. The leader gives her services freely and for
> no personal profit.

The circle, of which Haarhoff was a member, met every Thursday
evening. Mrs Lloyd spoke—or her control spoke through her—while she
was in deep trance; sometimes the message would be in a language she
could not speak in waking life, and afterwards she would have no
memory of what had been said.[50] 21 June 1947:

> I am so glad you saw Mrs L. But it's not enough. You must arrange a
> proper sitting with her. She will do it. You can prepare questions and
> ask her control (Tutu) who goes back ultimately to Egypt. Not all
> questions can be answered at once—but you may gain much
> enlightenment. The yellow aura means *inspiration*—how nice!

9 September 1947:

> Don't, if you can possibly help it, miss your chance with Mrs Lloyd.
> They are sailing back in October . . .

---

49. TJH to JK, 18 May 1947; Carleton Jones, op. cit. (n. 31) 89.
50. Haarhoff in *Rand Daily Mail* 8 Feb. 1952 (on her foreknowledge of the death
of George VI); TJH to JK, 2 April 1950; A. Howgrave-Graham, *The Dead
Companions* (London 1950) 103f., 198; *CLA* 288–96; 309–11 (two sittings
described).

23 October 1947:

> I am sorry indeed to hear that your attempt to see Mrs Lloyd came to
> nothing. I think you would have gained a lot from a sitting—this is
> quite different from the general run of 'mediums'. But perhaps we are
> to meet again and [be] given fresh opportunities. Curiously enough Mrs
> L. got the impression that *you* were not keen but that I was pushing
> you.

That certainly sounds plausible.

There were further developments after Mrs Lloyd had returned to
Johannesburg and her circle. Haarhoff writes on 29 November 1947:

> Mrs L.'s control Tutu said how sorry they were that they had not been
> able to speak direct to you. 'We could have helped him. He gets into
> worried and unhappy conditions sometimes. He is still in a mist. Later
> he will realise things more clearly. He gets inspiration from the other
> side but sometimes he doubts and his nervous condition increases his
> doubt.
>
> *But* a time is coming when he will be very successful in what he
> undertakes. There is a gateway opening for him—he must have faith
> and more confidence in himself. Since his contact with Medi (Mrs L.)
> there has been drawing nearer to him a guide—Do you know
> *Benjamin?*'
>
> Stupidly, I could only think of Benjamin Farrington.
>
> 'No, one who passed over some time ago.'
>
> 'Benjamin Jowett?'
>
> As I said that I felt a confirmatory touch on my head and the control
> agreed.

In later letters, Haarhoff quotes 'the Guides' as saying—presumably
through Mrs Lloyd—that Jowett is 'still working' with Jackson Knight as
his 'inspirer'. But mainly they are concerned about his health: he must
relax, take care about mental strain.[51]

Mrs Lloyd was back in London for a fortnight in the autumn of 1948.
Haarhoff was emphatic: '*DO TRY TO HAVE A SITTING.* I feel it is
important.' Again, it seems, the opportunity was neglected. But Jackson

---

51. TJH to JK, 29 February 1948, 2 April 1948 (naming Tutu).

Knight was evidently interested enough to enquire, a few months later, about the possibility of making posthumous contacts. Haarhoff replies:

> It would be hard to find those you mention without a strong link. If you were here in person or if some intimate article of theirs were here, it might be possible.

It is not known whom he wanted to contact. Nor what he had seen that prompted Haarhoff to add, in a laconic note at the end: 'Small, bald, rosy—was that Jowett? So they describe him.'[52]

There is no suggestion in any of Jackson Knight's writings that the supposed guidance of Jowett held any significance for him. But another, more startling, name that Haarhoff produced may have had some effect on him. Haarhoff believed that he himself had been, in an earlier life, Cornelius Gallus. At some time in London, probably in 1946, he had come to believe that Jackson Knight was a reincarnation of Marcus Agrippa. Tutu, Mrs Lloyd's control, gave 'acquiescent confirmation' of this in 1947 and 1948. It was a particularly odd idea for a classicist, since we know that Agrippa—a contemporary—took a poor view of Virgil's style: it was, he said, *nova cacozelia*. In *Roman Vergil*, Jackson Knight had rendered that phrase as 'an original kind of affectation', and gone on to attribute to Agrippa the view that Virgil's style was 'rather grotesque and dishonest'.[53] But Haarhoff was certain about it. In March 1950 he wrote:

> So many things I should like to talk about that won't go on paper. Tutu continues to take an interest in you. She says the London woman was wrong—you had only *two* incarnations—M. Agrippa and the present one. How I wish you were here to have direct experience!

The next time Jackson Knight had occasion to refer in print to Agrippa's criticism of Virgil, he did his best to explain it away. True, that was in the Haarhoff *Festschrift*, but the same embarrassment also appears elsewhere. In a public lecture in 1960, he went so far as to say that

---

52. TJH to JK, 16 October 1948, 15 August 1949.
53. TJH to JK, 29 November 1947, 2 April 1948; Donatus *vita Vergilii* 44; *Roman Vergil* (London 1944) 56f. = (Harmondsworth 1966) 79f., cf. 261 = 318.

'[Agrippa's] judgement has been considered the best description of Vergil's style ever recorded.'[54] It is not clear when this change of heart took place; probably not while the sceptical Mrs Knight was alive.

Jackson Knight's position in Virgilian scholarship at this time was an oddly equivocal one. *Roman Vergil* had been very well received, and could properly be described as a standard work. In 1949 an Italian translation appeared; in the same year Jackson Knight was elected President of the Virgil Society, and that September he took a prominent part in the 'constitutive assembly' of the Sodalitas Erasmiana in Rome. But in British academic circles he was not taken seriously, and one can see why. Here is a characteristic passage, from an essay boldly entitled 'New Principles in Vergilian Commentary' and dated December 1949:[55]

It is necessary to remember both Vergil's elaborate processes of thought and also the sometimes misleading success with which his poetry matches the perceived world, and to discover when his Muse is the daughter of Memory, and when she is the daughter of Observation. If, as I hope, I can eventually prepare a new edition of Vergil's works, I shall make the attempt . . . Of Vergil's purpose and intention, it is risky to speak. He must have understood to some extent how his own mind worked; but he was probably dominated by inspiration and visionary experience, presumably often anterior even to the derivations and combinations, especially if the dominance was on the spiritual or the psychic rather than on the psychological plane . . . If his purpose in the *Aeneid* has to be shortly guessed, perhaps the nearest guess to the truth may be found in some words quoted in *The New York Times* by Mr Murray Hickey Lee from Father Alan Watts, *Behold the Spirit*, New York, Pantheon Books, 1948,

'We do not have to attain union with God . . . Vision is given us now . . . Here and now God (who is not niggardly in his self-revelation) exposes himself right before our eyes. Now . . . the present moment (elusive image of eternity; so small that it has no temporal length and yet so long that we can never escape it) is Reality.'

54. *Acta Classica* 1 (1958) 43; 'Vergil's Conscious Art' (n. 89 below) 2.13.
55. *Humanitas* 3 (1950) 161–74, at p. 171; published by the University of Coimbra, Portugal. The first two omissions are mine, the last three Jackson Knight's.

He used the same quotation at the end of his Presidential Address to the Virgil Society on 21 January 1950. Father Watts and Murray Hickey Lee thus became two of the 138 names dropped on that occasion, for the address was an example of the 'saluting' style taken to grotesque lengths. It was published in a literary magazine, and a large number of offprints, with two corrections carefully pasted in, were 'distributed by Basil Blackwell, Oxford'. How many were printed, and how many sold, I do not know; but more than 300 were left over (and are still extant).[56]

The two publications present a melancholy contrast between aspiration and achievement. It is not surprising to discover that Jackson Knight's mental health was again uncertain. Wilson Knight refers to his neurotic obsession with cleanliness and the fear of contamination (amply confirmed by oral evidence), and reports that in 1950 he was again seeing the psychotherapist who had helped him in 1942.[57]

Early in 1950, Mrs Knight, who was 81, became seriously ill; at the same time, Jackson Knight received an invitation to spend two months at Witwatersrand that summer as a visiting lecturer. She insisted that he should go. Wilson Knight, who was now at Leeds, took charge of their mother and nursed her in her final illness. She died on 8 July; a month later Jackson Knight flew to Johannesburg.

'He was a great success', wrote Haarhoff later, 'although he was a difficult guest because he dissipated his energies in trying to help all sorts of people, including the Africans, and consequently overtaxed himself and lost documents and sat up till the early hours instead of packing.' That reticent obituary account may be supplemented by some first-hand memories of his visit to Cape Town in September. Mrs Rollo, whose husband was head of department there, remembers him insisting on paying for her platform ticket when she met his train, and struggling vainly to get a sixpence into the threepenny slot. Maurice Pope, then a young member of staff, recalls that 'he lectured continuously from quarter to nine until ten past one, not stopping between periods but being shepherded along the corridor to the next room and nudged, without ever very much success, towards the next advertised subject.' He also reports the enthusiasm Jackson Knight generated among the

---

56. 'Vergil and Homer', *The Wind and the Rain* 7.1 (Autumn 1950) 23–29 = *Many-Minded Homer* (London 1968) 189–210.
57. *JKB* 302f., 357.

students and the contrasting reactions of their elders, 'ranging from coldness or detached amusement to open outrage'.[58]

One of the enthusiastic students was Jean Gordon-Brown, now Dr Jean Branford. She remembers his time at Cape Town as 'a perfect riot . . . as if the Lord of Misrule had taken over'. It was an experience not to be forgotten:

> When J.K. left after his meteor-like passage through the Classics Department he left a gap out of proportion to the length of his stay. His capacity for recitation and bringing the verse alive was I think a revelation to all of us, and to him they were assuredly not 'dead languages'. It was a unique privilege to have known him.

Two details from Dr Branford's recollections show the way his own interests were developing. In a session on *Aeneid* II he referred to the appearance of Creusa's shade as *nota maior imago*, 'proving, he maintained, that the astral body is supposedly larger than the human body.' And when Field Marshal Smuts died during his visit, Jackson Knight went to the university memorial service and was very impressed; 'he was said, some days later, to have heard from Theo Haarhoff that Smuts was met on the other side by Queen Victoria.' That caused a good deal of innocent amusement among the students.[59]

Jackson Knight had flown to Johannesburg on or about 8 August. On 13 August he wrote to his brother about a sitting of Mrs Lloyd's circle which he had attended. It is likely that he went every week while he was in Johannesburg: references survive to the regular Thursday meetings on 24 and 31 August, 21 and 28 September, and to a private session with Mrs Lloyd on 4 September. Naturally, his mother was the main focus of his interest. Mrs Lloyd proved to be everything Haarhoff had said. So convincing were the messages from Mrs Knight achieved through her mediumship that from that time on neither Jackson Knight nor his brother had any doubts about the truth of spiritualism.[60]

---

58. Haarhoff, *Proc. Virg. Soc.* 4 (1964–5) 75; letters to the author from Mrs C.L. Rollo (19 June 1989) and Mr M. Pope (8 June 1989).
59. Letter to the author from Dr J. Branford (21 June 1989). Smuts died on 11 December 1950, the day Jackson Knight arrived in Cape Town; the service was on 15 September (information from Prof. Harold Baldry).
60. *CLA* 55–64, 75–79; *JKB* 340.

On Jackson Knight's return from Johannesburg, he and his brother began seriously exploring the psychic world. Wilson Knight, who had already begun collecting material for a biography of their mother, now systematically sought first-hand information from her, both via mediums and through his own 'automatic writing', a technique of communication that he took great pains to master.[61]

Haarhoff, with his much greater experience, gave help and advice. He emphasised particularly the need to distinguish

> between the speaking of the communicator in person and messages relayed, or reported, by a medium; and also, even when direct speaking was involved, between a 'deep trance' medium like Mrs Lloyd and a 'light trance' medium.

He insisted that communications transmitted by the latter means were not to be regarded as wholly authentic: 'the semi-trance people import their own thoughts into what they say. You must analyse and weigh up, before accepting.'[62]

As for Wilson Knight's difficulties with 'inspirational writing',

> that is to be expected at first. Thoughts are electrical forces and with a sensitive person may cause a movement of the hand. Until you are really attuned to your communicant and have eliminated disturbing factors, your own ideas, conscious or unconscious, tend to appear. I have been through all that. It takes time . . .

Haarhoff himself practised the technique every Sunday, when his communicant was Elizabeth Barrett Browning.[63]

It is clear that Mrs Lloyd's deep-trance mediumship was quite exceptional. She was in London in the autumn of 1951; Jackson Knight was unable to meet her for a sitting, but his brother did. Wilson Knight also had sessions with her when he in turn went to Johannesburg in the summer of 1952.[64] She died that October, and Haarhoff felt the loss for

---

61. *CLA* passim, esp. 147–90 on 'spirit-writing'.
62. *CLA* 86, 312; TJH to JK, 2 February 1951.
63. TJH to JK, 28 February 1951; cf. 20 May 1950 on Mrs Browning.
64. TJH to JK, 9 and 17 August 1951; *CLA* 216, 288–96, 309–11.

years afterwards: 'Nowhere, in London or here, have I found so pure a channel . . . We shall never have a medium like Margaret again.'[65]

Jackson Knight paid handsome tribute to her 'power, saintliness and integrity' in the spiritualist journal *Two Worlds*: 'I have to acknowledge my own immense private debt to her, and to Professor Haarhoff, through whom I met her.' It is clear that the breakthrough she achieved for him marked a turning point in his life. Another important stabilising influence, from the spring of 1951 onwards, was his collaboration and epistolary friendship with John D. Christie, a classicist at Edinburgh. At both levels, the help was timely. In 1951 Jackson Knight started work on what turned out to be, I think, his greatest achievement, the Penguin Classics translation of the *Aeneid*.[66]

Vergilius loquitur

Haarhoff's cautionary advice was very sensible, but it is doubtful whether he followed it himself. On a visit to Port Elizabeth in October 1951, he attended a séance at which the medium saw, and described, Virgil standing with his hand on Haarhoff's shoulder. It is not clear what sort of medium she was, but Haarhoff certainly believed that through her he was talking to Virgil:

> He confirmed my interpretation of his work and thanked me. He said that 'falsa ad caelum' could bear the meaning I gave; but he would later give a 'dissertation' in writing on the Gates of Sleep. The two levels of his writing—exoteric and esoteric—were confirmed . . .

Clearly Haarhoff was making the running in this conversation, and one naturally suspects that the medium was reacting to his leading questions. What 'Virgil' went on to communicate on his own account—including some rather lame English verses—was of merely general spiritualist interest.[67]

---

65. TJH to JK, 2 February 1958, 20 October 1958; also 16 November 1962, and TJH to WK, 5 September 1965.
66. *Two Worlds* 20 December 1952; *JKB* 350–4 (Christie), 377–81 (Penguin).
67. TJH to JK, 27 October 1951, Cf. 7 November 1951: 'tell me truly what you really think of the quality of the verse Vergil gave . . .'.

200	*Talking to Virgil*

Two years later Haarhoff met Mrs Emmy Vermey, an elderly lady both clairvoyant and clairaudient, who could see Virgil and hear him speak (in German). At his third sitting with her, in November 1953, 'V. said that the verses given at Port Elizabeth in his name were false. A heavy penalty awaits those who impersonate.' But the new contact made up for that disappointment. At his first sitting with Mrs Vermey, Haarhoff had asked about Jackson Knight:[68]

> I asked about you, Marcus Agrippa. To which he replied that there was a third name—Vipsanius. (Remarkable evidence coming through a woman who knows nothing whatsoever about Roman history.) Yes, he said, he is 'ein edeler Geist', and was closely associated with our circle. He will give you a message later. I asked him if my interpretation of *falsa ad caelum* was right and he said yes, I inspired that thought but people will not believe; however it will be recognised later . . .

The reading Haarhoff was so anxious about comes at the end of *Aeneid* VI (line 896), where Aeneas and the Sibyl come back to the living world by the ivory gate, through which 'falsa ad caelum mittunt insomnia Manes'. In order to avoid the natural inference, that the whole account of the Virgilian underworld is a 'false dream', Haarhoff had argued, implausibly enough, that the words *falsa ad caelum* should be taken closely together: 'false to the world above [but *really* true] are the visions sent through it by the Powers of the Spirit World'.[69] One suspects that for Haarhoff, confirmation of that reading was tantamount to proof that the communication was genuine. (Others may be tempted to draw the opposite conclusion.)

Haarhoff hastened to share the excitement of these revelations with his friend. In the last few weeks of 1953, five letters in quick succession arrived at Caroline House, Exeter, where Jackson Knight and his brother now had a permanent home (Plate VIII), with details, in translation, of Mrs Vermey's Virgilian communications. In mid-December, Haarhoff left Johannesburg for a visit to the Cape. On his return, late in February 1954, he immediately resumed:[70]

---

68. TJH to JK, 3 November 1953 (first session), 24 November 1953 (third).
69. Haarhoff, *Greece and Rome* 17 (1948) 88–90.
70. TJH to JK, 24 February 1954. For Euripides, cf. Haarhoff, loc. cit. 88: 'to Virgil as to Plato and perhaps to Euripides ('who knows if death be life or life be death?') the Spirit-World is the real world . . .'.

I managed, yesterday, to keep my appointment, *longo intervallo*, with Vergil. He came accompanied by Euripides and we had a brief preliminary talk. He sends his greeting to you as a busy and faithful collaborator and wishes you had been living in S. Africa. Are there any specific questions you would like me to ask him?

By this time Jackson Knight was about half-way through the *Aeneid*.[71] No doubt working on book VI made him even more than usually conscious of the Virgilian afterlife. At any rate, he took up the offer with alacrity. One of the points he wanted clearing up was evidently on I 661: 'quippe domum timet ambiguam Tyriosque bilingues'. Were the Tyrians 'two-tongued' in the treacherous sense, or merely bilingual? Haarhoff replied on 11 March:

I will put your questions to Vergil when I can. He is much interested in your Penguin effort and praises your industry. He thinks very highly of you. But you must not *worry* or overtire yourself. He sends his love and greeting.
I asked about Tyrios bilingues, and he said: people who have one language in their hearts and another on their lips.

But 'Virgil' then went on to speak about the Bible, and the obsolescence of Old Testament prophecies.
One would very much like to know what Mrs Vermey's reaction was to the prospect of putting to Virgil Jackson Knight's technical questions about his text and his meaning. Four weeks later (6 April 1954), Haarhoff writes:

At last I have had a session with Vergil. He wants me to tell you not to work late at night: the night is meant for rest.
I put your questions to him. He said: Yes, he read and studied continuously. 'God was always with me.' His great aim was to elevate people spiritually. But people laughed at him and his friends dissuaded him. Much that he wrote he either destroyed in despair or his friends destroyed it for him. His prose writings no longer exist: they were of a spiritual and philosophical nature . . .

71. *JKB* 379 (letter to Christie): at V 330 in July 1953.

And so on. Interesting, and perhaps plausible, to a convinced spiritualist, but no great help to a translator. Perhaps Haarhoff felt dissatisfied. At any rate, he tried another way, with spectacular success.

On 26 April 1954, he writes in great excitement: 'Vergil has broken through the veil and is writing for me in Latin!' The first message, written in a large, round hand quite unlike Haarhoff's own, ended with: 'Salutem Marco Agrippae nostro. Vale—tibi adsum—Vergilius Maro.' These messages had a classical as well as a spiritual content—on Gallus and Cytheris, on the authorship of the *Appendix Vergiliana* poems, and so on—and Haarhoff immediately transcribed them for Jackson Knight. On 28 May, he writes:

> I can now get corrections of things that were slightly distorted when
> orally communicated by Mrs Vermey . . . It would be possible to
> consult him on a point of reading, I think—tho' he says that he can
> sometimes hardly recognise our texts as his own.

As Haarhoff remarks in the same letter, at this stage Virgil's messages were 'mostly personal'. One is reminded of Hiram Corson, Professor of English at Cornell, whose spirit messages fifty years earlier from Tennyson, Browning and others were comfortingly familiar, almost cosy. Just as Tennyson told Corson not to worry about smoking his pipe, so Virgil told Haarhoff to watch his step getting on trains.[72] Jackson Knight, however, had serious questions to ask, and the sequence of about thirty letters from September 1954 to October 1955 is overwhelmingly concerned with problems of exegesis in the *Aeneid*. Every Tuesday, sitting by candlelight, Haarhoff made himself available for Virgil, through him, to write the answers.[73]

It is clear from his advice to Wilson Knight that Haarhoff was perfectly well aware of the fallibility of 'inspirational writing'. When the medium himself is well informed on the subject in hand, and interested in the answers, how can he be sure that his conscious mind has not affected the result? An early query, apparently on his own account, had been about 'pacique imponere morem' at *Aen.* VI 852. Virgil wrote that *imponere*

---

72. Hiram Corson, *Spirit Messages* (Rochester N.Y. 1911) 258f.; TJH to JK, 27
    July 1954.
73. *JKB* 382; Haarhoff in *Two Worlds* 16 March 1957, cf. *Psychic News* 16
    October 1971.

meant 'to plant': 'quasi de plantis arboribusque ut in Georgicis'. Haarhoff adds, in parenthesis, 'an old idea of mine. Perhaps here wishful thinking? I will check up.' But later Virgil confirmed to him that that was what it meant.[74] On 'Aequos Faliscos' at VII 695, the first answer had been 'locum in aequore positum, non in montibus'. A fortnight later Haarhoff wrote again:[75]

> A mistake crept in with Falerii. The main point was that Aequi Falerii [*sic*] was a place name. V. now says—Falerii ad Aequos (the people) pertinentes. The other was 'per errorem'—perhaps a thought in my mind.

But such doubts and corrections are very rare. Evidently Haarhoff was confident that his conscious mind was *not* contributing, and that what his hand wrote was authoritatively Virgilian.

How much of it did Jackson Knight believe? There is a phrase of Wilson Knight's, in a different context, which may sum up the attitude of both men: 'As regards the messages—as usual, it's a mixture of what is convincing with just a shade of doubt.'[76] In general, Jackson Knight believed in their authenticity, as is shown by his dedication of the translation to Haarhoff, and the coded reference in the acknowledgements to the nature of his help and guidance: 'how authentic his direction has been must be left to appear hereafter.'[77] In detail, however, he kept his independence. A comparison of the correspondence with the finished translation shows how many of the Haarhoff readings were accepted, and how many were not.

It will come as no surprise that agreement was commonest in the last section of Book VI, where Anchises explains the nature of the universe and the mystery of reincarnation.

> 'Principio caelum ac terras camposque liquentis
> lucentemque globum lunae Titaniaque astra
> spiritus intus alit . . .'

---

74. TJH to JK, 28 July 1954, 17 August 1955.
75. TJH to JK, 23 February 1955, 9 March 1955.
76. Letter of 22 September 1951 quoted by van Domelen, op. cit. (n. 7 above) 153. *JKB* 383 on the Haarhoff messages.
77. *Virgil: the Aeneid* (Harmondsworth 1956) 10; explained in *JKB* 392f.

On *principio*, Haarhoff's Virgil wrote: 'duae significationes. Anglice *firstly* sed etiam "in the beginning there is a spirit that sustains".' Haarhoff himself added in brackets 'perh. "first" could cover both', and that is what Jackson Knight wrote. In the next line he accepted the emendation 'Titanaque et astra', making explicit the reference to the sun. Haarhoff's Virgil had written: 'Titanaque et. ita scripsi. recte poeta.' Haarhoff notes that the allusion was to Dryden's phrase 'both the radiant lights'—i.e. moon *and* sun. Jackson Knight translates 'the moon's gleaming face, the Titanic Sun and the stars'.[78]

At line 747, on the soul's return to the *aether*, 'aurai simplicis ignem' had been translated by Jackson Knight in *Roman Vergil* as 'fire of air's purity', with *aura* meaning, as usual, 'breath'. But now he translates it 'spark of elemental fire', and the correspondence shows us why. Haarhoff's Virgil had written:

> Aura bis in Aen. VI significat 'lux', vibratio vel sonis vel lucis. Aurai simplicis ignem = spark of elemental light. Nosti sane quomodo vocabulo 'aura' in scientia psychica homines utantur.

Despite the alleged parallel (VI 204 'aura refulsit', of the golden bough), Jackson Knight was evidently not prepared to translate *aura* as 'light'. But his version comes very close to it.[79]

At line 852, 'pacique imponere morem', where Haarhoff himself had momentarily wondered about wishful thinking, Jackson Knight accepts the horticultural sense of *imponere*: his Anchises tells the Romans 'to graft tradition onto peace'. And at the all-important line 896, on the ivory gate, his version—'the Spirits send visions which are false in the light of day'—is based on the Haarhoff interpretation of *falsa ad caelum*. When the translation was published, Haarhoff's Virgil wrote for him: 'bonum est quod Agrippa sententiam tuam de Somni portis accepit.'[80] (One can't help feeling that the real Virgil, commenting on such a crucial passage, would have said not just 'I'm glad he takes your view', but 'I'm glad he got it *right*'.)

---

78. Virg. *Aen*. VI 724–6; TJH to JK, 19 October and 29 November 1954; for the text at line 725, see p. 340 of the translation.

79. *Roman Vergil* (n. 10 above) 215 = 263; TJH to JK, 30 September 1954, 17 August 1955.

80. TJH to JK, 29 September 1956. See notes 69 and 74 above.

There are four passages elsewhere in the poem where Jackson Knight followed the Haarhoff-Virgil version against the reading of the Oxford text:[81]

    I 636, munera laetitiamque *dei*;
  IV 54, *incensum* animum *inflammavit* amore;
   X 850, *exsilium* infelix;
 XII 916, *telum*que instare tremescit.

But did he choose those readings because they were guaranteed by the author, or because he had made up his own mind? Was he following Haarhoff as a medium, or as a fallible fellow-scholar? The disagreements suggest that it was mainly the latter.

For 'Aequos Faliscos' at VII 695, Jackson Knight translates 'the Faliscans, plain-dwellers now', in the version Haarhoff's Virgil had repudiated as an error. At VII 543 he translates 'caeli convexa per auras' as 'she rode across the airs of the sky', preferring his own interpretation of the phrase to the one Haarhoff said Virgil had indicated (which is also Servius' explanation). Even in Anchises' speech in book VI, where one would expect him to be most receptive, Jackson Knight ignored the explicit statement of a lacuna after line 796.[82]

Of the 57 incompleted half-lines in the *Aeneid*, there is only one that does not give a complete sense: III 340 on Ascanius, 'quem tibi iam Troia . . .'. Haarhoff's Virgil commented on it as follows:

> verba ipsissima evanuerunt sed sic fortasse: Quem tibi iam Troia fovit flagrante Creusa.

Haarhoff added a reference to Creusa's appeal to Aeneas at II 673–8. His next letter began: 'You don't say what you think of the restored line at III 340. Is it worth publishing?' Jackson Knight did not of course translate the restoration, and it is clear from his version of the half-line ('You had

81. TJH to JK, 9 February 1955 (contrast *Roman Vergil* 215 = 264); 29 June 1955; 9 February 1955; 20 November 1954.
82. TJH to JK, 9 March 1955 (n. 75 above); 9 February 1955, cf. *Class. Quart.* 34 (1940) 129f. and *Roman Vergil* 212 = 260; 19 October 1954, 'versus desunt'.

him with you in Troy . . .') that he was not even convinced by the suggested sense.[83]

When we add to these explicit disagreements the places where Haarhoff's Virgil suggested an English translation which was subsequently ignored,[84] we can see clearly enough that Jackson Knight had not abandoned his critical faculty. He was excited, impressed, and in many cases prepared to believe. But he followed Haarhoff's own advice, analysing and weighing up before accepting. As he put it later, it is difficult to get a certain result, to be absolutely sure that a message is being transmitted from one world to the other.[85]

The translation was published in the autumn of 1956, to general acclaim. Wilson Knight quotes many letters of appreciation, and adds drily:[86]

> The general reader may be assured that nowhere are authorities less prone to excited and exuberant praise than in the field of classical learning. The consensus is impressive . . .

An even better index of success is the way it has lasted. At the time of its thirty-first reprinting, in 1988, well over 400,000 copies had been sold.

Speaking openly

Jackson Knight was now sixty. The University College of the South-West had become the University of Exeter; he retired in 1961 from his Readership there, and in December 1964 he died.

In the last eight years of his life, which he spent with Wilson Knight at Caroline House, his state of health was better, but still not good. Two letters to John Christie in 1962 give both sides:

> I am afraid it is my shell-shock (obsolete and tendentious term); I forget things within seconds, and, worse, remember wrong . . .

---

83. TJH to JK, 9 and 23 February 1955.
84. E.g. TJH to JK, 7 December 1954 (XI 514 'by surmounting the ridge'); 26 April 1955 (VII 791 'symbol of a mighty story'); 17 August 1955 (I 244 'won his way to').
85. *Orpheus* 9 (1962) 10; n. 62 above.
86. *JKB* 387–91.

My brain feels as if it can't work at all, but it isn't so bad as all that really, and I believe (when not overworked) I am really far better than for ?30?40? years.

He refers to 'this perpetual blur in the mind', which must be the 'daze' first mentioned in 1939.[87] But we hear no more of 'horrors'. One thing at least spiritualism did for him: it freed him from the Furies.

Again, his state of mind is reflected in the style of his scholarly work. Two good Virgil essays, one for the Haarhoff *Festschrift* and one for the Virgil Society, deserved their later republication in the new edition of *Roman Vergil*; these, and his piece on Ovid's metre and rhythm for a bimillennary publication, show little sign of the diffuseness, the name-dropping allusiveness and the portentous over-reaching which characterise his worst manner.[88] But when he was invited to give three lectures at the University of Newcastle in 1960, what he produced was largely an updated expansion of his 1946 booklet on poetic inspiration, complete with all the talismanic names receiving their regular salute. Apparently there was the possibility of publication; it is not surprising that that came to nothing.[89]

In the first of the Newcastle lectures, Jackson Knight distinguished three types of inspiration: mystical, psychic, and psychological. He did not make any great claims for the second of these, but his own view was presented without apology:

> That discarnate spirits have psychically inspired some poets is hard to doubt. They have almost certainly inspired musicians; for this there is strong evidence. But psychic inspiration is usually hard to identify and prove in poetry . . .

Wilson Knight was sure that that was why the lectures were not published. (It is certainly why the University of Michigan Press later

87. *JKB* 430, cf. 219.
88. *Acta Classica* 1 (1958) 31–44 = *Roman Vergil*³ (Harmondsworth 1966) 399–418; *Proc. Virg. Soc.* 1 (1962) 1–14 = *Riv. cultura classica e medio-evale* 6 (1964) 12–39 = *Roman Vergil*³ 419–39 = *Meminisse Iuvabit* (ed. F. Robertson, Bristol 1988) 9–23; *Ovidiana: recherches sur Ovide* (ed. N.I. Herescu, Paris 1958) 106–120.
89. 'Vergil's Conscious Art' (typescript, Exeter University Library); *JKB* 417f., 425f. I am grateful to Professor David West for information from the Newcastle end.

turned them down.) Once convinced of the truth and relevance of spiritualism, Jackson Knight discussed it openly, and brought it into his scholarly work wherever he thought it appropriate. His brother comments:

> Few had a greater respect than Jack for the formalities. He believed in exact manners, titles, and honours, and put his friends' honorific letters on envelopes. He had a firm respect for the 'respectable', above all for established scholarship. It is accordingly to his credit that, when spiritualistic truth became his concern, he swerved not at all, as most careerists in the academic or ecclesiastical professions regularly do, from public avowal and use of what he knew to be relevant truth.

That seems to me absolutely just.[90]

The Penguin translation had won Jackson Knight some, at least, of the recognition he always felt had been denied him. Now spiritualism, and his own honesty about it, kept him marginalised in the eyes of the academic world.

A few years ago, I had occasion to telephone a very distinguished Oxford classicist. At first he thought I was speaking from Exeter *College*. I explained that I meant the city and university of that name. 'Ah yes, isn't that where they have memorial lectures for an old second-rater called Jackson Knight?' Well, Jackson Knight never got a Regius chair, or a knighthood. But thanks to his brother he got something that was perhaps as good as either—what George Steiner has called

> one of the major acts of insight, of active sensibility, in our time; a masterpiece comparable to the autobiography of John Cowper Powys, with which it has many points of contact; a book that brings a life to life as almost no other modern biography has done.

That was said in a Jackson Knight Memorial lecture, and in the presence of Wilson Knight.[91] But it is no less true for that.

---

90. *JKB* 426. E.g. 'Vergil's Conscious Art' 1.4–7; *Folklore* 69 (1958) 227f., 236, and 74 (1963) 301f.; *Orpheus* 9 (1962) 10, 18f.; *Elysion* (London 1970), passim.

91. George Steiner, *Antigones* (The Twelfth J.K. Memorial Lecture, Exeter 1979) 3, referring to *JKB*.

'An extraordinary document, and a somewhat melancholy one' is how Jackson Knight's first head of department reacted to the biography. He found in it no evidence from either Bloxham or Exeter that Jackson Knight had ever maintained a 'steady equable workaday relationship' with adults; nevertheless, 'I am still convinced in spite of all the grousing I had to listen to from sundry colleagues that his appointment at Exeter was desirable and justified by the results.'[92] That measured judgement on a difficult colleague may be set against the plentiful evidence, from ex-students, of Jackson Knight as a brilliantly inspiring teacher.

His published work too reflects the complexities of a many-sided personality. The shortcomings are obvious enough, but they are honourable ones. The ingenuous will to believe, the constant striving to make contact with the mind of Virgil, may be thought more admirable than an academic idiom that denies the reality of the author, insists that texts are inevitably ambiguous and undecidable, and has to put words like 'truth' and 'meaning' into ironical inverted commas.

I give the last word to Wilson Knight, as spokesman for them both (and for their mother):[93]

> What I would say in defence is, that in a cultural period of defeatism, cynicism, satire, and general negation, we have, all three in our different ways, put what abilities we had, in uncompromising and unwavering trust, to service of the brighter and kindlier powers. As Nietzsche puts it: 'Many a one that cannot see the sublime in mankind calleth it virtue to see too well what is base: thus he calleth his evil eye virtue' (*Thus Spake Zarathustra*, II.5). That at least we avoided.

92. G.V.M. Heap to J.R.T. Pollard, 28 April 1976: *Pegasus* 33 (1990) 25–6.
93. *JKB* 249.

10

UNCIVIL DISCOURSE

First, a piece of polemic. It was written in the 'consultation period' before the publication of the Education Reform Bill in November 1987. Only the footnotes have been added.[1]

On the absence of classical subjects from the National Curriculum

It's the name that does it, of course. For many people, the very word 'Classics' irresistibly conjures up the picture of old Crocker-Harris, with his mortarboard and his rusty gown, flogging the Remove through a construe of Livy, while from outside, in the long Edwardian summer, comes the distant sound of leather on willow. Only some such atavistic stereotype can account for the headline 'Classics to Classics, Dust to Dust' over a lively defence of the subject by Peter Walsh in the *Times Higher Education Supplement*, or for David Cannadine's anguished plea to his fellow-historians to face 'the very worst that might happen . . . that history may become the Classics of the twenty-first century: self-absorbed and self-enclosed, and thus doomed to self-destruction.'[2] It isn't like that any more. But myths are potent, and mere evidence cannot exorcise them.

'The classics' is an eighteenth-century phrase embodying an eighteenth-century ideal—'a set of selected texts from a golden age

---

1. *Perspectives on the National Curriculum* (ed. M. Golby, University of Exeter School of Education, October 1987) 82–6.
2. *THES* 20 Sept. 1985 p. 15; *Times Lit. Supp.* 10 October 1986 p. 1140.

which present a model of life and letters for posterity: a balanced, rational life, traditional letters'.[3] But the study of the ancient world is more than that, and always has been. It matters as much for Marx and Freud as for Gibbon and Matthew Arnold. And the way it is taught in today's schools is as far from Crocker-Harris as Tony Harrison's translations are from Gilbert Murray's. The trouble is, the name's the same.

The old classical education was indefensible, simply because of the amount of teaching time it monopolised. But the reaction against it was largely on non-educational grounds. Because the languages and literature of Greece and Rome had been considered appropriate for the education of the British imperial élite, to an idealistic post-war generation they were something to be swept away along with the rest of the bad old days. Those who persisted in believing in their value were forced to rethink the subject *ab initio*, produce new teaching materials and methods, and set about convincing a sceptical public that the Greeks and Romans were, after all, relevant to the modern world. Thanks largely to JACT (Joint Association of Classical Teachers) and the Cambridge Classics Project, that programme was carried out with considerable success. But by now there was much more competition for time in the school curriculum, and new pressures against subjects which were perceived, however wrongly, as divisive.

The confusion about the nature of the subject was memorably illustrated in March 1987, when the effect on Latin of ILEA's abolition of sixth forms (by the introduction of tertiary colleges) became a subject of debate in *The Times*. In a brilliant diversionary tactic, Frances Morrell, then leader of ILEA, wrote a letter to the editor in Latin—real Ciceronian Latin, as in Crocker-Harris's prose composition class (though even he might have thought it a bit pretentious to have *two* 'quin'-clauses in adjacent sentences). That hit the headlines—'A Classic Reply for the archives of The Times'—but it was all beside the point. The protesters weren't asking for the old public-school regime of ten years' intensive Latin, which you need if you're going to be able to write like Cicero—and which the 'friends in County Hall' who helped Mrs Morrell had presumably been through.[4]

A much less conspicuous letter to *The Times* a few days later, from Mrs Jessica Yates, was much closer to the reality of things:[5]

---

3. Lord Dacre's formulation: *Sunday Times* 11 Dec. 1977 p. 39.
4. *Times* 21 March 1987 pp. 1, 9.
5. *Times* 1 April 1987 p. 13.

'Sir, it is all very well to write to *The Times* in Latin and promise that somewhere some children in ILEA schools will continue to study Latin, but Frances Morrell's letter and interview do not tell me that she understands the pleasure and usefulness of classics for the many who couldn't write or understand such a letter.

As an ILEA librarian in the 1970's I stood by while year after year enthusiastic, able arts (and science) pupils at my school were deprived of their cultural heritage and the key to modern European languages. There was too much fear of setting up an elite group and arousing jealousy; and in the fourth year there wasn't room for an extra option . . .'

That's it in a nutshell—on the one hand, the fear of elitism and pressure on the timetable; on the other, the basis of western civilisation. It sounds such a pompous phrase, but it is still a true one. The origins of all critical enquiry—physical science, ethics, political theory, historiography, medicine, law—and a corpus of mythology and literary and dramatic texts which infuse our entire culture, in art, music and language. It's a big responsibility to deny children access to that.

There's no need to fear elitism: classical civilisation is a subject demonstrably accessible to every range of ability. And those whose imaginations are caught by it, and want to go on to the languages, are *not* like Crocker-Harris's unwilling conscripts in the Remove. All classicists are familiar with the conversational gambit commonly heard from the over-forties—'Oh yes, I had to do Latin at school, and hated it.' They are now becoming equally familiar with a very different refrain from the under-thirties—'I loved Class. Civ. at school, and I wish I'd been able to go on with it.' Which brings us to the other problem, finding the time.

If parents, head teachers and educational administrators are sufficiently convinced of the value of a subject, then room can be found for it in the timetable. But the myths are strong, and ideology exerts a double bind. On the left, you can call it Latin and dismiss it as elitist; on the right, you can call it a 'studies' subject and sneer at it as insufficiently rigorous; whatever your prejudice, the unexamined assumption that nothing from so long ago can be relevant to the modern world provides a spurious justification. Those who have actually read Sophocles and Catullus, Plato and Tacitus, whether in English or the original, *know* how 'relevant' the subject is. But those who don't want to know find it easy not to.

In this context, one may reasonably ask how the contents of the proposed foundation curriculum were arrived at. How much serious thought went into deciding which subjects are so essential to children's education that they must occupy 85% of the available time, and which are so peripheral that they can be left to fight over the other 15%?[6] It is hard to imagine the nature of the arguments (if there *were* any arguments) which resulted in putting the study of the ancient world, its literature and languages, in the second category.

I don't suppose the present Government is much exercised by ILEA's fear of appearing elitist. As for pressure on the timetable, that's the whole point of the exercise—to make sure that there *is* room in the timetable for the subjects that matter most. And yet what might have been the ideal opportunity for the confirmation of classical subjects in the curriculum has resulted instead in their exclusion. Why? Just think how much advice and expertise the Secretary of State has at his command, from educationists, civil servants and politicians. All those well-educated and well-informed men and women can't be wrong, can they? And when Sir Ernst Gombrich describes the exclusion of Latin from the foundation curriculum as cutting loose our civilisation from its moorings,[7] we don't need to take him seriously, do we? What do people like him know about it?

What is inexplicable, and infuriating, is the absence of any awareness that the exclusion even needs to be justified. It seems to be simply taken for granted that no case exists for considering the languages and civilisation of the ancient world as fundamental. And all because of the spectre of Crocker-Harris.

There is now good evidence from the USA that Latin, introduced into literacy programmes at the elementary or primary school level, has a dramatic effect on the performance of pupils in standardised tests in English. This information is not hard to find; there was an article on it in the top people's paper,[8] so the politicians and civil servants can be expected to know about it. But when my Newcastle colleague Peter Jones referred to it in a letter to Angela Rumbold recently, he was given the brush-off:[9] 'I do not believe the case for classical languages could or should hinge on controversial claims about their contribution to the learning of English or other subjects; they should stand or fall in their own right.'

---

6. These percentages were suggested by government spokesmen, but not specified in the text of the Act.
7. *TLS* 7 August 1987 p. 899.
8. *Times* 17 April 1987 p. 12.
9. Mrs A. Rumbold (Minister of State, Department of Education and Science) to Dr P.V. Jones, 23 July 1987.

But if 'their own right' consists precisely in the fact that by their nature classical subjects are basic to English, the Romance languages, and a range of other subjects from civics to art-history, then what sort of evidence *would* Mrs Rumbold accept?

The study of the ancient world, with or without its languages, is educationally important because it gets children outside the confines of their own experience and the value-system of their own society, while at the same time introducing them to our own world in embryo. For every level of age and ability, from the household of Caecilius Iucundus in Unit 1 of the Cambridge Classics Course to the arguments on censorship and totalitarianism in Plato's *Republic*, it is both alien enough to stretch the imagination and familiar enough to be relevant to the issues of our own time. And it is fascinating in itself. How many times has *I Claudius* been repeated on television? For that matter, how many times have Penguin Classics reprinted Thucydides' *History of the Peloponnesian War*? Look it up next time you're in a bookshop.[10] Thucydides isn't easy reading, but what he has to say on power politics he says to *us*. By anybody's definition, the subject *is* fundamental. Not in the core curriculum, fair enough. But not in the foundation curriculum either? Ten subjects, and no room for this one? The baby has been thrown out with the Crocker-Harris bathwater.

The proposal is that 'Classics' should be available at the option stage in years 4 and 5. Presumably that means the languages, Latin and/or Greek. Now, that would be fine, if all pupils had had the benefit of classical civilisation courses in the first three years; then they would know what Latin and Greek are about, and why it is worth studying them; the option would be an informed choice. The Cambridge Classics Project was itself based, very successfully, on that strategy. But without the necessary 'Class. Civ. for everyone' component, how many are going to opt for Latin and/or Greek? Those whose parents happen to believe in it, at schools where the head happens to think it worth offering. The result—tiny groups vulnerable to economies, and the whole subject precariously dependent on the devotion of a handful of dedicated teachers who can't expect to be replaced when they retire.

In effect, whether deliberately or by inadvertence, the exclusion of classical studies from the foundation curriculum is an announcement that the subject is not important enough to protect. It will have to take

---

10. Rex Warner's translation, first published in 1954, had its twenty-fourth reprinting in 1990.

its chance with the inessentials, competing for scarce resources of time and support without being able to show the customers why it is worth spending time on. That, it seems to me, is either a gross blunder or an abdication of educational responsibility.

Inconsistent messages

In July 1988, the Education Reform Bill became the Education Reform Act. Naturally, a government with strong opinions and an unassailable majority in the Commons did not take much notice of what its critics said. But two years later, in the light of experience, even its supporters began to think the opposition might be right in demanding much more flexibility in the non-core subjects of the National Curriculum.[11]

Meanwhile, the classicists had been fortified by two welcome statements of support from independent sources. First, Her Majesty's Inspectors devoted the twelfth booklet in their 'Curriculum Matters' series to classics and classical studies, emphasising the way the subject inculcates sensitivity to language, respect for reason, independence of thought and a readiness to enter into other cultures' attitudes and experience. Then a survey of major employers revealed their high opinion of classics graduates, whose discipline they thought produced intellectual rigour, breadth of view, logical and analytical skills and clarity of expression.[12]

In the schools, however, conditions were not promising. Head teachers, burdened by LMS (Local Management of Schools) and the government's financial pressure on local authorities, naturally concentrated their resources on the National Curriculum subjects which they were legally obliged to teach and test. The subject was, and still is, in serious danger of being squeezed out entirely.

Yet this was not at all what the government wanted. The Prime Minister went on record as saying 'we do need more Greek', and urging the teaching of Latin as a way of improving language skills.[13] Her

---

11. E.g. John Clare, 'Education: Does Labour Know Best?', *Daily Telegraph* 24 May 1990 p. 16.
12. *Classics from 5 to 16* (Curriculum Matters 12, HMSO 1988); *Classics in the Market Place* (CUCD 1990, available from Central Services Unit, Precinct Centre, Manchester M13 9EP).
13. *Times Educational Supplement* 7 July 1989 p. 4; *Sunday Telegraph* 15 April 1990 p. iii ('Me, I believe in grammar').

Secretary of State for Education, the architect of the Reform Act itself, wrote an article for the Joint Association of Classical Teachers in which he declared:

> I attach importance to the study of Classics in schools. It is a particularly rich and stimulating part of the educational experience. That is why Classics will continue to have an important role both within the framework of the National Curriculum and outside it.

Within? Yes, because 'the unique strength of classical studies is their ability to inform many other subjects'—notably English and History, whose National Curriculum working groups were invited to consider the contribution of classical studies.[14]

But somehow it did not work out like that. Mr Baker made a particular point about 'new and exciting developments' in the teaching of the subject, including the training of teachers for classical studies in primary schools. That was presumably a reference to the classical studies subject specialism at St Mary's College Twickenham, a course which Mr Baker's successor, literally within weeks of the appearance of his article, decided not to approve. The reason was that it was not a National Curriculum subject.

In a speech to the Society of Education Officers in January 1990, and again to the National Association of Head Teachers six months later, the new Secretary of State announced that the curriculum for 14- to 16-year-olds ('key stage 4') had to be made more flexible. Why? 'Because we must make space for the child who wants to take, for example, classics, a second foreign language, or economics, to be able to do so.' Thus Mr MacGregor made the very point that had been repeatedly urged, and consistently ignored, while the Education Reform Act was being drafted. Better late than never, though it might have been sensible to build in the flexibility to start with. Mr MacGregor insisted, however, that the change was 'in no sense a retreat'; his predecessor's policies were being pursued 'with great vigour and absolutely in accordance with the planned timetable.'[15]

---

14. Rt. Hon. Kenneth Baker, 'The National Curriculum and Classics', *JACT Bulletin* 5 (Summer 1989) 2–3.
15. *The Independent* 3 August 1990 (a letter to the Editor).

All this showed an inconsistency between aim and effect which was evident also in a more general context in the government's attitude to the humanities. Mr Baker's 1987 White Paper on higher education stated firmly in its 'aims and purposes' section that

> the encouragement of a high level of scholarship in the arts, humanities and social sciences is an essential feature of a civilised and cultured society.

The message was repeated in the Secretary of State's speech to the Annual General Meeting of the British Academy in July 1988: celebrating 'a tradition of unequalled richness and diversity', Mr Baker announced that 'every civilised society, in order to remain civilised, needs to instil in its citizens the aptitudes and intuitions provided by the humanities.'[16]

The Education Reform Act introduced new arrangements for the funding of higher education. A Universities Funding Council (UFC) was set up, consisting of fifteen members of whom no fewer than six and no more than nine would be non-academics with experience in 'industrial, commercial or financial matters'. It is said that Sir John Harvey-Jones was proposed as chairman and agreed to serve, but the nomination was turned down by the Prime Minister herself.[17] On the first page of his book *Making it Happen* (London 1988), Sir John remarks: 'Everything I have learnt teaches me that it is only when you work with rather than against people that achievement and lasting success are possible.' Perhaps that was why he was thought unsuitable.

Lord Chilver was appointed to the position, and gave an interview to the *Times Higher Education Supplement*. In his opinion, students in all subjects, including the humanities, should be funded wholly by the market:

> The decaying parts of the university system are those which lose their contact with the real world; they're really armchair things. [Either] they really are *relevant* and people support them or else they're not and they fade away.

---

16. *Higher Education: Meeting the Challenge* (HMSO April 1987) para. 2.1. For the Academy speech (not published, as far as I know), cf. *TLS* 22–28 July 1988 p. 804.
17. *The Independent* 27 June 1988.

So history students, for instance, should be paid for by the museums and theatres (*sic*) which benefit directly from their knowledge.[18] To be fair, Lord Chilver was talking off the cuff, a good six months before taking up his duties. Even so, as a policy statement it was pretty staggering, and not easily to be reconciled with the Secretary of State's views on the humanities. But others too held the same 'market forces' view of higher education.

When Mr Norman Tebbit was interviewed by *The Independent* in the spring of 1988, he reckoned there was a long way to go before Mr Baker's education reforms were fully implemented:

> Mr Tebbit thought for a moment and then added: 'The university sector is, I think, determined to remain as unreformed as possible for as long as possible. Yes, we have a long way to go there,' he said with quiet menace.

A polite enquiry as to the nature of the reforms he thought necessary brought the following reply:[19]

> I think the principal reform which is necessary is that there should be a clear connection between the interests of those who finance universities and those who benefit from the finance by working or studying in them. As you will know, universities today produce many graduates in disciplines for which there is no economic demand and too few in disciplines for which there is a demand.

What we know, in fact, is that humanities graduates (classicists among them) are highly employable. And universities cannot force students to read Engineering or Computer Science if there is a shortage of graduates in those subjects.

The pursuit of government attitudes to the humanities has brought us to the bigger question of the 'reform' of the university system as a whole. That too deserves examination. It is a very strange story.

---

18. *THES* 14 October 1988 p. 9.
19. *Independent* 4 April 1988; Rt. Hon. Norman Tebbit CH MP to T.P. Wiseman, 14 April 1988.

A rancorous relationship

Before the Reform Act changed the system, public funds for higher education were distributed by the University Grants Committee, a body set up in 1919 'as a device in recognition of the autonomy of the universities', manned by senior academics but served by Treasury officials.[20]

In the summer of 1979, four months after Mrs Thatcher's first election victory, the UGC advised universities to plan in the expectation of substantially reduced funding. In December 1980 they reported a reduction of £30m in the previously announced grant for 1981–2; that was a 3.5 per cent cut, but taking into account the anticipated loss of income as a result of the government's policy on overseas students' fees, the UGC forecast a loss of between 5 and 6 per cent. That was the first stage. On 15 May 1981 the UGC told the universities:

> The Secretary of State has now informed the Committee that it should plan on the basis of an 8½ per cent cut in grant for home students by 1983–84. To this reduction must be added the loss of income from overseas students (not accurately predictable) which, in the Committee's view, will result in a total loss of income by 1983–84 as compared with 1979–80 of at least 11 per cent and possibly significantly more.

Individual universities were told on 1 July 1981 what their own grants would be. Exeter, for example, whose 1980–81 grant had been £11.94m, was given £10.77m for 1981–82, with provisional grants (expressed in 1981–82 prices) of £10.15m for 1982–83 and £9.69m for 1983–84.[21]

Throughout the system, the effects were devastating. Since salaries are the biggest single item in university expenditure, staff numbers had to be reduced very rapidly; since no university could risk the expense of testing in the courts the compulsory redundancy of tenured staff, it had to be done by early retirement and non-replacement. It was impossible to plan on criteria of academic desirability. Effectively, what mattered

---

20. J. Carswell, *Government and the Universities in Britain* (Cambridge 1985) 10–12.
21. *University of Exeter Annual Report 1980–81* (Exeter 1982) 4. (The UGC had agreed in 1979 that Exeter was 'historically underfunded'.)

was the size and age structure of departments; small units with a high proportion of staff near retirement age had to be sacrificed if there was to be any hope of balancing the books. At Exeter, a university with a strong Faculty of Arts and an excellent tradition of teaching and research in the humanities, the Department of Philosophy was wound up—an absurdity in academic terms, but typical of the decisions that were being forced on universities throughout the country.

Well, government policy can be a blunt instrument at the best of times, and in her first term Mrs Thatcher had a serious economic crisis to contend with. The universities could console themselves with the reflection that they were just part of an overall strategy that depended on the drastic reduction of public spending. They might not agree with the policy, but at least they could understand what it was for. But the economy picked up. The government, quite justifiably, claimed credit for the success of its policies. Perhaps now the austerity programme in higher education could be reduced?

In September 1984, after a year of careful consultation, the UGC published its advice to Sir Keith Joseph, the Secretary of State for Education and Science, on the financing of the universities:

> For several years the Committee has hoped, with some encouragement from the Government . . . that the cuts of July 1981 would be followed by a period of level funding. It is on this basis that we have formulated our policy and our advice to universities. The Government's actions and its spending plans to 1986–87 have not borne out their hopes.

The UGC warned that if resources continued to decline at the rate of 1.5 per cent per year, 'the total fall between now and the end of the decade will be of the same order as the 1981 cuts'.[22]

The Secretary of State disregarded the advice, and the UGC Chairman therefore told universities in May 1985 that they must expect, as a working hypothesis, an annual decline of two per cent per annum in the UGC's recurrent grant.[23] In its advice to Sir Keith, the UGC said of a 1.5 per cent decline that 'substantial damage to the system and to national interests would be unavoidable'. The government, now in its second term of office, either thought it knew better or was prepared to allow the damage to happen.

---

22. *A Strategy for Higher Education into the 1990's* (HMSO 1984).
23. Sir Peter Swinnerton-Dyer, circular to Vice-Chancellors 9 May 1985.

Cuts in a general context of austerity; a promise of level funding, not honoured; then more cuts in a period of economic prosperity. The universities were both angry and bewildered. What had they done to deserve this?

The answer was given in the austere pages of the *Times Literary Supplement*. A review by T.J. Reed sparked off a correspondence on government and education.[24] One of the contributors was the Conservative MP for Wantage, Mr Robert Jackson. He wrote as follows:

> In relation to the universities the issues were at first too narrowly conceived by the government, simply as one field and one application of its wider programme of reducing the burden of public expenditure. But more and more it has been understood that the universities are central to the strategic design of Britain's economic revival, and that if they are to make the contribution they must, the apparatus and ethos of the self-regarding academic producer-monopoly must be dismantled.

Earlier in the correspondence, the then minister for higher education, Mr George Walden, had referred to 'inefficiency and lax management'; Mr Jackson now added 'the latent corruptions of the parson's freehold'.[25] Neither gave any examples of what he meant, but clearly the government had decided that for some reason the universities *deserved* the treatment they were getting.

In July 1987, after the election which returned Mrs Thatcher for a third time, Mr Jackson was appointed to the post Mr Walden had laid down. As Parliamentary Under-Secretary, he continued to comment freely on what he saw as the shortcomings of those who work in universities. 'Academics', he announced to a management conference, 'should stop cowering in the secret garden of knowledge and get to grips with the real world. Knowledge for its own sake is no longer the prime concern.'[26] At a conference on the funding and management of higher education, he identified the 'pathologies' generated by a centrally funded system as

---

24. T.J. Reed, 'A cause for indignation', *TLS* 13 March 1987 p. 262; correspondence, *TLS* 27 March–15 May 1987.
25. Mr Walden: *TLS* 27 March 1987 p. 324. Mr Jackson: *TLS* 8 May 1987 p. 491.
26. *THES* 17 June 1988 p. 6; in *THES* 1 July 1988 p. 12, Mr Jackson asserted that the phrases quoted were 'not his own'.

'complacency, evasions and vested interests' (again, no explanation or examples were given), and in a later speech he referred to his academic critics as 'those who conceive their professional life as a species of holy mystery'.[27] That gives the intellectual background, as it were, to Mr Tebbit's remark about the necessity for reforming the universities.

At all times, but particularly in her triumphant third term, the policies of Mrs Thatcher's government reflected her own strongly held convictions. Those convictions, and the determination with which she held them (what her opponents called her tunnel vision), were both her strength and her weakness.

> I am in politics because of the conflict between good and evil, and I believe that in the end good will triumph.
>
> You first sort out what you believe in. You then apply it. You don't compromise on things that matter.
>
> Do you know, there are still people in my party who believe in consensus politics . . . I regard them as quislings, as traitors.

That is an attitude both admirable (in a way) and perilous.[28]

It is clear enough, I think, where the universities were in the Prime Minister's demonology. In May 1988, Mrs Thatcher told *The Sunday Times* about 'academics and intellectuals . . . [who] are putting out what I call poison. Some young people, who were thrilled to bits to get to university, had every decent value pounded out of them.' And in *The Scotsman*:

> The rules of a civilised society are politeness and good-neighbour-liness . . . This business of breaking the rules began in the universities, where most of these theoretical philosophies always start. They never start with ordinary people.

And in *Reader's Digest*:

> Socialism did not come from the people. It is a doctrine of intellectuals who had the arrogance to believe they could better plan everyone's life. You will see it in our left-wing Labour authorities and in some university groups . . .

---

27. Speech at L.S.E. conference, 20 Sept. 1988; speech to Centre for Policy Studies, 9 May 1989.
28. Quotations taken from Hugo Young, *One of Us* (London 1989) 352, 4, 223.

It is not surprising that the minister for higher education felt free to be offensive about academics.[29]

Mr Jackson's style attracted some criticism in the House of Lords. Lord Beloff was 'very worried about the inability of Her Majesty's Government to heal the breach that has developed between them and the universities.' Lord Peston referred to academics' sense of frustration: 'it seems impossible to persuade the Government to understand the damage they are doing. Not only does one get no response, but one has to read the most absurd arguments which are put forward'—exemplified by a remark of Mr Jackson's which was 'not unique in its vulgarity'. The *Times Higher Educational Supplement* was even provoked to an editorial on 'the pitfalls of rudeness'.[30]

The minister reacted with a derogatory reference to ' "Establishment" opinion in the universities—the kind of thinking represented by the *THES* and in the House of Lords.' A few weeks later, on the death of a distinguished philosopher, he wrote to *The Independent* about 'the voice of a dethroned hegemony—dethroned largely because of the poverty and superficiality of its thinking.' Rebuked by the Oxford Professor of Jurisprudence for this 'parade of untutored arrogance', Mr Jackson replied:

> Constructive polemic is a valuable antidote to academic torpor. Would that the 'established orthodoxies' of academe—including those of Professor Dworkin himself—were open to 'invigoration' as he implies they should be!

The correspondence closed with the comment (from an academic) that Mr Jackson's letter, 'even by the low standards of modern public debate, was exceptionally foolish.' The Secretary of State, meanwhile, was telling the Vice-Chancellors 'We want you with us, not against us'.[31] Needling

---

29. *Sunday Times* 8 May 1988; *Scotsman* 2 May 1988; *Readers Digest* 134 (May 1989) 31. For the background, see Young (n. 28) ch. 18, 'The treason of the intellectuals'.
30. *Hansard* (Lords) 28 June 1988, cols. 1397, 1530; n. 26 above for the remark referred to. *THES* 25 Feb. 1989 p. 48.
31. *The Independent* 30 June (on the death of A.J. Ayer), 3, 4 and 5 July 1989; Kenneth Baker, speech to Committee of Vice-Chancellors and Principals, 28 September 1988.

the dons is good fun, no doubt, but as a means of achieving co-operation
with government policies it does leave something to be desired.

For those who work in higher education, both Mrs Thatcher's vision of
universities as bastions of the hard left and Mr Jackson's idea of
complacent torpor in an entrenched establishment are equally grotesque
caricatures. The trouble is, caricature is precisely the way most people
derive their notion of universities. Everyone knows what academics are
like: you've only to read a novel or watch television. For Mrs Thatcher's
view, see *The History Man*; for Mr Jackson's, see *Porterhouse Blue*; for
that of their opponents, see *A Very Peculiar Practice*.[32] As Raymond
Williams pointed out, 'trivial fictions, in the comic novels of academia,
have been received by many as sober documentation of some authentic
inner story.'[33]

Academics are good at self-parody; they are not good at anticipating
political fall-out. An excellent recent study of 'campus fiction' blames the
university novelists for 'preparing the ground for Thatcherite higher
education policy'.[34] Professor Carter's analysis is both entertaining and
convincing. He rightly castigates Malcolm Bradbury and Tom Sharpe for
playing into their opponent's hands—and yet he calls his own book
Ancient Cultures of Conceit! God protect us from our friends . . .

It takes an effort to remember how highly British universities and
British academics were regarded elsewhere. The French newspaper
Libération organised a 'peer review' by 600 European academics to find
out which were the best universities in the twelve countries of the EEC.
British Universities came top in seven of the eleven subjects, and in *every*
category there were one, two or three British names in the top five.[35] In
North America, admiration was expressed in more practical ways, by
recruiting as many British academics as possible. American university
presidents were quite open about this, and the process went far enough

---

32. Novels by Malcolm Bradbury (1975), Tom Sharpe (1974) and Andrew Davies
    (1986), respectively; all three were televised between 1981 and 1988.
33. *THES* 5 June 1987 p. 13.
34. Ian Carter, *Ancient Cultures of Conceit: British university fiction in the post-
    war years* (London 1990); quotation from p. 274.
35. *Les 100 meilleurs universités en Europe* (Les guides *Libération* no. 1, Dec.
    1989).

to cause some irritation and hostility among American academics.[36] That was unfortunate, but at least it disproved one of the caricatures; for why should hardheaded deans of faculty want to hire the torpid, the complacent and the self-regarding?[37]

Sir Keith Joseph had been anxious about the 'brain drain' as early as 1985. But Mr Jackson did not believe in it.[38] He thought it was mere rhetoric, and he told the Vice-Chancellors so:

> As far as I can see there is little convincing evidence to substantiate these claims. In the meantime you will doubtless share my concern about the damaging effect such stories can have both on morale and on universities' reputations both at home and abroad.

So *that* was what caused low morale! Sir Edward Parkes, the chairman of the Committee of Vice-Chancellors and Principals, replied to this piece of effrontery by pointing out what was really doing the damage: academics were leaving 'because they feel the government is hostile to the universities'.[39] The record shows that they had some reason to feel that.

Envoi

In this imbroglio of confusion, sophistry and malice, the humanities were particularly vulnerable. The most conspicuous case was that of philosophy, subject of a 'debate' between Simon Blackburn and Robert Jackson in 1988; the two papers and the resulting correspondence are necessary reading for cultural historians.[40] But other disciplines suffered as well. For example, university Classics departments were closed, and

36. See for instance N.F. Cantor, *TLS* 3–9 Feb. 1989, p. 109; R. Trumbach, *TLS* 17–23 Feb. 1989, p. 165; well-informed analysis by R. Janko, *TLS* 24 Feb.–2 March 1989 p. 194f.
37. According to Mr Jackson (*Independent* 31 May 1990), 'some of these people are extinct volcanoes'. That's all right, then.
38. Sir Keith: *Hansard* (Commons) 14 June 1985 cols. 1127, 1140. Mr Jackson: *TLS* 10–16 March 1989 p. 249, and frequently elsewhere.
39. *THES* 14 July 1989 p. 3.
40. *TLS* 30 Dec. 1988–5 Jan. 1989 pp. 1442, 1452–3; correspondence from *TLS* 13–19 Jan. to 7–13 April 1989. See also S. Blackburn, *Cambridge Review* 110 (March 1989) 12–15.

Arts faculties consequently impoverished, at Aberdeen,[41] Aberystwyth, Bangor, Birkbeck, Cardiff, Hull, Lancaster, Leicester, Sheffield, Southampton and Sussex. Was that policy, or just accident? Mr Tebbit's views suggest the former; Mr Baker's, the latter. Who can say?

In small things as in great, for good or ill, the achievements of Mrs Thatcher's government did not, on the whole, fulfil the prayer of her first day in office: 'where there is discord, may we bring harmony.' For the study of the ancient world, and for the virtues (p. 215 above) attributed to it by employers and educationalists alike, the hectoring 'conviction politics' of the 1980s produced a deeply uncongenial environment. Whatever happens next, it is a real pleasure to see those days in their turn pass into history.

---

41. Thus ending a tradition of very nearly 500 years.

APPENDICES

1. The world survey: Latin texts

(a) Inscription on the Cornwall map (p. 24):
Orientalis plaga anticodoxo[1] dimensa habet maria septem. Insulas novem.
Montes triginta unum. Provincias decem. Oppida sexaginta sex. Flumina viginiti
duo. Gentes quinquaginta unum. A polliclito meridiana pars dimensa habet maria
duo. Insulas septemdecim. Montes sex. Provincias duodecim. Oppida sexaginta
quatuor. Flumina duo. Gentesque plurimas. A theodoto septemtrionalis et
occidentalis pars dimensa habet maria undecim. Insulas quadraginta. Montes
viginti duo. Provincias viginti quatuor. Oppida centum viginti quinque. Flumina
viginti unum. Gentesque multas.

In hoc vero libello quasi in quadam brevi tabella quasdam celi causas situs
terrarum et maris spacia annotavimus ut in modico lector ea percurrat et
compendiosa brevitate Ethimologias eorum causas cognoscat.[2]

(b) Inscription on the Ebstorf map (p. 25):
Mappa dicitur forma. Inde mappa mundi id est forma mundi. Quam Iulius Cesar
missis legatis per totius orbis amplitudinem primus instituit; regiones, provincias,
insulas, civitates, syrtes, paludes, equora, montes, flumina quasi sub unius
paginae visione coadunavit; que scilicet non parvam prestat legentibus utilitatem,
viantibus directionem rerumque viarum[3] gratissime speculationis directionem.[4]

(c) Julius Honorius (p. 26):
Iulio Caesare et Marco Antonio consulibus omnis orbis peragratus est per
sapientissimos et electos viros quattuor: Nicodomo[5] orientis, Didymo
occidentalis, Theudoto septemtrionalis, Polyclito meridiani.

---

1. Read 'a nicodoxo'?
2. The last four words are displaced two lines up.
3. Evidently garbled: Professor M.D. Reeve suggests 'variarum'.
4. No doubt a dittography. Read 'lectionem' (Destombes)? or 'descriptionem' (Reeve)?
5. According to Riese's apparatus, the MSS read 'Nicodomo', 'Nichodomo', 'Nicodoro',
   'Nicodoso'. He prints 'Nicodemo' in his text, which seems arbitrary.

A consulibus supra scriptis usque in consulatum Augusti IIII et Crassi annis XXI mensibus quinque diebus novem oriens dimensa est. Et a consulibus supra scriptis usque in consulatum Augusti VII et Agrippae annis XXVI mensibus III diebus XVII occidui pars dimensa est. A consulibus supra scriptis usque in consulatum Augusti X annis XXVIIII mensibus VIII septemtrionalis pars dimensa est. A consulibus supra scriptis usque in consulatum Saturnini et Cinnae annis XXXII mense I diebus XX meridiana pars dimensa est.

(d) 'Aethicus' (p. 26f.):

Lectionum pervigili cura comperimus, senatum populumque Romanum totius mundi dominos, domitores orbis et praesules, cum quidquid subiacet caelo penetrarent triumphis, omnem terram oceani limbo circumdatam invenisse atque eam ne incognitam posteris reliquissent, subiugato virtute sua orbe totum qua terra protenditur proprio limite signavisse. Et ne divinam eorum mentem omnium rerum magistram aliquid praeteriret, quam vicerant, quadripertito caeli cardine investigarunt et intellectu aetherio totum quod ab oceano cingitur tres partes esse dixerunt, Asiam Europam et Africam reputantes . . .

Itaque Iulius Caesar bissextilis rationis inventor divinis humanisque rebus singulariter instructus cum consulatus sui fasces regeret, ex senatus consulto censuit omnem orbem iam Romani nominis admetiri per prudentissimos viros et omni philosophiae munere decoratos. Ergo a Iulio Caesare et M. Antonio consulibus orbis terrarum metiri coepit, id est: a consulatu supra scripto usque in consulatum Augusti tertium et Crassi annis XXI mensibus V diebus VIIII a Nicodoxo[6] omnis oriens dimensus est, sicut inferius demonstratur. A consulatu item Iulii Caesaris et M. Antonii usque in consulatum Augusti septimum et Agrippae a Didymo occidui pars dimensa est annis numero XXXI mensibus III diebus XII, sicut aperietur stilo. A consulatu item Iulii Caesaris et M. Antonii usque in consulatum Augusti decimum annis XXVIIII mensibus VIII diebus X a Theodoto septemtrionalis pars dimensa est, ut evidenter ostenditur. A consulatu similiter Iulii Caesaris usque in consulatum Saturnini et Cinnae a Polyclito meridiana pars dimensa est annis XXXII mense I diebus XX, sicut definita monstratur. Ac sic omnis orbis terrae intra annos XXXII a dimensoribus peragratus est, et de omni eius continentia perlatum est ad senatum.

(e) Historia Pseudoisidoriana (p. 28 n. 12):

Iulius Cesar . . . a Pireneis montibus ad Ispali usque callem sub tecto fieri praecepit totumque mundum in longitudine et latitudine circuivit, ac duos consules Marcum et Cathonem ad hoc praefecit. Postea mensuravit a Roma usque in orientem et occidentem et austrum et septentrionem. Nochodoxus prepositus praefuit illis qui mensuraverunt terram a Roma in orientem; Ridimus

---

6. Variant readings: 'anocodoxo' (*V*), 'anno procodoxo' (*L*), 'a natodoxo' (*R*).

occidentalibus praefuit; prepositus in mensuratione austri Pelagius; prepositus in mensuratione septentrionalis plage Todora. De qua satis mensuratione dictum est in geometria.[7] Mensuratio orientalis facta fuit XXXVI annis ac tribus mensibus et XVII diebus, mensuratio occidentis in XXIX annis et VIII mensibus, mensuracio septentrionis XXIII annis et mense et XX diebus, mensuracio austri XXI anno et quinque mensibus et VIIII diebus.

(f) Lambert of St Omer (p. 28f.):
Post haec cum triumpho Romam reversus a senatu cum honore excipitur; deinde regna orientis et meridiani ac septentrionis occidentisque et provincias insulasque per tres viros prudentissimos videlicet Nicodoxum et Pollyclitonem atque Theodotum metiri praecepit . . .
   Europa mundi pars quarta. Iulio Cesare imperante a Theodoto dimensa nominatur pars tercia, sed vere est quarta, nam Asia continet partes duas et Affrica terciam, Europa quartam. Habet Europa maria XI, insulas XL, provincias XX, montes XXI. Habet autem oppida CXX, flumina XXI gentesque diversas numero XXXIII.

(g) Albertus Magnus (p. 29f.):
Volumus autem in hac descriptione praecipue imitari descriptionem, quae facta est sub AUGUSTO CAESARE, qui primus mandavit 'ut totus orbis describeretur'; licet enim etiam aliqui ante ipsum imperatores attemptaverint, tamen ipse descriptionem perfici fecit per quattuor partes habitabiles mittens legatos, qui orbem metirentur et describerent. Cuius orientales partes descripsit NOCODOXUS quidam philosophus, septentrionales autem THEODOTUS alius philosophus, POLYCLITUS autem sapiens meridianas descripsit partes, occidentales autem per itineraria sua Romani sciverunt, eo quod in occidente praecipue erant dominia et viae eorum. Facta est autem totius orbis descriptio in annis triginta duobus, et omnis mundi continentia, quae tunc erat, perlata est ad senatum.

(h) Hemmerlein 'Malleolus' (p. 30f.):
Exhinc fuerunt consules usque ad tempus Iulii Cesaris inclusive, qui bisextilis rationis inventor divinisque humanis rebus singulariter plus ceteris imbutus et naturali magnificentia decoratus et senatoris urbis consultus senatus[8] censuit omnem orbem iam Romani nominis imperio parentem per prudentissimos viros et omni philosophie munere redimitos conscribi. Et ita tempore suo laudabiliter incepit et post mortem suam Octavianus Augustus diligenter consumavit ita ut

---

7. I.e., in the *Cosmographia* of Julius Honorius or 'Aethicus'?
8. Evidently garbled from (e.g.) 'ex senatus consulto'.

ducentis dimessoribus omnis orbis terre per annos XXXII peragratus est. Et de omni eius continentia perlatum est ad Octavianum et senatum predictos. Qui quidem Augustus ex eorundem dimessorum fidelis rationis et descriptionis pronuntiatione emisit edictum, ut describeretur universis[9] orbis. Et hec descriptio prima facta est a presidie[10] Syrie Cirino Luc. c. II ne traderentur oblivioni tam miro et inestimabili conatu conquesita, unde non tantum loca, sed locorum habitatores scire volentes.[11] Et iuxta dictam evangelicam veritatem ibant omnes ut profiterentur singuli in suam civitatem. Unde per predictos peragratores et inter tres principales mundi plagas conscripta fuerunt nominatim primum maria, quorum XXX fuerunt in numero, item insule LXXII, item montes prominentes XL, item provincie LXXVIII . . .

Item invenerunt dicti peragratores civitates et oppida elegantiores CCLXX. Item invenerunt flumina famosiora LXII, item gentes centum nonaginta, de quibus alique annumerate sunt in Actibus Apostolorum c. II . . . Et hec omnia videlicet maria, insule, montes, provincie, civitates, oppida, flumina et gentes singulariter singuli et singule propriis nominibus sunt in Itinerario urbis Rome notabiliter conscripta prout diligenter vidi et prospexi, etiam cum leucis et miliaribus distantiarum de locorum locis[12] propriissime designata.

2. Thomas Jones and the Villa Negroni excavations

In 1988 the Whitworth Art Gallery in Manchester held an exhibition based on Thomas Jones' journals, with an excellent catalogue by Francis W. Hawcroft (*Travels in Italy 1776–1783*). Item 48 (p. 46 f.) is Jones' painting of the Villa Negroni excavation, done in oil on paper 'over black crayon under-drawing'. On the back is inscribed:

> No. 2   An Antique Building discovered in a Cava
> in the Villa Negroni at Rome in ye Year 1779
> T. Jones

In fact, as we know from his journal and other sources, the excavation was in July 1777. Item 113 (p. 101), also oil on paper, bears a similar inscription:

> No. 3 Mount Vesuvius from Torre dell'Annunziata near Naples

---

9. A slip for 'universus'.
10. A slip for 'pr(a)eside'.
11. Verb missing: 'invenirent'?
12. Evidently garbled, but the meaning is clear enough.

As Hawcroft points out, Jones was at Torre Annunziata from 25 to 31 July 1783 (see pp. 124–5 of his journal); but 'the artist's few days there were so busy with expeditions . . . that there would have been little time for him to work on a painting.'

Both paintings are now in the Tate Gallery. They are clearly a pair, or two in a series (to judge by the numbers on the back). Jones seems to have used the same palette of colours for both, with a green unexpectedly lush for Italy in July. The natural assumption, which Hawcroft makes tentatively for the Vesuvius view only, is that both scenes were sketched on the spot and then painted much later, after Jones' return to Radnorshire in 1789. That would explain the mistaken date of his visit to Villa Negroni, and the colours more reminiscent of the Welsh border country than of Rome or Campania.

It would also explain the otherwise baffling church in the background of the Villa Negroni scene. The only identification suggested by Hawcroft is that of Lindsay Stainton in the Iveagh Bequest catalogue *British Artists in Rome 1700–1800* (Kenwood, London 1974): 'possibly the convent of S. Eusebio seen from the north-east.' But that seems incompatible with the shadows, and would place the artist's viewpoint completely outside the grounds of the Villa. The excavation was in the *garden* of the Villa Negroni (Hawcroft p. 46, citing Thomas Egerton's *Journal*, 19 March 1785), and if the Roman house was indeed the *casa sotteranea* of the Cappelletti vineyard, as assumed above (p. 85), then the position—though not the orientation—of the mysterious church would be that of the Villa Negroni *palazzo*.

My guess is that Jones' original sketch, naturally concentrating on the excavation itself, gave only the vaguest indication of a large building in the background; and that when he later worked up the scene into an oil painting, he elaborated it into something vaguely appropriate which would correspond with the house in the equivalent position on the Vesuvius scene.

3. Howes, Crawfords and Terrys: genealogy and bibliography

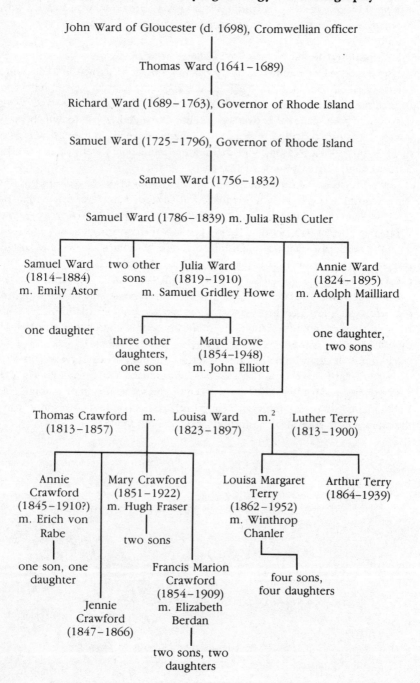

Family memoirs:

Julia Ward Howe, *Reminiscences 1819–1899* (Boston and New York 1899)

Mrs Hugh Fraser, *A Diplomatist's Wife in Many Lands*, two volumes (London 1911)

Mrs Hugh Fraser, *Further Reminiscences of a Diplomatist's Wife* (London 1912)

Maud Howe Elliott, *Three Generations* (London 1925)

Maud Howe Elliott, *My Cousin F. Marion Crawford* (New York 1934)

Mrs Winthrop Chanler, *Roman Spring: Memoirs* (Boston 1934)

Maud Howe Elliott, *Uncle Sam Ward and his Circle* (New York 1938)

Biographies based on documentary sources:

Louise Hall Tharp, *Three Saints and a Sinner: Julia Ward Howe, Louisa, Annie and Sam Ward* (Boston 1956)

Robert L. Gale, *Thomas Crawford: American Sculptor* (Pittsburgh 1964)

John Pilkington jr, *Francis Marion Crawford* (New York 1964)

4. G. McN. Rushforth: a provisional bibliography

This list makes no claim to completeness, and information about missing items (especially for the early years) would be very welcome. Abbreviations:

Ant. J.: Antiquaries Journal

JBSMGP: Journal of the British Society of Master Glass Painters

JRS: Journal of Roman Studies

TBGAS: Transactions of the Bristol and Gloucester Archaeological Society

1891 'Melber's Dio Cassius' (review of Teubner Dio Cassius, ed. Joannes Melber, vol. 1), *Classical Review* 5 (1891), 27–9.

1893 *Latin Historical Inscriptions illustrating the History of the Early Empire*, Oxford, Clarendon Press, 1893: pp. xxvii + 144.

1895 'Melber's Edition of Dio Cassius' (notice of vol. 2 of Teubner Dio), *Classical Review* 9 (1895), 367.

1900 'The Temple of the Clitumnus and the Proto-Renaissance in Umbria', *The Guardian*, 24 January 1900, 135–6.

Carlo Crivelli, London, Bell, 1900: pp. xi + 122.

1902 'Art', in F.P. Barnard (ed.), *Companion to English History (Middle Ages)* (Oxford, Clarendon Press, 1902), 329–52.

'The Church of Santa Maria Antiqua', *Papers of the British School at Rome* 1 (1902), 1–123.

1910 (translated) G.T. Rivoira, *Lombardic Architecture, its Origin, Development and Derivatives*, London, Heinemann, 1910 (2 vols.): pp. xii + 250, 368.

1911 'Two Pictures by Giambono', *Burlington Magazine* 20 (November 1911), 101–6.
'The Incantations of Medea', ibid. (December 1911), 172–5.
1912 'Stained Glass from Malvern', *Notes and Queries* (11th series), 6 (7 September 1912), 188.
1914 'The Wheel of the Ten Ages of Life in Leominster Church', *Proceedings of the Society of Antiquaries* 26 (1913–14), 47–60.
Review of Ethel Ross Barker, *Rome of the Pilgrims and Martyrs*, *JRS* 4 (1914), 188–9.
1915 'A Note on the Mosaic from the Roman Villa at Robato, Malta', *JRS* 5 (1915), 79–80.
'Funeral Lights in Roman Sepulchral Monuments', ibid. 149–64.
1916 *The Stained Glass of Great Malvern Priory Church*, photographed by Sydney A. Pitcher, with descriptive notes by G. McN. Rushforth, F.S.A.: vol. 1, The Windows of the North Clerestory of the Quire. Gloucester, Sydney A. Pitcher, 1916: 1 p. of text.
1917 *The Stained Glass of Great Malvern Priory Church* (see 1916), vol. 2, The East Window. Gloucester, Sydney A. Pitcher, 1917: 3 pp. of text.
1918 (translated) G.T. Rivoira, *Moslem Architecture, its Origins and Development*, London, Oxford U.P., 1918: pp. xvi + 383.
'An Account of Some Painted Glass from a House in Leicester', *Archaeological Journal* 75 (1918), 47–68.
1919 *The Stained Glass of Great Malvern Priory Church* (see 1916), vol. 5, The Windows of the North Transept. Gloucester, Sydney A. Pitcher, 1919: 3 pp. of text.
'Magister Gregorius de mirabilibus urbis Romae', *JRS* 9 (1919), 14–58.
1920 *The Stained Glass of Great Malvern Priory Church* (see 1916), vol. 4, The Windows of the South Clerestory of the Quire and the West Window. Gloucester, Sydney A. Pitcher, 1920: 2 pp. of text.
'A Sketch of the History of Malvern and its Owners', *TBGAS* 42 (1920), 41–57.
1921 'The Glass of the East Window of the Lady Chapel in Gloucester Cathedral', *TBGAS* 43 (1921), 191–218.
'A Royal Portrait from Malvern', *Malvern Gazette*, 14 January 1921.
1922 'The Great East Window of Gloucester Cathedral', *TBGAS* 44 (1922), 293–304.
'Inscription at Clapton', ibid. 305–7.
1923 *Little Malvern Church*, Worcester n.d. (1923 according to the Society of Antiquaries Library): 4 pp., unnumbered.
'Architecture and Art', in Cyril Bailey (ed.), *The Legacy of Rome* (Oxford, Clarendon Press, 1923), 385–427.
'An Indulgence Inscription in Clapton Church, Gloucestershire', *Ant. J.* 3 (1923), 338–42.

Review of Grant Showerman, *Eternal Rome, JRS* 13 (1923), 197.

Review of Helen H. Tanzer, *The Villas of Pliny the Younger*, ibid. 201.

1924 'Medieval Tiles in the Church of Llangattock-nigh-Usk', *Ant. J.* 4 (1924), 382-7.

'The Glass in the Quire Clerestory of Tewkesbury Abbey', *TBGAS* 46 (1924), 289-324.

Review of Eugenie Strong, *La Chiesa Nuova (Santa Maria in Vallicella)*, *Ant. J.* 4 (1924), 183.

1925 (translated) G.T. Rivoira, *Roman Architecture and its Principles of Construction under the Empire, with an Appendix on the Evolution of the Dome up to the XVIIth Century*, Oxford, Clarendon Press, 1925: pp. xxxvii + 310.

'The Burials of Lancastrian Notables in Tewkesbury Abbey after the Battle, AD 1471', *TBGAS* 47 (1925), 131-49.

'Tewkesbury Abbey: The Wakeman Cenotaph and the Starved Monk', ibid. 150-2.

Review of Alfred C. Fryer, *Wooden Monumental Effigies in England and Wales*, *Ant. J.* 5 (1925), 297.

Review of H. Dragendorff and E. Krüger, *Das Grabmal von Igel, JRS* 15 (1925), 131-3.

Review of Eugenia Strong, *La scultura romana da Augusto a Constantino*, ibid. 281-3.

Obituary of Giacomo Boni, *Ant. J.* 5 (1925), 441-3.

Biographical note on G.T. Rivoira, in G.T. Rivoira, *Roman Architecture* (see above), xxi-xxvi.

1926 'The Baptism of St Christopher', *Ant. J.* 6 (1926), 152-8.

'Lord Cromwell's Rebus in Tattershall Castle', ibid. 163-5.

Review of *Atti della Pontificia Accademia romana di archeologia, serie III, Memorie I, Rendiconti I and II*, ibid. 94-7.

1927 *The Stained Glass of Great Malvern Priory Church* (see 1916), vol. 6, The Windows of the North Aisles. Gloucester, Sydney A. Pitcher, 1927: 3 pp. of text.

'A Lily-crucifix and an Unidentified Saint in Kenn Church, Devon', *Ant. J.* 7 (1927), 72.

'The Painted Windows in the Chapel of the Vyne in Hampshire', *Archaeological Journal* 84 (1927), 105-13.

'Herefordshire' (Presidential Address), *TBGAS* 49 (1927), 43-62.

'The Painted Glass in the Lord Mayor's Chapel, Bristol', ibid. 301-31.

'The Painted Windows in the Chapel of the Vyne in Hampshire', *Walpole Society* 15 (1926-7), 1-20.

'The Kirkham Monument in Paignton Church, Devon: a Study in Medieval Iconography and in Particular of the Mass of St Gregory', *Transactions of the Exeter Diocesan Architectural and Archaeological Society* 15 (3rd series, vol. 4, 1927), 1–37.

Review of W.J. Anderson and R. Phené Spiers, *The Architecture of Ancient Rome*, *JRS* 17 (1927), 128–9.

Review of Herbert Read, *English Stained Glass, JBSMGP* 2. 1 (April 1927), 45–8.

Biographical note on J.D. Le Couteur, in J.D. Le Couteur, *English Medieval Painted Glass* (London, S.P.C.K., 1927), vii–x.

1928 'The Painted Glass in Birtsmorton Church', *Worcestershire Archaeological Society Transactions for 1926–7* (Worcester 1928), 91–9.

'The Story of Dauntsey', *TBGAS* 50 (1928), 325–51.

Review of Rudolph Schultze, *Basilika*, *JRS* 18 (1928), 105–6.

Review of *Recherches à Salone* vol. I, ibid. 114–17.

Review of F. Harrison, *The Painted Glass of York*, *JBSMGP*, 2. 3 (April 1928), 152–6.

1929 'Seven Sacraments Compositions in English Medieval Art', *Ant. J.* 9 (1929), 83–100.

'The Font in Elmley Castle Church', *Worcestershire Archaeological Society Transactions for 1927–8* (Worcester, 1929), 92–5.

Review of S.B. Platner and Thomas Ashby, *Topographical Dictionary of Ancient Rome*, *Ant. J.* 9 (1929), 396–8.

1930 *Latin Historical Inscriptions illustrating the History of the Early Empire*, 2nd ed., London, Oxford U.P., 1930: pp. xxxi + 144.

'Mediaeval Glass in Oriel College Chapel: St Margaret and the Dragon', *JBSMGP* 3. 3 (April 1930), 108–11.

'Warkworth', *TBGAS* 52 (1930), 265–74.

1931 'A 14th-century Tomb from Little Malvern Priory Church', *Ant. J.* 11 (1931), 169.

Review of I.A. Richmond, *The City Wall of Imperial Rome*, ibid. 180–2.

1932 'The Arms of St Augustine's Abbey, Bristol', *TBGAS* 54 (1932), 129–30.

'The Arms of St Mark's or the Gaunts' Hospital, Bristol', ibid. 131–2.

'The Sacraments Window in Crudwell Church', *Wiltshire Archaeological and Natural History Magazine* 45 (1932), 68–72.

Review of Tancred Borenius, *St Thomas Becket in Art*, *Ant. J.* 12 (1932), 461–3.

1933 (translated) G.T. Rivoira, *Lombardic Architecture, its Origin, Development and Derivatives*, re-edited with additional notes, Oxford, Clarendon Press, 1933 (2 vols.): pp. xxviii + 283, xv + 401.

'A Missing Roman Inscription at Exeter', *Devon and Cornwall Notes and Queries* 17 (1932–3), 55.

'Late Medieval Paintings in Exeter Cathedral', ibid. 249–53.

'The Rev. Benjamin Foster and the Windows of St Neot', ibid. 224–6.

'St Urith', ibid. 290–1.

Review of F. Sydney Eden, *Ancient Stained and Painted Glass, Ant. J.* 13 (1933), 321–3.

1935 *The Stained Glass of Great Malvern Priory Church* (see 1916), vol. 3. Gloucester, Sydney A. Pitcher, 1935: 2 pp. of text.

'Nettlecombe Church: Glass in the Trevelyan Chapel', *Proceedings of the Somersetshire Archaeological and Natural History Society* 80 (1935), 63–6.

'St Cecilia', *Notes and Queries* 169 (30 November 1935), 382–4.

1936 *Medieval Christian Imagery, as illustrated by the Painted Windows of Great Malvern Priory Church, Worcestershire, together with a Description and Explanation of all the Ancient Glass in the Church*, Oxford, Clarendon Press, 1936: pp. xx + 456.

(translated) P. Borchardt, 'The Sculpture in Front of the Lateran as Described by Benjamin of Tudela and Magister Gregorius', *JRS* 26 (1936), 68–70.

Obituary of Montague Rhodes James, *Great Malvern Parochial Magazine*, July 1936.

1937 'Additional Note to the Painted Windows in the Chapel of the Vyne', *Walpole Society* 25 (1936–7), 167–9.

'A Rock Crystal Intaglio by Giovanni Bernardi', *Burlington Magazine* 71 (1937), 284–5.

'St Cecilia', *JBSMGP* 6. 4 (April 1937), 180–3.

'The Windows of the Church of St Neot, Cornwall', *Transactions of the Exeter Diocesan Architectural and Archaeological Society* 15 (3rd series, vol. 4, Part 3, 1937), 150–90.

1938 'The Bacton Glass at Atcham in Shropshire', *Transactions of the Woolhope Naturalists' Field Club, Hereford*, volume for 1933–5 (1938), 157–62.

n.d. *A Short Guide to the Painted Windows in the Church of St Neot*, London, S.P.C.K.: pp. 16.

Rushforth left his 'professional' correspondence, papers and notebooks to the Rev. E.P. Baker, who in February 1982 generously donated them to the Exeter University Library. The collection includes offprints (from Huelsen and Ashby, among many others), the manuscript of an unfinished article on Cardinal York, evidently abandoned in 1906, and the texts of four lectures: untitled (on mosaics), given at King's College London in 1918; 'Roman Art and Architecture', given to the Glasgow and West of Scotland Centre of the Classical Association of Scotland on 30 November 1920; 'Rome in the Middle Ages', given at Cambridge on 8 August 1922; and 'Madresfield and its Owners', evidently given in 1936. 'Rome in the Middle Ages' was published in *Pegasus* 25 (1982) 11–20.

INDEX

Accius, L., playwright, 6, 8
Aeneas, 17, 173, 180, 181, 205
'Aethicus', geographical text, 26–8, 31–2, 33, 37, 228
Agrippa, king of Judaea, 10
Agrippa, M., 74, 194–5; world map of, 38–42; reincarnation of, 194, 200, 202, 204
Agrippina, empress, 77
Albertus Magnus, on world survey, 29–31, 229
Alexander the Great, 33–4, 63, 64
Alfred, king and translator, 41
Alfieri, Vittorio, 83
Allecto, 191
Anchises, 203, 204, 205
Andromeda, 58
Annius Vinicianus, L., 2, 11
Apollonius of Tyana, 13
aqueducts, 74, 77–80
art as physiognomy, 66–7
Ashby, Thomas, 117–22, 134–5, 139, 142–3, 156, 159–61, 237
astrology, 54
Atreus, see Thyestes
Augustus, 3, 4, 7, 38, 41–2; dynasty of, 1–2; on *mappa mundi*, 23–4, 29–31, 41
Avernus, entrance to Hades, 17, 181

Baccelli, On. Guido, 121, 124–5, 128, 134, 148
Baddeley, Edmund, 116, 126, 127, 140, 146–7
Baddeley, Helen, 115–16, 120, 126, 147
Baddeley, W. St Clair, 111–48 passim, 153, 154, 155–6, 161; character and abilities of, 114, 132, 138, 143, 147–8
Baiae, etymology of, 17
Baker, Rev. E.P., 162, 169, 237

Baker, Rt Hon. Kenneth (Secretary of State for Education and Science, 1986–89), 216, 217–18, 223, 226
'Basilica Aemilia', excavation of, 124, 131, 133, 136, 139, 140–1, 154
Beckford, William, of Fonthill, 83, 84
Bloxham School, 171, 172, 174, 179, 209
Boni, Giacomo, 111, 115, 121, 123–43 passim, 146–7, 154, 155–6, 158
Branford, Dr Jean, 197
Bridges, Robert, 50
Bristol and Gloucester Archaeological Society, 131, 145–6, 161–2
British School at Rome, 143, 155–8, 170; foundation of, 134–5, 139, 152–5; *Papers* of, 137, 140, 156–7
Brutus, L., 7
Brutus, M., tyrannicide, 7, 12
Bulwer, Miss D.E., photographer, 117–18, 121–2
Burton-Brown, Mrs E., guidebook author, 142
Byron, in Anthony Powell, 55, 61

Caesar, see Iulius
Caligula, see Gaius
Campania, 14–23 passim
Campus Martius, 35, 38–9
Candaules, king of Lydia, 60, 63, 65
Cape Town, Jackson Knight in, 196–7
Cassiodorus, 27
Cassius of Parma, tyrannicide, 8
Cassius Chaerea, Guards officer, 1–3, 5, 8–11
Cassius Dio, historian, 2, 4, 20
Catullus, on ends of earth, 35
centaurs, 52, 54, 60
Chilver, Lord, 217–18
Christie, John D., 199, 206

Christy, Edmund, 112–13, 116, 140
Cicero, M., 4, 6–7, 35
Cimmerians, at Cumae, 181
Circe, 54
Claudius Caesar, 2, 10–12, 72, 77
collective unconscious, 182–3, 189
Committee of Vice-Chancellors and Principals, 225
Cornelius Sabinus, Guards officer, 2, 9, 11
Cornwall, Duchy of, 24
Cornwall *mappa mundi*, 24–5, 27, 32, 42, 227
Corson, Prof. Hiram, 202
Crassus, M., 4, 34–5, 36–7
Crawford, Annie, 88, 96–100 passim
Crawford, Francis Marion, 90, 96–100 passim, 106; as novelist, 93–4, 99, 113
Crawford, Jennie, 88, 96, 97
Crawford, Mary, see Fraser
Crawford, Thomas, sculptor, 88–90, 92, 96
Croce, Benedetto, 131
Cumae, 14, 18, 179, 181
Cunedda, 68, 69
Currie, Lord, ambassador in Rome, 124–6, 136
Cyclopes, 181

Dance to the Music of Time, A, 51–70 passim
Day-Lewis, Cecil, 178
Deane, Rev. A.C., 163–4
Dicuil, learned monk, 28, 32
Didymus, Alexandrian author, 33
Dio, see Cassius
Diodorus Siculus, on Herakles, 16–17
Dionysius of Halicarnassus, on Herakles, 17
Dionysus, 55–6, 64
Diotima, Platonic wise woman, 47, 49
Drusus, brother of Tiberius, 4–5

Ebstorf *mappa mundi*, 25, 32, 227
Education Reform Act, 215, 216, 219
Eliot, T.S., 176, 188–9
Eratosthenes, 33, 34
Evander, 14, 17
Evans, Sir John, 159–60
Exeter, blitzed, 166, 170, 188; Cathedral, 164, 165; University College of the South West, 149, 165–7, 168–9, 178–9, 206, 209

Exeter University, 169–70, 206, 219–20; Roborough Library, 166, 167, 169–70
Exmouth, 165, 169, 189

Fannius Caepio, republican, 7
Flavius Josephus, historian, 2, 3, 8, 10
Fontana, Domenico, architect, 79–80, 82, 109, 110
Franciscans, Platonic doctrine of, 46, 47
Fraser, Hugh, 97–100 passim
Fraser, Hugh, son of above, 98, 101
Fraser, John, 98, 99, 101
Fraser, Mary Crawford ('Mimoli'), 90, 96–101 passim; as author, 100–9
Fuller, Margaret, 88–9
Furies, 56–7, 187, 191, 207

Gaius Caesar ('Caligula'), 1–13 passim, 75–6; favourite quotation of, 8
Galba, rebel and emperor, 12
genealogy, 67–9, 162
Germanicus Caesar, 5
Getty, John Paul, benefactor, 22
Giants, 14–17, 20–1
gladiators, 70
Globe, Baddeley writes for, 126–7, 129–36 passim, 138, 156
Gloucester, 111, 162, 164
Gracchus, playwright, 8
Gracchus, Ti., death of, 5
Greek colonists in Italy, 14, 17–18
Greek writers on Italy, 14–18
Gregorovius, Ferdinand, 87, 92, 93
Güntert, Hermann 180–1, 185
Gyges, 60, 63, 65

Haarhoff, T.J., 178–9, 183, 186, 188, 191–206 passim
Hailes Abbey, 131, 145, 146
Hare, Augustus, 93, 140, 157
Harris, J. Rendel, 177, 181
Harvey-Jones, Sir John, 217
Haverfield, F.J., 119, 150, 151, 155
Hemmerlein, Felix, on world survey, 30–2, 41
Heraclitus, 44–6, 191
Herakles (Hercules), 59, 63–4; defeats Giants, 14, 16–17, 20

Herculaneum, 14, 17, 18, 21
Hercynian forest, 34
Hereford Cathedral, 22, 42
Hereford *mappa mundi*, 22–5, 27, 30, 31,
   32, 37, 42
Hopkins, Gerard Manley, 43–50 passim
Horace, on the Esquiline, 74, 80
Horti Lolliani, 72–4, 77, 85–6, 110
horti of Lucullus, 72, 74, 75, 77; of
   Maecenas, 74, 76; of Sallust, 72, 74, 76; of
   Taurus, 74
Howe, Julia Ward, 88, 93, 96, 97; poetry of,
   89–90, 97
Howe, Maud, 101
Huelsen, Chr., archaeologist, 129, 141, 145,
   237

ILEA (Inner London Education Authority),
   211–12, 213
imperialism, Roman, 33–40 passim
initiations, 53–4, 61
Iphigenia, 63
Iulius Caesar, C., 4, 6–7, 9–10, 34–7;
   world map project, 23–42 passim
Iulius Honorius, geographical author, 26–8,
   31, 33, 40, 227–8
Iulius Vestinus, M., republican, 12

Jackson, Robert (Parliamentary Under-
   Secretary of State, Dept. of Education and
   Science, 1987–90), 221–5
James, Henry, 87, 89, 97, 98, 100, 158
James, Montague Rhodes, 161, 163
Janiculum, discoveries on, 145
Jenkins, Thomas, entrepreneur, 84
Johannesburg, 166, 188, 193, 196, 197–8
Jones, Thomas, painter, 84–5, 230–1
Josephus, see Flavius
Jowett, Benjamin, 47, 193–4
Julius, see Iulius
Jung, Carl Gustav, 182–3, 189, 191

Knight, Mrs Caroline, 172–3, 187, 189,
   191, 195, 196, 197–8, 209
Knight, G. Wilson, 172, 174–5, 177–8,
   187, 188, 198, 202, 203, 206, 209; as biographer, 177, 179, 184, 185, 196, 207–8

Knight, W.F. Jackson, 171–209 passim;
   Cumaean Gates 179–83, 185, 188, 190;
   Homeric Poetry, 184, 187; *Roman
   Vergil*, 176, 184, 185, 187, 195, 204, 207;
   Vergil's Troy, 173–7

Lambert of St Omer, on world survey,
   28–9, 31, 229
Lanciani, Rodolfo, 111–12, 117–23 passim,
   126–30, 132–3, 137–8, 142–3, 146–7
laws, as guarantee of liberty, 2–3, 9–10, 12,
   13
Le Couteur, J.D., 160
liberty, 2–5, 9–10, 13
Livius, T. ('Livy'), 3
Lloyd, Mrs M., trance medium, 192–194,
   197–9
Llywarch the Old, 68, 69
Lollia Paullina, 75–7, 110
Lollia Saturnina, 75
Lollius, M., 74–5, 79, 86
Luke's Gospel, as evidence for world
   survey, 23–4, 29, 31, 41

MacGregor, Rt Hon. John (Secretary of State
   of Education and Science, 1989–90), 216
Malvern, 158, 168; Priory Church, 161,
   163–4
maps, ancient, 32, 33–6, 38–42
maps, medieval, 22–5, 36, 41
Marsyas, 7, 58
Massimo, Prince, 88, 93, 108
Memmius Regulus, P., 75
Messallina, empress, 77
Mithras, 55, 64
Mommsen, Theodor, 150
Morrell, Mrs Frances, 211–12
Murray, John, Principal of UCSW, 165–7,
   169, 178–9
Myres, J.L. 173–4

Naples, Angevin, 115–17, 146
Naples, Bay of, 14–23 passim, 65
National Curriculum, 210–16 passim
Nero Caesar, 12, 62
Norton, Prof. Richard, 122, 124, 127, 138
Nuceria, 19
nymphs, 57–8, 64

Octavia (play), date of, 12
Orchard, Miss, teacher, v, 56–7, 70
Orosius, historian, 26, 27, 28, 41

Painswick, Glos., 116, 117, 127, 140, 145, 146
Parthenope, 17, 65
Pelham, Prof. H.F., 119, 134, 150, 151, 152, 155, 157
Peretti, Felice, see Sixtus V
Perrins, C.W. Dyson, collector, 159, 167
Persephone, 59
Petronius, 62
Peutinger Table, 36, 40
Phillips, Lionel, benefactor, 124–5, 134, 136, 141, 142
Piso, C., conspirator, 12
Pitcher, Sydney A., photographer, 164–5, 169
Pius IX, Pope, 72, 87, 88, 89, 106–7, 109
Plato, in Hopkins, 46–50
Plinius Secundus, C. ('the elder Pliny'), 40, 41, 75–6
Plinius Caecilius Secundus, C. ('the younger Pliny'), 21
Pluto, 59
Pompeii, 14–21 passim, 65
Pompeius, Cn. ('Pompey'), 4, 6–7, 34
Pomponius Secundus, P., playwright, 8
Pomponius Secundus, Q., consul AD 41, 9, 11
Porcius, M., benefactor at Pompeii, 19, 20
Pope, Maurice, 196–7
Powell, Anthony, 51–2, 69–70
Pozzuoli (Puteoli), 14, 18
Praetorian Guard, 1, 2, 10–12
principate, nature of, 4–5, 7, 9, 12–13

Quinctius Valgus, C., benefactor at Pompeii, 19
Quintilia, showgirl, 1

Rabe, Eric von, 97, 98–9
reincarnation, 183, 194, 203
republic, surviving idea of, 3–5, 9–13

Richard of Haldingham, carographer, 22
Rivoira, Gian Teresio, 160, 161, 163
Roman Campagna, 83–4, 93, 104, 107, 109, 122, 148; Lanciani's exploration of, 117–21 passim, 126, 139
Roman Forum, excavations in, 111, 112, 117, 121–43 passim, 148, 154
Rome, climate of, 102, 112, 157–8; walls of, 71, 73, 80, 91, 109–10; papal city, 78, 80, 83–4, 86, 95, 105–6, 111; capital of united Italy, 71–2, 93–4, 108, 111; modernisation and building boom, 93–5, 99, 111, 113–14
Romulus, death of, 6
Rumbold, Rt Hon. Angela (Minister of State, Dept. of Education and Science, 1986–90), 213–14
Rushforth, Collingwood McNeil, 149, 165
Rushforth, Francis McNeil, 149, 165, 168
Rushforth, Gordon McNeil, 137, 139, 146, 149–70 passim; library of, 149–50, 152, 166, 168–70; bibliography of, 233–7
Rushforth, Janet McNeil, 149, 165, 168, 169
Ruskin, John, 125, 131

Sacra Via, removal of, 128, 129, 133–4, 137–8, 142–3
St Andrews, 130, 133, 147
'saluting soldier' syndrome, 185, 189, 196, 207
S. Stefano, Roman villa at, 121–2, 123, 127, 143–4
satyrs, 58
Scribonianus, L., rebel general, 11, 12
Seneca, L., 6, 8
Sentius Saturninus, Cn., consul AD 41, 9–10
Servius Tullius, king of Rome, 3, 71, 91
Shakespeare, on Antony, 64
Sixtus V, Pope, 79–83, 91, 107
Society of Antiquaries, 158–9, 168
Socrates, 47, 49, 63
sorcery, 54–6
Steed, Wickham, 123, 125, 141, 156
'stone-folk', 180–1, 185
Story, William W., sculptor, 88–9, 90–1, 97, 105, 113
Strabo, geographer, 15, 20, 40
Stuart Jones, H., 150, 158, 161
Suetonius, 2
Sulla, L., 6, 18–19, 20

Tacitus, historian, 2, 3, 5, 12, 19
Tartarus, 59, 178
Tea, Eva, biographer, 111, 115, 124, 142, 147
Tebbit, Rt Hon. Norman (Chairman of the Conservative Party, 1985–87), 218, 222, 226
Termini, Piazza di, 78, 80, 82, 91, 106, 108, 109; railway station, 93, 109
Terry, Arthur, 97
Terry, Louisa Ward (Crawford), 88, 96–8, 101, 102
Terry, Luther, painter, 88, 97, 99, 101
Terry, Margaret, 97, 99
Thatcher, Rt Hon. Margaret, 215, 217, 219, 220, 221–2, 224, 226
Theocritus, 63
Theodosius, emperor, 32
Theophrastus, philosopher, 33
Thyestes (and Atreus) as theme for drama, 6, 8
Tiberius Caesar, 4–5
Times, reporting Roman archaeology, 122, 123, 124, 137, 139, 141, 145, 156
Tiresias, 54
trash, Platonic, 49
trees in love, 63
Triads of Britain, The, 69
Trimalchio, 62
tritons, 57, 60, 69, 110
triumphs, 34, 37, 38
Trojan War, as historical event, 176
tyrannicide, justifiable, 5–8, 10, 12

Umberto I, king of Italy, 125, 138
universities, caricatured, 224
Universities Funding Council, 217
University Grants Committee, 219, 220

Valerius Asiaticus, D., 9, 75, 77
Varro of Atax, poet, 34
Venus, goddess of Pompeii, 19, 20
Vermey, Mrs E., medium, 200–1
Vespasian, emperor, 13
Vesuvius, 15, 19–21, 36
Victor Emmanuel III, king of Italy, 141
Villa Montalto-Negroni-Massimo, 79–92 passim, 102–10 passim, 230–1; destruction of, 72, 93, 99
Vinicianus, see Annius
Virgil, 16, 17, 171–2, 173, 178, 180–3, 189–91; hexameters of, 172, 175–6, 190; communication with, 199–206 passim
Virgil Society, 189, 195, 196
Vortigern, 68, 69

Walden, George (Parliamentary Under-Secretary of State, Dept. of Education and Science, 1985–87), 221
Ward, see also Howe, Terry
Ward, Samuel, 97, 99
Washington, Crawford sculpture in, 90, 96
wooden horse, meaning of, 176–7